British Civilization

An introduction

FOURTH EDITION

▪ John Oakland

First published 1989
by Routledge
11 New Fetter Lane,
London EC4P 4EE

Simultaneously published in the USA
and Canada
by Routledge
29 West 35th Street, New York
NY 10001

Second edition 1991
Third edition 1995
Reprinted 1996
Fourth edition 1998
Reprinted 1999, 2000

Routledge is an imprint of the Taylor & Francis Group

© 1989, 1991, 1995, 1996, 1998
John Oakland

Text design: Barker/Hilsdon

Typeset in Sabon and Futura by The Florence Group, Stoodleigh, Devon

Printed and bound in Great Britain by Biddles Ltd, Guildford and King's Lynn

All rights reserved. No part of this book may be reprinted or reproduced or utilized in any form or by any electronic, mechanical, or other means, now known or hereafter invented, including photocopying and recording, or in any information storage or retrieval system, without permission in writing from the publishers.

British Library Cataloguing in Publication Data

A catalogue record for this book is available from the British Library

Library of Congress Cataloguing in Publication Data

Oakland, John
British civilization: an introduction
p. cm.
Includes bibliographical references (p.) and index
1. Great Britain–Civilization I. Title
DA110.025 1998
94–dc21

ISBN 0–415–16569–5

Contents

Plates

Figures

Tables

Preface and acknowledgements

This book is largely concerned with institutional features of British civilization. It combines factual, descriptive and analytical approaches within a historical context and gives information on recent developments in Britain. Contrasting critical views and the people's attitudes to institutions are presented, which should allow students to develop their own responses to British life.

A book of this type is necessarily indebted to many sources for its facts, ideas and statistics, to which acknowledgement is gratefully made (see Bibliography and Suggested further reading). Particular thanks are due to *Britain: An Official Handbook* (the current edition of which contains the latest information); *British Social Attitudes*; and Market and Opinion Research International (MORI).

Chronology of significant dates in British history

800 BC	continuing settlement of Celts
55–54 BC	Julius Caesar's exploratory expeditions
AD 43	Roman conquest begins under Claudius
122–38	Hadrian's Wall built between Scotland and England
409	Roman army withdraws from Britain
410	Anglo-Saxon invasions; Anglo-Saxon kingdoms created
597	St Augustine brings Christianity to the Anglo-Saxons
664	Synod of Whitby chooses Roman Catholic Church model
789–95	Scandinavian raids begin
844	union of the Celts in Scotland
878	Vikings defeated in England by King Alfred
1014	Vikings defeated in Ireland
1066	William the Conqueror defeats King Harold at Hastings and ascends the English throne
1172	Henry II invades Ireland
1215	King John signs Magna Carta, which protects feudal rights against royal abuse

1265	first English Parliamentary Council meets (de Montfort)
1295	the Model Parliament (first regular English Parliament)
1314	battle of Bannockburn ensures Scottish independence
1326	first Scottish Parliament
1337	Hundred Years War between England and France begins
1348–49	Black Death (bubonic plague) destroys a third of England's population
1362	English replaces French as the official language
1381	Peasants' Revolt in England
1402	Welsh independence under Owen Glendower for five years
1407	the House of Commons becomes responsible for taxation
1415	the Battle of Agincourt; France defeated
1455–87	Wars of the Roses between Yorkists and Lancastrians
1477	first book to be printed in England, by William Caxton
1534–40	English Reformation; Henry VIII breaks with Papacy and becomes Head of the English Church
1536–42	Acts of Union integrate England and Wales
1547–53	Protestantism becomes official religion in England under Edward VI
1553–58	Catholic reaction under Mary I
1558	Calais, England's last possession in France, lost
1558–1603	Elizabeth I; moderate Protestantism established
1560	establishment of Church of Scotland by John Knox
1564	William Shakespeare born
1584	first English colony (Virginia) in North America
1587	Mary Stuart, Queen of Scots, executed in London
1588	defeat of Spanish Armada
1590–1613	plays of Shakespeare written

1600	East India Company founded
1603	union of the two crowns under James VI of Scotland
1607	Plantation of Ulster; Scots and English settle in northern Ireland
1611	the Authorized Version of the Bible issued
1642–51	Civil Wars between King and Parliament
1649	execution of Charles I, monarchy abolished
1653–58	Oliver Cromwell rules as Lord Protector
1660	monarchy restored under Charles II
1666	the Great Fire of London
1679	Habeus Corpus Act passed; party political system grows
1688	Glorious Revolution: accession of William I and Mary
1689	the Declaration of Rights
1690	Irish defeated by William III at the Boyne
1707	Act of Union unites England and Scotland as Great Britain
1721	Walpole becomes Britain's first Prime Minister
1760s-1830s	Industrial Revolution
1761	opening of the Bridgewater Canal begins the Canal Age
1769	the steam engine and the spinning machine invented
1775–83	American War for Independence; loss of thirteen Colonies
1793–1815	Revolutionary and Napoleonic Wars
1801	Act of Union unites Great Britain and Ireland as the United Kingdom
1805	Battle of Trafalgar
1807	abolition of the slave trade
1815	Napoleon defeated at the battle of Waterloo
1825	opening of the Stockton and Darlington Railway, the world's first passenger railway
1829	Catholic emancipation
1832	First Reform Act extends the franchise

1838	the People's Charter and the beginning of official trade unions
1845	disastrous harvest failure in Ireland
1851	first trade unions appear (New Model Unionism)
1868	Trade Union Congress (TUC) established
1870	compulsory elementary education introduced
1871	legal recognition of trade unions
1884	universal male suffrage
1911	political power of the House of Lords restricted
1914–18	First World War
1916	Easter Rising against Britain in Dublin
1921	Anglo-Irish Treaty establishes the Irish Free State; Northern Ireland remains part of the United Kingdom
1924	the first Labour government
1926	General Strike
1928	universal suffrage for women
1939–45	Second World War
1944	Butler Education Act
1945	United Nations formed
1949	Irish Free State becomes Republic of Eire; NATO created
1952	accession of Elizabeth II
1956	the Suez Crisis
1960	Britain joins EFTA
1973	Britain enters European Community (European Union)
1979	Margaret Thatcher becomes Britain's first woman Prime Minister
1997	Referendums on devolution for Scotland and Wales

Introduction

THE FOLLOWING CHAPTERS mainly examine the historical development and contemporary roles of British institutions. Institutions are organizations that have been constructed over varying periods of time and encompass actual practices in society. They take many different forms and sizes; operate on both national and local levels; may be public or private in character; can be formal or informal; and may embrace different attitudes and values.

The major formal elements, such as Parliament, monarchy, law and government, are concerned with state and public business. They have a top–down structure (with policies originating at the top of hierarchies) and have been conditioned by the military power, economic strength, political development and imperial status of Britain's past. But there are also other institutional features, such as sports, families, leisure activities, neighbourhoods and forms of popular and elite culture, that have

their own particular organizations and values. They may reveal more localized, individualistic, informal and often private characteristics.

The 'British way of life' is determined by how people function within and react to institutions on both these levels, whether negatively or positively. Institutions are not remote abstractions. They directly influence individuals in their daily lives. Changes in interest rates by the Bank of England affect savers and borrowers of money; commercial and media organizations manipulate consumers of popular culture in areas such as music, clothes and fashion; sponsorship may determine the nature of sports activities; changes in central government policies affect old age pensioners, schoolchildren, employees and employers; and local government conditions community life. Institutions cover a range of practices and identities and embrace both high and popular cultural expressions. The number and variety of such organizations means that there are many different 'ways of life' in Britain and all contribute to the diversity of contemporary society.

Institutions must adapt if they are to survive. They provide frameworks for new situations and their present roles may be very different from their original functions. State institutions concerned with political, legal, economic and religious matters have evolved slowly and pragmatically over many centuries. This has particularly been the case since 1707, when England and Wales were united with Scotland as Great Britain, and since 1801, when the United Kingdom (England, Scotland, Wales and Ireland) was formed. The latest stage in this process will be the devolution (1999–2000) of some political power from the London Parliament to a Scottish Parliament and a Welsh Assembly, following referendums in 1997. Such evolutionary developments have formed British society generally and change has mainly occurred through compromise within the law, rather than by radical upheaval.

These characteristics have often been attributed to the allegedly insular and conservative mentalities of the island peoples who comprise the British Isles, with their supposed preference for traditional habits and structures. Although some influences have come from abroad, the absence of any successful external military invasion since the Norman Conquest of AD 1066 has allowed institutions to develop internally in distinctive ways. The resulting institutional principles, like parliamentary democracy and religion, have frequently been imitated by other countries, or exported through the creation of a colonial empire and a commercial need to establish worldwide markets for British products.

The development of the British state and its empire historically was aided by increasing military and economic strength, so that by the nineteenth century Britain had become a dominant world power. But the country has experienced substantial changes since the earlier imperial period and from the mid-twentieth century. Today it is a complex society in which diversity has produced problems as well as advantages.

Britain today may give a surface impression of uniform or homogeneous behaviour, which is influenced by an English norm centred on the dominant role of London as the centre of political and economic life. But there is also considerable heterogeneity or difference in British life, such as the cultural distinctiveness and separate identities of Wales, Scotland and Northern Ireland; demands for greater local autonomy in the English regions; disparities between affluent and economically depressed areas throughout the country (including the decay of inner-city locations); alleged cultural gaps between north and south; political variety (reflected in support for different political parties in different parts of Britain); debates on the positions of women, minority groups and ethnic communities; campaigns for individual and collective rights; and a gulf between rich and poor (with a growing underclass of disadvantaged people).

Such features illustrate some of the present divisions in British society. They suggest a decline in the traditional respect for and deference to established authority, consensus views and national institutions. They indicate that the people are now more nonconformist and individualistic than in the past. Opinion polls report periodically that the British feel that they have become more aggressive, more selfish, less tolerant, less kind, less moral, less honest and less polite. A Leeds University research survey in

1997 portrayed a society riddled with mistrust and cynicism in which materialism, possessions and physical looks constitute the new standards.

Arguably, such developments have led to an increase in anti-social behaviour, yobbishness, alchohol and drug abuse, disputes between neighbours and public disorder. The tolerant civic image of individual liberty and sense of community that foreigners and the British often have of the country (rightly or wrongly) has suffered. Politicians and commentators argue for a return to community values, social responsibility, consensus politics and a caring society in which individuals feel that they have a place.

Many Britons are worried about the quality of contemporary life. A MORI poll conducted in May 1997 found that the following issues were most important for them: health care (68 per cent); education (61); law and order (51); unemployment (49); pensions (39); taxation (33); the economy (30); Europe (22); housing (22); the environment (20); public transport (18); defence (12); Northern Ireland (12); animal welfare (10); trade unions (9); and constitutional issues (7). These findings show that institutional issues are of concern to and affect British people.

Pressures are consequently placed on institutions and the national leadership to reflect and respond more adequately to current differences and conditions. The performances of state and local institutions in Britain are vigorously debated and many are found wanting. Questions are asked as to whether the existing structures can satisfactorily cope with the needs and demands of contemporary life, and whether (and how) they might be reformed in order to operate more efficiently and responsively. Such questioning is also linked to debates about the nature of British national identity and how the country should be organized socially, politically and economically.

This domestic situation has been influenced by external pressures. Since the Second World War (1939–45), Britain has had to adjust with considerable difficulty to the consequences of a withdrawal from empire; a reduction in world status; a series of global economic recessions; increased competition from abroad; and the growth of a different geo-political world order. Britain has been forced into a reluctant search for a new identity and direction. It has moved from empire and the Commonwealth towards an economic and political commitment to Europe, mainly through membership of the European Union (EU). This impetus will inevitably increase as the EU expands and develops further integrated institutions and policies.

In recent centuries, Britain rarely saw itself as part of mainland Europe. It sheltered behind the barrier of the English Channel, and its outlook was westwards and worldwide. Today, the psychological and physical isolation from Europe is changing, as illustrated by increased cooperation between Britain and other European countries and by the opening (1994) of a Channel rail tunnel between England and France. But the relationship between Britain and its European partners continues to be difficult, and new associations have been forced by circumstances and events, rather than wholeheartedly sought. Britain also still maintains many of its traditional worldwide commercial and cultural links.

Despite such developments and more internal social diversity, there is still a conservatism in some areas of British life that regards change with suspicion. This attitude can result in a tension between the often enforced need for reform and a nostalgia for an assumed ideal past. It can cause difficulties for national progress and the evolution of institutions. Historical fact demonstrates that the past in Britain was not as idyllic as is sometimes imagined. But the myth and traditional patterns of behaviour still hold considerable force and attraction for many people.

Fundamental change does not come easily to old cultures such as Britain, and institutions (or the human beings who operate them) are often resistant to major alteration. The countries that avoid decline are those that are capable of political progress, social innovation, economic development and institutional reform. Critics maintain that Britain since the 1950s has been unwilling to face large-scale reassessment and embrace fundamental change. It has avoided hard decisions; continued the tradition of pragmatic evolution; lurched from one economic crisis to another; revealed mismanagement at all levels of society; complacently persisted with its ancient institutions and ways of doing things; and ignored lessons that could have been learned from abroad.

It has been frequently argued that a long-term relative economic decline since the late nineteenth century was joined to a political constitution and national mentality that could not cope with the reality or needs of the post-industrial and culturally-diverse society that Britain had become. Much of this decline could be explained by long-term and global events that were not reversible. But critics insist that the country still suffers from structural and institutional defects that need to be remedied by radical rethinking.

Britain does have its problems. There is evidence of continuing instability, such as relatively high unemployment; a gap between rich and poor; fear of crime; increased violence against the person; industrial and technological change; inadequacies in some social institutions; alleged lack of governmental vision; political volatility; and an apparent decline in national cohesion and identity.

Despite the often lurid picture painted by some commentators and the media, however, these features do not mean that the essential fabric of society is falling apart, nor should Britain be seen as a country in terminal decline. Biased ideological views and a British capacity for self-denigration and complaint can encourage unbalanced, sensational views, and isolated incidents may be exaggerated beyond their national importance. Most British people now enjoy greater prosperity and opportunities and the economy is strong and competitive (1997) in international terms. A Gallup International poll in January 1997 showed that Britain had become the most optimistic nation in Europe and that a majority of Britons were (for the first time in 10 years) enthusiastic about their economic prospects. But a MORI poll in August 1997 found that economic optimism among the middle class had declined sharply since the May 1997 general election. Existing structural and social problems therefore warn against undue complacency.

Assumptions about British life have been questioned recently and change has occurred. Conservative governments (1979–97) tried to reform institutional structures and promote new attitudes. The term 'Thatcherism' (after the Conservative Prime Minister, Margaret Thatcher 1979–90) described these developments, such as the reduction of the state's role in national affairs and its replacement by 'market forces'; the creation of jobs by the 'market'; the restoration of economic stability and growth by control of inflation; encouragement of competition, business activity and investment; proposed cuts in taxes and public spending; privatization programmes where state concerns are transferred to the private sector; the reduction in the influence of trade unions and some monopolistic professions; the creation of greater choice, accountability and higher standards in the educational, health and social security systems; and the attack upon an alleged local government inefficiency and monopoly. People were encouraged to be more responsible for their own affairs without automatic reliance on the state for support (the 'dependency culture') and urged to adopt more individual competitiveness and efficiency (the 'enterprise culture').

Such policies were relatively successful on the economic level, but there was public resistance to others. While some people applauded the freedoms of an enterprise culture, others wished for more intervention in social areas of national life. Indeed, a 1990 MORI poll showed that 54 per cent of interviewees regarded themselves as 'socialists'; 34 per cent as 'Thatcherists'; and 12 per cent did not know. Such views, repeated in later polls such as *British Social Attitudes: 1997–98*, were probably influenced by a severe economic recession and high unemployment from 1989 to 1993. They suggest that it is difficult to change Britons' attitudes, and that many people still look to the state for support in areas such as health, education and social security. Nevertheless, free market policies continued under the Conservative Prime Minister John Major (1990–97), and the Labour government (1997–) under Tony Blair will not depart radically from them.

The Labour government has modernized its policies and moved to the political centre ground. It is addressing the social and economic realities of the modern state, accepts the need for personal initiative and stresses that hard choices have to be made.

In areas such as social security, health, employment and tight control of public spending, the government's policies mark a departure from the Labour past and the dependency culture.

Opposition to some government programmes and acceptance of others demonstrate that institutional change can occur in various, often interconnected, ways. Some institutions wither away because they are no longer used. Others are reformed internally as new situations arise. Additional forces that contribute to change are opposition political parties parading their alternative programmes; interest or pressure groups exerting their influence upon formal decision makers; grassroots movements protesting at some action or lack of action; campaigns by the media to promote reform or uncover scandals; and the weight of public opinion for or against official plans. However, government initiatives are the single most important factor in determining institutional change as governments implement their policies or respond to events.

The British allow their governments a great deal of power in the running of the country; but there is a limit to their tolerance. Most politicians are sensitive to the views of the people, since their hold upon political power is dependent upon the electorate at each general election. Governments usually govern with at least one eye on public opinion and generally attempt to gain acceptance for their policies. They sometimes have to move cautiously (even with big majorities in the House of Commons like the present Labour government) and may suffer setbacks in some of their programmes.

The British assume, rightly or wrongly, that they have an individual independence and liberty within the framework of the national institutions and are quick to voice disapproval if their interests are threatened. Protest is a natural and traditional reaction, as well as being a safety valve against more serious social and political disruption. But dissension may be neutralized by the promise of reform, or ignored by the central government. Adequate responses may not come from the authorities, and there is always the danger of more serious conflict. However, peaceful evolution continues to characterize most of British life, and gradualist changes reflect the diverse nature of the society and its attitudes.

The British do, however, have a healthy cynicism about their institutions and political leaders. *British Social Attitudes: 1988–89* suggested that

> the British electorate is far from being compliant or deferential. For all Britain's political and social stability over the years . . . the British reveal an uncompromisingly irreverent and critical streak. . . . The public's trust in the pillars of the British establishment is at best highly qualified. . . . [they] seem intuitively to have discovered that the surest protection against disillusionment with their public figures and powerful institutions is to avoid developing illusions about them in the first place.
>
> (*British Social Attitudes: 1988–89*, pp.121–2)

The British today are confronting different cultural and economic realities than those of the past. They no longer have the benefits of their earlier industrial revolutions, such as cheap raw materials, cheap labour and an uncompetitive world market. Their society has become more diverse, individualistic and mobile. The old pragmatic methods of innovation, which illustrate the British tendency to muddle through difficulties without long-term planning or fundamental reform, may no longer be sufficient for an era in which specialized education and training, high-technology competence and a need to respond to international competition are the main determinants. Britain is still seen among export markets as traditional, 'historical', backward-looking and conventional, despite Labour government rhetoric to create a 'new, young and modern' society. Yet, in the past, evolutionary methods showed an instinct for survival on institutional, individual and national levels and promoted successful adaptation to new conditions.

EXERCISES

■ Explain and examine the following terms:

tolerance	insular	grassroots	pragmatic
deference	conservative	inner-city	diversity
norm	recession	heterogeneous	ethnic
nostalgia	homogeneous	post-industrial	autonomy
myth	dependency	nonconformist	evolution
enterprise	Thatcherism	yobbishness	high-technology

■ Write short essays on the following topics:

1 Try to define the term 'institutions' and examine its possible usages.

2 What are some of the characteristics that you would associate with the British people and their society? Why?

Chapter 1

The country

THE COUNTRY'S FULL TITLE for constitutional and political purposes is the United Kingdom of Great Britain and Northern Ireland, although the short terms 'UK' and 'Britain' are normally used for convenience. It is part of that group of islands, described geographically as the British Isles, that lie off the north-west coast of continental Europe. The mainlands of England, Scotland and Wales form the largest island and are known politically as Great Britain. Northern Ireland shares the second-largest island with the Republic of Ireland (Ireland or Eire), which has been independent of Britain since 1921. Smaller islands, such as Anglesey, the Isle of Wight, the Orkneys, Shetlands, Hebrides and Scillies, lie off the coasts and are part of the British political union.

The Isle of Man in the Irish Sea and the Channel Islands off the French west coast are not, however, part of the United Kingdom. They are self-governing Crown Dependencies that have a historical relationship with the British Crown and possess their own independent legal systems, legislatures and administrative structures. However, the British government is responsible for their defence and foreign relations and can interfere if good administration is not maintained.

Britain is often discussed and divided up according to 'regions'. 'Regionalism' can mean several things, such as political and geographical identification; assistance and development aid areas; and the provision of services like gas, water, electricity and health to specific places. It should not be confused with formal local government structures (see chapter 4) and is often based, as in figure 1.3, on former economic planning regions.

'Regionalism', as a cultural factor, is important in British life. It illustrates a sense of local identity that becomes stronger with increasing distance from London. It also reflects a reduction in the influence of the central government on local populations and a determination by these people to assert their individual liberty and choice. National feelings may intensify with the establishment of a Scottish Parliament in Edinburgh and a Welsh Assembly in Cardiff. But this could also lead to increased regionalism within Scotland and Wales themselves (as areas react to Edinburgh and Cardiff) and provoke demands for greater local autonomy in English regions.

Physical features

Historically, Britain's physical features have influenced human settlement, population movements, military conquest and political union. They have also conditioned the location and exploitation of industry, transport systems, agriculture, fisheries, woodlands, energy supplies and communications. Today they continue to influence such activities and are tied to public concerns about pollution and the quality of the natural environment. Some have been controversially affected by government policies (such as privatization) and directives on agriculture and fisheries from the European Union.

Britain's geographical position is marked by 0° longitude, which passes through the international time zone of Greenwich east of London; by latitude 50°N in south-west England; and by latitude 60°N across the Shetlands. Britain thus lies within only 10° of latitude and has a small and compact size when compared with some European countries. Yet it also possesses a great diversity of physical features, which surprises those visitors who expect a mainly urban and industrialized country. The many beauty spots and recreation areas, such as the 10 National Parks in England and Wales and areas of natural beauty in Scotland and Northern Ireland, may be easily reached without much expenditure of time or effort.

Britain's physical area amounts to some 93,025 sq. miles (242,842 sq. km). Most of this is land and the rest comprises inland water such as lakes and rivers. England has 50,052 sq. miles (129,634 sq. km), Wales has 7,968 (20,637), Scotland has 29,799 (77,179) and Northern Ireland has 5,206 (13,438).

England is therefore much larger than the other countries. It also has a bigger population of 48,708,000 out of a UK total of 58,395,000. These factors partly explain the English dominance in British history.

The distance from the south coast of England to the most northerly tip of the Scottish mainland is 600 miles (955 km), and the English east coast and the Welsh west coast are 300 miles (483 km) apart at their widest points. These relatively small distances have aided the development of political union and communications and contributed to standardized social, economic and institutional norms. But, prior to the eighteenth century, there were considerable obstacles to this progress, such as difficult terrain and inadequate transportation.

Britain's varied physical characteristics are the result of a long geological and climatic history. Over time, earth movements have caused mountain chains to rise from the sea-bed to form the oldest parts of Britain. Warmer, sub-tropical periods intervened between the earth movements, and during these times large swamp forests covered most lowland zones. These, in their turn, were buried by sand, soil and mud, so that the forests' fossil remains became the coal deposits of modern Britain. Later, the climate alternated between warmth and sub-Arctic temperatures. During these latter Ice Age periods, ice-sheets or glaciers moved southwards over most of the British Isles, leaving only southern England free from their effects.

The raised land areas were gradually worn away by weathering agents such as wind, ice and water. This process rounded off the mountain peaks and moved waste materials into lowland zones, where they were pressed into new rocks and where the scenery became softer and less folded than the mountain areas. The geological and weathering changes shaped the details of valleys and plains and dictated the siting of Britain's major rivers, such as the Clyde, Forth and Tweed in Scotland; the Tyne, Trent, Humber, Severn and Thames in England and Wales; and the Bann and Lagan in Northern Ireland.

Natural forces have also affected the coastlines as the seas have moved backwards and forwards over time. Parts of the

FIGURE 1.1 The British Isles

coastal area have either sunk under the sea or risen above it. These processes continue today, particularly on the English east and south coasts. The sea's retreat has created chalk and limestone uplands, and sand beaches along many coasts, while erosion has resulted in the loss of land in some places.

Britain was originally part of the European mainland, but the melting of the glaciers in the last Ice Age caused the sea level to rise. The country was separated from the continent by the North Sea at its widest point, and by the English Channel at its narrowest point. The shortest stretch of water between the two land masses is now the Strait of Dover between Dover in southern England and Calais in France (20 miles, 32 km).

There are many bays, inlets, peninsulas and estuaries along the coasts and most places in Britain are less than 75 miles (120 km) from some kind of tidal water. Tides on the coasts and in inland rivers can cause flooding in many parts of the country. Substantial financial resources are needed by water companies and local authorities, particularly on the English east and south coasts, to enable them to construct defences against this threat. For example, a London flood barrier was completed in 1984 across the River Thames.

The coastal seas are not deep and are often less than 300 feet (90 m) because the greater part of the British Isles lies on the Continental Shelf, or raised sea-bed adjacent to the mainland. The warm North Atlantic Current (Gulf Stream) heats the sea and air as it travels from the Atlantic Ocean across the Shelf. This gives the British Isles a more temperate climate than would otherwise be the case, when one considers their northerly position. It also influences the coastal waters, which are important fish breeding grounds, on which the national fishing industry is considerably dependent.

Britain's physical relief can be divided into highland and lowland Britain (see figure 1.2). The highest ground is mainly in the north and west. Most of the lowland zones, except for the Scottish Lowlands and central areas of Northern Ireland, are in the south and east of the country, where only a few points reach 1,000 feet (305 m) above sea level.

1 North-West Highlands
2 Central Highlands (Grampians)
3 Southern Uplands
4 Sperrin Mountains
5 Antrim Mountains
6 Mourne Mountains
7 Cumbrian Mountains
8 Pennines
9 Peak District
10 Welsh Massif (Cambrians)

FIGURE 1.2 Highland and lowland Britain

The north and west consist of the older, harder rocks created by the ancient earth movements, which are generally unsuitable for cultivation. The south and east comprise younger, softer materials formed by weathering processes that have produced fertile soils and good agricultural conditions. Much of the lowland area, except for regions of urban settlement and industrial usage, has been cultivated and farmed. It is largely composed of fields, which are normally divided by fences or hedges. Animal grazing land in upland zones is separated either by moorland or stone walls.

England

England (population 48,708,000) consists largely of undulating or flat lowland countryside, with highland areas in the north and south-west. Eastern England has the low-lying flat lands of the Norfolk Broads, the Cambridgeshire and Lincolnshire Fens and the Suffolk Marshes. Low hill ranges stretch over much of the country, such as the North Yorkshire Moors, the Cotswolds, the Kent and Sussex Downs and the Chiltern Hills.

Highland zones are marked by the Cheviot Hills (between England and Scotland); the north-western mountain region of the Lake District and the Cumbrian Mountains; the northern plateau belt of the Pennines forming a backbone across north-west England; the Peak District at the southern reaches of the Pennines; and the south-western plateau of Devon and Cornwall.

The heaviest population concentrations centre on the largest towns and cities, such as London and in south-east England generally; the West Midlands region around Birmingham; the Yorkshire cities of Leeds, Bradford and Sheffield; the north-western industrial area around Liverpool and Manchester; and the north-east region comprising Newcastle and Sunderland.

Wales

Wales (population 2,913,000) is mainly a highland country, with long stretches of moorland plateau, hills and mountains, which are often broken by deep valleys, such as those created by the

PLATE 1.1 Welsh countryside *(Brenda Prince/Format)*

rivers Dee, Wye and Severn. This upland mass contains the Cambrian Mountains and descends eastwards into the English counties of Shropshire and Hereford and Worcester. The highest mountains are in Snowdonia in the north-west, where the dominant peak is that of Snowdon (3,560 feet, 1,085 m).

The lowland zones are restricted to the narrow coastal belts and to the lower parts of the river valleys in south Wales, where two-thirds of the Welsh population live. The chief urban concentrations of people and industry are around the bigger southern cities, such as the capital Cardiff, Swansea and Newport, and to a lesser extent in the north-east of the country. In the past, the highland nature of Wales has hindered conquest, agriculture and the settlement of people.

Scotland

Scotland (population 5,132,000) may be divided into three main areas. The first is the North-West and Central Highlands (Grampians), together with a large number of islands off the west and north-east coasts. These areas are thinly populated, but comprise half the country's land mass. The second is the Central Lowlands, which contain one-fifth of the land area but three-quarters of the Scottish population, most of the industrial and commercial centres and much of the cultivated land. The third is the Southern Uplands, which cover a number of hill ranges stretching towards the border with England.

The Highlands, with their inland lochs and fiord coastlines, and the Southern Uplands are now smooth, rounded areas since the originally jagged mountains formed by earth movements have been worn down over time. The highest point in the Central Highlands is Ben Nevis (4,406 feet, 1,342 m), which is also the highest place in Britain.

The main population concentrations are around the administrative centre and capital of Edinburgh; the commercial and industrial area of Glasgow; and the regional centres of Aberdeen (an oil industry city) and Dundee. The climate, isolation and harsh physical conditions in much of Scotland have made conquest, settlement and agriculture difficult.

Northern Ireland

Northern Ireland (population 1,642,000) has a north-east tip that is only 13 miles (21 km) from the Scottish coast, a fact that has encouraged both Irish and Scottish migration. Since 1921, Northern Ireland has had a 303-mile (488-km) border in the south and west with the Republic of Ireland. It has a rocky northern coastline, a south-central fertile plain and mountainous areas in the west, north-east and south-east. The south-eastern Mourne Mountains include the highest peak, Slieve Donard, which is 2,796 feet (853 m) high. Lough Neagh (147 sq. miles, 381 sq. km.) is Britain's largest freshwater lake and lies at the centre of the country.

Most of the large towns, like the capital Belfast, are situated in valleys that lead from the Lough. Belfast lies at the mouth of the river Lagan and has the biggest population concentration. But Northern Ireland generally has a sparse and scattered population and is a largely rural country.

Climate

Temperature

The relative smallness of the country and the influences of a warm sea and westerly winds mean that there are no extreme contrasts in temperature throughout Britain. The climate is mainly temperate, but with variations between coolness and mildness. Altitude modifies temperatures, so that much of Scotland and highland areas of Wales and England are cool in summer and cold in winter compared with most of England.

Temperatures rarely reach 32°C (90°F) in the summer or fall below –10°C (14°F) in the winter. But the average monthly temperature in the Shetlands ranges from 3°C (37°F) during the winter months to 11°C (52°F) in the summer months, while the corresponding measurements for the Isle of Wight are 5°C (41°F) and 16°C (61°F). There may be exceptions to these average figures throughout the year and throughout the country.

Rainfall

The main factors affecting rainfall in Britain are depressions (low pressure areas) that travel eastwards across the Atlantic Ocean; prevailing south-westerly winds throughout much of the year; exposure of western coasts to the Atlantic Ocean; and the fact that most high ground lies in the west.

As a result, the heaviest annual rainfalls are in the west and north (over 60 inches, 1,600 mm), with an autumn or winter maximum. The high ground in the west protects the lowlands of the south and east, so that annual rainfall here is moderate (30 inches, 800 mm), with a slight summer maximum. The total national rainfall average is over 40 inches (1,100 mm) annually; March to June tend to be the driest months; September to January the wettest; and drought conditions are infrequent, although they do occur and can cause problems for farmers, water companies and consumers.

Low pressure systems normally pass over the northern British Isles and may produce windy, wet and unstable conditions. But high pressure systems, which also occur throughout the year, are relatively stable and move more slowly, resulting in light winds and settled weather. They can give fine and dry effects, both in the winter and summer.

Sunshine

The amount of sunshine in Britain varies between regions. It decreases from south to north; inland from the coastal belts; and with altitude. In summer, the average daily sunshine varies from five hours in northern Scotland to eight hours on the Isle of Wight. In winter, it averages one hour in northern Scotland and two hours on the English south coast.

These average statistics indicate that Britain is not a particularly sunny country, although there are periods of relief from the general greyness. The frequent cloud-cover over the British Isles is a complicating factor, so that even on a hot summer's day there may be little sunshine breaking through the clouds. This may result in humid, sticky conditions. Sunshine can frequently mix with pollutants to give poor air quality in both the cities and rural areas.

Such climatic features give the British weather its changeability and what some regard as its stimulating variety. Discrepancies between weather forecasts and actual results often occur and words such as 'changeable' and 'unsettled' are generously employed. The weather is virtually a national institution, a topic of daily conversation and for some a conditioning factor in the national character. Britons tend to think that they live in a more temperate climate than is the case. But many escape abroad in both winter and summer.

Agriculture, fisheries and forestry

Agriculture

Britain's long agricultural history includes a series of revolutions in farming methods. Today, agriculture (including horticultural products such as apples, berries and flowers) is an important industry and covers most of the country. It is very productive, efficient, mechanized and specialized. Technical advances have increased crop and animal yields and income from farming has risen considerably since 1995, although some small farmers do have difficulty in surviving.

Soils vary in quality from the thin, poor ones of highland Britain to the rich, fertile land of low-lying areas in eastern and southern England. The climate usually allows a long, productive growing season without undue drought or extreme cold. But weather conditions can create problems for farmers because of droughts or when there is too much rain and too little sunshine at ripening time.

There are 235,000 farm units, varying in size from small farms to huge business concerns, and many of them are owner-occupied. They use 77 per cent of the land area, although there is concern that farmland is being increasingly used for building and recreational purposes. Only some 600,000 people (2.1 per cent of the workforce) are engaged in farming. But agriculture provides two-thirds of Britain's food needs, agricultural products and machinery contribute 1.5 per cent to the GDP (Gross Domestic Product) and exports continue to grow.

Half the full-time farms specialize in dairy farming, beef cattle and sheep herds in Scotland, Northern Ireland, Wales and northern and south-western England. The tradition of sheep farming, on which Britain's prosperity was once based, continues. Dairy herds and milk yields have increased and two-thirds of beef consumption comes from the national stock. But concerns about BSE (Bovine Spongiform Encephalopathy) in cows and its possible link to CJD (Creutzfeldt-Jakob Disease) in humans led to a European Union worldwide ban (1996) on British beef and consequent damage to the beef market. After government action and selective culling of the beef herd, the number of new cases of BSE has declined considerably. Further doubts about the safety of beef and beef products continue to plague farmers, however, and in 1997 the government banned the sale of beef meat on the bone.

Some farms concentrate on pig production, particularly in eastern and northern England and Northern Ireland. The poultry meat and egg industries are also widespread and have increased their production levels in recent years, due largely to intensive 'factory farming', so that Britain is now almost self-sufficient in these foodstuffs.

Most of the other farms (mainly in southern and eastern England and in eastern Scotland) tend to specialize in arable crops and have increased their production, despite occasional bad harvests. Wheat, barley, oats, potatoes, oilseed rape, sugar beet and vegetables are widely cultivated.

The agricultural industry is a well-organized interest group. But the Common Agricultural Policy (CAP) of the European Union (EU), which accounts for 48 per cent of the EU's budget, has affected British farmers. It represents a protectionist intervention in farming. Its original aims were to increase productivity and efficiency; stabilize the market by ensuring regular supplies of essential food; give farmers a reasonable standard of living for their work by providing them with subsidies; and produce goods at fair prices. The CAP set minimum guaranteed prices for food products, such as wheat, beef, eggs and butter, by operating a price support system. It also standardized the quality and size of produce and imposed import duties on foreign goods coming into the EU.

The British attitude to the original CAP system was negative on the grounds that it was unwieldy, bureaucratic, expensive, open to fraud and resulted in surplus foodstuffs. British consumers suffered because prices rose as a result of the market support system. Farmers had to curb production under EU quota systems in order to become less competitive, at a time when the country could have aimed for self-sufficiency in cheap agricultural produce.

PLATE 1.2 Barley fields in Devon, England *(Ken Lambert/Barnaby)*

Price support mechanisms remain part of the CAP, but reforms in 1992 reduced these and intervention measures. British farmers now receive most of their funding directly from the government under various schemes. In order to control production, conditions such as quotas or 'set-aside' programmes (farmers receive funds to divert their land from agriculture) are levied on producers receiving such payments. The government then claims reimbursement on this expenditure from the EU budget, to which Britain is a net contributor.

British governments pressurize the EU to reform the CAP further, arguing that it is still too costly for consumers and too restrictive for producers. They maintain that supply and demand should reflect the real needs of the market and meet consumers' demands. The aim is to phase out production controls, eliminate bureaucratic burdens on producers, prevent over-production and cut support levels and subsidies.

High EU farm prices and the export of subsidized food have concerned non-EU nations. GATT (General Agreement on Tariffs and Trade) reforms have reduced subsidies in order to reflect market forces and permit greater access to the EU by foreign countries. GATT restrictions on levels of subsidized exports are likely to become tighter in future and the aim is further to liberalize international agricultural trade. Future enlargement of the EU to include Eastern European countries will also promote pressures for change to the CAP.

Fisheries

Britain is one of Europe's leading fishing nations and operates in the North Sea, the Irish Sea and the Atlantic. The fishing industry is important to the national economy and is centred on a number of ports around the British coasts.

However, employment in and income from fishing have declined substantially in recent years. This is partly due to fluctuations in fish breeding patterns and a reduction in fish stocks because of overfishing. Many fishermen have become unemployed and fishing towns, such as Grimsby and the Scottish ports, have suffered. But the fishing industry still accounts for 59 per cent of Britain's fish consumption. Fishermen now number about 17,000, with some 5,000 occasionally employed and three jobs in associated occupations for every one fisherman.

The fishing industry has also been affected by the EU's Common Fisheries Policy (CFP) and British government policies, which have affected the fishermen's old freedom of operation. The need to conserve fish resources and prevent overfishing is stressed. Zones have been established in which fishermen may operate and EU countries can fish up to Britain's 6-mile (10-km) fishing limit. Quota systems are in force inside and beyond the zones in order to restrict fish catches. British government measures to limit the time fishing vessels spend at sea and to decommission (take out of operation) fishing boats have further restricted employment and the fishing fleet.

The conflicting interests of EU members and other nations have gradually been improved by fishing agreements. But there are continuing problems and critics argue that British governments have not acted in the best interests of their own national fisheries. Fishermen have been angry with government policies, the EU quotas and fishing zones, 'quota-hoppers' (other EU fishermen who buy British-registered ships to avoid quota limits in their own countries) and their resulting loss of livelihood. But without fish conservation, there will be reduced supplies in the future.

The most important British fish catches are cod, haddock, whiting, herring, mackerel, plaice and sole, which are caught by the 9,313 registered vessels of the fishing fleet. The fish farming industry is a large and expanding business, particularly in Scotland, and is chiefly concerned with salmon, trout and shellfish. Fish meal and fish oil are important by-products of the fishing industry and fish imports continue. But the import of whale products has been banned since 1982 in order to protect the whale population.

Forestry

Woodlands cover an estimated 5.9 million acres (2.4 million hectares) of Britain and comprise 7 per cent of England, 15 per cent of Scotland, 12 per cent of Wales and 6 per cent of Northern Ireland. These figures amount to some 10 per cent of total land area, which is considerably below the European average. Some 37 per cent of productive national forests are managed by the state Forestry Commission or government departments and the rest by private owners. About 34,000 people are employed in the state and private forestry industries and 10,000 are engaged in timber processing.

However, these activities contribute only 15 per cent to the national consumption of wood and associated timber products, which means that the country is heavily dependent upon wood imports. The government has encouraged tree planting programmes, particularly in Scotland and Wales, and allowed the sale of state woodlands to private owners in order to reduce public expenditure and to encourage productivity. New plantings, controlled felling, the expansion of timber industries and a profitable private sector may reduce Britain's present dependence upon imports and benefit the environment.

Forestry policy is supposed to take environmental and conservation factors into account in the development of timber facilities. But such aims are not always achieved and there is disquiet about some government programmes. Environmentalists campaign against the destruction of woodlands for road building, advocate increased tree planting to combat global warming and pollution and try to preserve the quality of the existing woodlands. These in recent years have been badly affected by disease, unreasonable felling and substantial storm damage in October 1987 and January 1990.

Energy resources

Britain has considerable energy resources and its primary sources are oil, gas, nuclear power, coal and water. The most important secondary source is electricity. Some 200,000 people work in the energy production business, which accounts for 5 per cent of the GDP, and three of Britain's largest companies (Shell, BP and British Gas) are in this sector. But there are problems associated with energy sources and concerns about pollution and environmental damage. Many energy industries have also been privatized in recent years, leading to criticisms about their services, effectiveness and regulation.

Since 1980, Britain has produced an increased amount of its energy needs and is largely self-sufficient. This is due to the growth in offshore oil and gas supplies, which make a crucial contribution to the economy. Multinational companies operate under government licence and extract these fuels from the North Sea and newly discovered West Atlantic fields. Gas and oil distribution in Britain is now in the private sector.

Because governments encourage high extraction rates, however, large supplies of oil and gas (even with the discovery of new reserves) will continue only into the early twenty-first century. Development of existing resources and the search for alternative forms of energy are crucial for Britain and its economy. As oil and gas decline, the positions of coal and nuclear power are debated and further research is needed into renewable energy such as solar, wind, wave and tidal power.

Coal is an important natural energy resource, but there are objections to its use on pollution and cost grounds. The coal industry is now privatized, extraction is by private companies and Britain produces most of its own coal needs. Conservative governments tried to develop a competitive coal industry by reducing the workforce and closing uneconomic pits. After trade union opposition to these policies, the workforce was cut, mines were closed and productivity and profitability improved. But British coal remains expensive and suffers from a lack of demand from big consumers, such as electricity power stations, which have moved to fuels like gas, oil and cheap coal imports. More pit closures have occurred and the future of the coal industry is uncertain.

Electricity generation and distribution is now privatized and mainly provided by coal-, gas- and oil-fired power stations, in addition to a small amount of hydro-electricity. But 27 per cent of electricity is produced by thirteen nuclear power stations of various types. Conservative governments originally encouraged the growth of nuclear power to satisfy Britain's energy needs. But further expansion is unlikely and a partial privatization of the nuclear industry occurred in 1996.

Alternative forms of renewable energy are becoming more important. Electricity generation by wind power is already operative, although there is public opposition to wind farms in the countryside. The possibilities of extracting heat from underground rocks are being explored and the potential use of tidal and wave power is being examined on the Severn (Bristol) and Mersey (Liverpool) estuaries. Some solar energy is already provided, with plans for more research. These and other forms of renewable

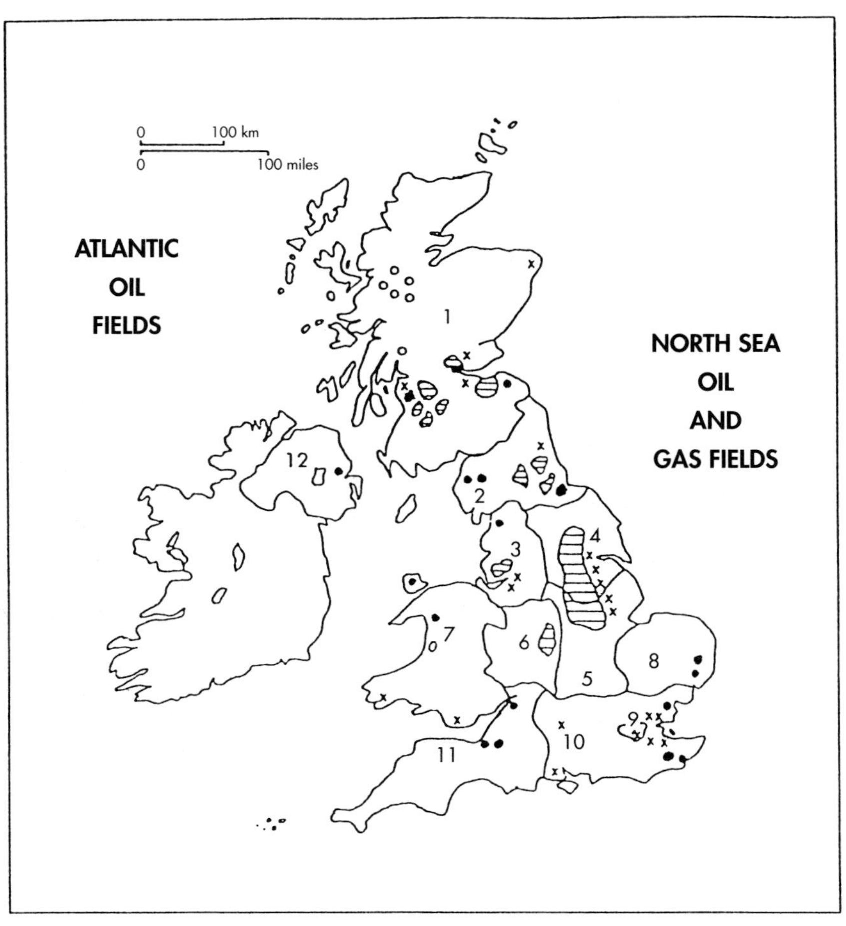

1 Scotland
2 North
3 North-west
4 Yorkshire and Humberside
5 East Midlands
6 West Midlands
7 Wales
8 East Anglia
9 Greater London
10 South-east
11 South-west
12 Northern Ireland

• Nuclear power stations
x Coal-, gas- or oil-fired power stations
Active coalfields
o Hydro-electric power stations

FIGURE 1.3 The British regions and energy sources

PLATE 1.3 Battersea Power Station (disused), London
(Bernard Gerard/The Hutchison Library)

energy are important for Britain's future energy needs, particularly as environmental concerns grow. But their functioning capacity will be limited, possibly to about 10 per cent of total electricity production.

Critics argue that insufficient work and research money is being devoted to potential alternative supplies; that too much reliance has been placed on nuclear power; that oil and gas have been wasted rather than extracted more slowly; and that not enough consideration has been given to the coal industry. British domestic and industrial energy users are extravagant when compared to other European countries. But energy consumption has shown a decline recently because of better building insulation and the relative success of government energy savings campaigns. However, the provision of cheap and environmentally suitable energy for both domestic and industrial use will be a problem for Britain in the future.

Transport and communications

Transport and communications are divided between the public and private sectors of the economy, although many state businesses have now been privatized. Roads, railways, shipping and civil aviation provide the country's transport system. British Telecom, competing telecommunications companies and the Post Office supply most communications needs.

Transport

Central and local government are responsible for the *road network* in Britain. Various types of public roads make up most of the highway system. The rest are motorways and trunk roads, which nevertheless carry most of the passenger traffic and heavy goods vehicles. Some roads are in bad condition and unable to handle the number of vehicles on them, leading to traffic congestion. Expansion, modernization and repair of roads are environmentally damaging and may also be inadequate to meet the estimated future number of vehicles. The Labour government has cancelled some controversial road building programmes in an attempt to cut the demand for road space and to persuade drivers to adopt alternative methods of transport.

There are 25 million licensed vehicles, of which 21 million are private cars; 2.2 million light goods vehicles; 421,000 heavier commercial lorries; 594,000 motor cycles, scooters and mopeds; and 74,000 buses, coaches and taxis. Car transport is most popular and accounts for 86 per cent of passenger mileage, while

PLATE 1.4 A London bus *(Jeremy Horner/The Hutchison Library)*

buses and coaches take 6 per cent. Britain has one of the highest densities of road traffic in the world, but also a relatively good safety record in which road accidents continue to decrease.

Private road haulage has a dominant position in the movement of inland freight. Lorries have become larger and account for 80 per cent of this market. Critics campaign to transfer road haulage to the railways and the publicly owned inland waterways (canals). But the waterways are used for only a small amount of freight transportation because of expense, although they are popular for recreational purposes. Rail freight, however, is increasing for bulk commodities.

Public passenger services have declined in Britain because of increased private car usage. Conservative governments deregulated bus operations and most local bus companies have now been privatized, although some services are still operated by local government authorities. There has been a considerable expansion in private long-distance express coach services, which have attracted increased numbers of passengers because they are cheaper than the railways.

The world's first public passenger steam *railway* opened in 1825 between Stockton and Darlington in north-east England. After 100 years of private operation, the railways became state-owned in 1947, only to be privatized in 1997. One company (Railtrack) owns the railway lines and stations; the actual trains are owned and operated by regional companies; and rail accounts for 5 per cent of passenger mileage.

Rail passenger services consist of a fast inter-city network, linking all the main British centres; local trains that supply regional needs; and commuter services in and around the large areas of population, particularly London and south-east England. Increased electrification of lines and the introduction of fast diesel trains such as the Intercity 125s travelling at a maximum speed of 125 mph (201 km/h), have improved rail journeys considerably. But such speeds and facilities are still inferior to those in other countries.

Many railway lines and trains are old and need replacing. Privatization appears to be coming to terms with some of the problems. But there is still much criticism by passengers, particularly in south-east England, about fare increases, overcrowding, delays, cancellations, staffing and poor services. Similar complaints are also made about the London Underground system (the Tube), which covers 254 miles (408 km) of railway line in the capital. Critics argue that the inadequate state of Britain's railways is due to a failure to realize that rail could be part of a modernized and integrated transport system (including roads and air facilities) catering for both passengers and freight. This would arguably ease road congestion, satisfy demand and improve the environment.

The *Channel Tunnel*, privately run by a French/British company (Eurotunnel), opened for commercial use in 1994. It was meant to improve passenger and freight rail travel between Britain and mainland Europe and has succeeded in taking business from sea/ferry services. The system has two main tunnels and a smaller service tunnel. It provides a drive-on, drive-off service (Le Shuttle) for cars, coaches and freight vehicles, as well as passenger trains (Eurostar). The two terminals, Folkstone and Coquelles, are 31 miles (50 km) apart. But a new high-speed rail connection between Folkestone and London will not be finished before 2003.

Although there are over 300 *ports* in Britain, most are small concerns that do not handle much cargo or passenger shipping. The bigger ports, such as Clyde, Dover, Tees, London, Southampton, Grimsby, Hull, Felixstowe, Liverpool, Cardiff and Swansea, service most of the country's trade and travel requirements. But there has been a big decline in work and labour since the great days of the ports in the past.

The British shipping fleet has been greatly reduced from its peak year in 1975, due to increased competition and a world shipping recession. The cargo market is now dominated by a small number of large private sector groups. But 77 per cent of Britain's overseas trade is still carried by sea, although passenger mileage has been much reduced. Both may decline further because of competition with the Channel Tunnel.

Britain's *civil aviation* system accounts for 1 per cent of passenger mileage and is in the private sector following the privatization of the former state airline, British Airways, in 1987. There are other carriers, such as British Midland, Britannia Airways and Virgin Atlantic, that run scheduled and charter passenger

PLATE 1.5 Waterloo International train terminal, London
(Jeremy Horner/The Hutchison Library)

services on domestic and international routes. All are controlled by the Civil Aviation Authority (CAA), an independent body that regulates the industry and air traffic control, and which may be privatized. The airlines also provide air cargo and freight services.

There are 142 licensed civil aerodromes in Britain, varying considerably in size. Heathrow and Gatwick Airports outside London are the largest. These airports, together with Stansted in south-east England and Glasgow, Edinburgh and Aberdeen in Scotland, are owned and managed by the private sector British Airports Authority (BAA). They deal with about 73 per cent of air passengers and 84 per cent of air cargo in Britain. Most of the other larger regional airports, such as Manchester (which threatens Gatwick's status as Britain's second largest airport), Birmingham, Luton, Belfast, Newcastle and East Midlands, are controlled by local authorities and cater for the country's remaining passenger and cargo needs.

Expansion of existing airports (particularly regional facilities) and the provision of new ones will be necessary if Britain is to cope with increased consumer demand and competition from Europe. But such projects are very expensive and controversial because of environmental problems, such as construction work, noise and traffic. Some disquiet also exists about plane congestion in the skies over Britain.

There is concern about the adequacy of British transport systems and the lack of an integrated public transport infrastructure of roads, railways and airports. But improvements involve considerable expense and Britain invests less in transport than any other European country. Government initiatives and investment are ideally needed to remedy the existing problems, not only domestically but also in terms of European trade and competition. But governments are reluctant to spend more public money, although the Labour government hopes to persuade the private sector to invest in the transport infrastructure in partnership with the state.

Communications

Communications systems in Britain are also divided between the public and private sectors. The main suppliers are the private British Telecom and the public Post Office.

British Telecom (BT) was privatized in 1984 and provides telephone and telecommunications systems domestically and internationally. It is responsible for 20 million domestic and 6 million business telephone subscribers, public payphones, telephone exchanges and telex connections. Following privatization, there was disquiet about BT's performance. But most of the initial problems have been solved and it is operating efficiently and profitably as one of the world's largest and most influential telecommunications systems. The private company, Mercury, competes fiercely with British Telecom, and other competitors, such as cable networks, have also been licensed to provide telecommunications facilities.

The *Post Office*, established in 1635, is a state industry and is responsible for collecting, handling and delivering some 70 million letters and parcels every day. It has sorting offices throughout the country with sophisticated handling equipment, based on the postcodes allotted to every address in Britain. Local post offices throughout the country provide postal and other services. The Post Office has a monopoly on the collection and delivery of letters. But the government can suspend this monopoly and allow competition. It is possible that the service may be privatized in some form, although there are fears that privatization would reduce rural facilities and increase costs. The Post Office is also facing substantial competition from e-mail, Internet and mobile phone users.

ATTITUDES

Attitudes to the environment

There is public concern about pollution, traffic congestion, the quality of the natural habitat, the use of energy sources and the safety of agricultural products.

A 1997 MORI poll found that 60 per cent of respondents felt that environmental problems were damaging their health (an increase from 53 per cent in 1992). A majority stated that protection of the environment should rate higher than economic growth; environmental problems should be tackled; and they were prepared to make sacrifices to see the environment cleaned up and wildlife conserved. But such views do not always lead to environmentally-sensitive behaviour.

Awareness of these issues coincided with the rise of the Green movement in the 1980s and the adoption of 'green' policies by all political parties. Governments have introduced

Environmental Protection Acts and other measures to safeguard the environment, reduce pollution levels and penalize polluters. European Union legislation also makes very stringent demands.

Critics argue, however, that government action is insufficient and often ineffective. Controls and protection are not strict enough; polluters can evade regulations or suffer only minor fines; insufficient pressure is put on companies to modernize their facilities; tension exists between local and central government in environmental matters; and there is a conflict between the cost of protection and the government's privatization policies (such as water, coal and electricity).

Some of the worst polluters are Britain's top companies, according to the government's Environmental Agency. Factories and power stations discharge pollutants into the air that can cause acid rain in Britain and abroad. Emissions from cars, buses and lorries seriously affect urban centres, despite the introduction of unleaded petrol and catalytic converters in new cars. However, of the 20 countries that promised to reduce carbon dioxide emissions by the year 2000 at an Earth Summit (1992), Britain is one of only three still on target. But this is due more to the decline of mining than active government policy, although the Labour government intends to cut emissions by a further 20 per cent by 2010.

Air pollution in Britain is a threat to people's health, particularly asthmatics and those suffering from respiratory problems. Traffic pollution was also linked for the first time to heart attacks in 1997 medical reports. Although pollution was reduced by Clean Air Acts in the 1950s and 1960s, air pollution reaches harmful levels in many areas of the country, particularly in summer when pollutants mix with sunshine and still, humid conditions to produce high ozone levels.

The situation will worsen as the deterioration in public transport encourages more people to use private vehicles. Britain's transport policy is overly dependent on the car and alternatives have been neglected. The car is now seen as the greatest transport problem and the Labour government intends to curb its unnecessary use, ration road space in favour of buses, increase taxes or charges on car usage in cities and give funding to local schemes that improve public transport.

Governments have not, however, provided an integrated public transport system (roads, rail and air) that would relieve environmental pressures. The problem arises because of the varied geography of Britain's cities, the devolution of control to local authorities and an increase in privatization schemes. It is thus difficult to implement one overall plan and the question is one of who will pay for the alternatives.

Increased freight and private transport has resulted in traffic congestion, noise and damage to roads and property. Pressures upon the road system will increase as competition among road users grows, car ownership increases and the European Union's internal market develops. The Channel Tunnel and its rail links have also attracted opposition from environmentalists, although landscaping and noise suppression have alleviated some damage. Fears have also been raised about safety in the Tunnel (outbreaks of fire in 1996 and 1997 forced the cancellation of services) and about the transmission of rabies.

A 1997 Autoglass/Audience Selection poll asked respondents about their preferred transport priorities. The results were: better public transport (52 per cent); cutting pollution (46); reducing congestion (33); getting freight off the roads (27); keeping cars out of towns (26); building new roads (11) and banning cars completely (5). On asked how to tackle congestion, the results were: better public transport (77 per cent); encouraging work from home (27); taxing lorries (24); taxing company cars (23); building more roads (20); encouraging telephone shopping (17) and road tolls (16).

There are other forms of environmental damage. Sea and beach pollution is partly caused by untreated sewage and toxic industrial waste being pumped by commercial companies into the sea, particularly the North Sea. Britain is committed to reducing discharge levels but, although 90 per cent of beaches met European quality standards in 1996, pollution levels on 51 beaches in 1997 still exceeded safety levels. Some rivers are polluted by industrial waste, toxic fertilizers, pesticides and farm silage. This has caused public concern about the safety of drinking water and the privatized water companies have been pressurized to raise the quality of their services. Many polluted rivers, lakes and estuaries have now been cleaned up and more stringent controls of the oil and shipping industries in the North Sea have reduced pollution levels.

Problems have been experienced with the exploitation of energy resources, for example expense, capacity and availability, and there are environmental concerns about the burning of fossil fuels (coal, oil and gas), global warming and the damage to the countryside caused by new developments. Nuclear expansion was halted briefly because of public opposition to nuclear facilities, the danger of radioactive leaks, the reprocessing of nuclear waste at the Thorp and Sellafield plants in north-west England and the dumping of radioactive waste. There is still much debate about the future of nuclear power.

Considerable public worry surrounds the agricultural industry because of its widespread use of fertilizers and pesticides, its methods of animal feeding and the effects of intensive farming on the environment. Much hedgerow, which is important for many forms of animal and vegetable life, has been lost in recent years as fields have become bigger and farming more mechanized. The quality and standards of food products, particularly those concerned with intensive farming techniques, are of concern. Cases of food poisoning have risen sharply in the past decade and there are worries about standards of hygiene in the food and farming businesses. The BSE scare seriously affected the consumption of beef and other meats and led to a drop in

PLATE 1.6 Sellafield nuclear reprocessing plant, Windscale
(P. Wolmuth/The Hutchison Library)

demand for traditional foods. Yet the success of organic farming in Britain has been small, largely because of the cost of such goods and the lack of adequate government subsidies.

Environmentalists are also concerned about protection of the countryside. Agricultural land is used for building and recreational purposes; there has been an increase in urban and suburban sprawl as house building encroaches into rural areas; new towns are proposed to cater for an estimated need of 4.4 million new homes; and giant supermarkets or shopping centres are increasingly located in the countryside. The amount of agricultural, forestry and other greenfield

ATTITUDES

land lost to building developments rose considerably between 1984 and 1990. A Research Survey of Great Britain (1997) found that 80 per cent of people were worried about the future of the countryside and 69 per cent wanted to stop housing and road schemes that damaged the environment.

EXERCISES

- **Explain and examine the following terms:**

Britain	Heathrow	Intercity 125	Post Office
weathering	Highland Britain	Lough Neagh	Ben Nevis
arable	Channel Islands	horticulture	BT
CAP	earth movements	the Tube	drought
Eire	British Telecom	postcodes	Greenwich
BSE	global warming	CFP	tidal

- **Write short essays on the following topics:**

1 Does Britain have an energy crisis? If so, why?

2 Examine the impact of Britain's membership of the European Union upon its agricultural and fisheries industries.

3 What are the reasons for environmental concerns in Britain?

Chapter 2

The people

THE BRITISH ISLES have attracted settlers and immigrants throughout most of their history. The contemporary British are consequently composed of people from worldwide origins. They are mainly divided into the English, Scots, Welsh and Irish, who themselves have mixed roots derived from early settlement and invasion patterns. There are also immigrant minorities with their own cultures who have come to Britain over the centuries. Even the English language, which binds most of these people together linguistically, is a blend of Germanic, Romance and other world languages. This historical development has created a contemporary society with multinational and multiracial characteristics. But it also raises questions about the meaning of 'Britishness' and national identity.

Early settlement to AD 1066

There is no accurate picture of what the early settlement of Britain was actually like. Historians and archaeologists are constantly revising traditional theories about the gradual growth of the country as new evidence comes to light.

The earliest human bones found (1994) in Britain are 500,000 years old. The first people were Palaeolithic (Old Stone Age) nomads from mainland Europe, who were characterized by their use of rudimentary stone implements. They travelled to Britain by land and sea, especially at those times when the country was joined to the European land mass.

Later settlers in the Mesolithic and Neolithic (New Stone Age) periods between 8300 and 2000 BC had more advanced skills in stone carving. Some came from north-central Europe and settled in eastern Britain. Others arrived by sea from Iberian (Spanish-Portuguese) areas and populated south-west England, Ireland,

Wales, the Isle of Man and western Scotland. Arguably these are the oldest large sections of British society, whose descendants live today in the same western parts. Neolithic groups built large wood and stone monuments, like Stonehenge, and later arrivals introduced a Bronze Age culture.

Between 800 and 200 BC there was a movement of Celtic peoples into Britain from mainland Europe, who brought an Iron Age civilization with them. This Celtic population was then overcome by Belgic tribes (also of Celtic origin) around 200 BC, when the first major armed invasions of Britain took place. The Belgic tribes (or Britons) were in their turn subjected to a series of Roman expeditions from 55 BC.

The Roman military occupation of much of Britain lasted from AD 43 until AD 409. After Roman withdrawal, Angles and Saxons from north-central Europe invaded the country. They either mixed with the existing population or pushed it westwards. The country was divided into mainly Anglo-Saxon zones in England, with Celtic areas in Wales, Scotland and Ireland. All regions suffered from Scandinavian military invasions in the eighth and ninth centuries AD.

This early history was completed when the Anglo-Saxons were defeated by French-Norman invaders at the Battle of Hastings in AD 1066 and England was subjected to their rule. The Norman Conquest was an important watershed in English history that greatly influenced the English people and their language, marked the last successful external military invasion of the country and initiated many of the social and institutional frameworks, like a feudal system, that were to characterize future British society. However, Celtic civilizations continued in Wales, Scotland and Ireland.

People have entered the British Isles from the south-west, the east and the north. But settlement was often hindered by climatic and geographical obstacles, particularly in the north and west, so that many newcomers tended to concentrate initially in southern England and settlement patterns were not uniform over all of Britain at the same time. Despite some intermixture between the various settlers, there were racial differences between the

English and the people of Ireland, Wales and Scotland, as well as varying identities between groups in the English regions. It is this mixture, increased by later immigration, that has produced the present ethnic and national diversity in Britain.

The early settlement and invasion movements substantially affected the developing fabric of British life and formed the first foundations of the modern state. The newcomers often imposed their cultures on the existing society, as well as adopting some of the native characteristics. Today, there are few British towns that lack any physical evidence of the successive changes. The newcomers also profoundly influenced social, legal, economic, political, agricultural and administrative institutions and contributed to the evolving language.

TABLE 2.1 Early settlement to AD 1066

500,000–8300 BC	Palaeolithic (Old Stone Age)
8300 BC	Mesolithic
4000 BC	Neolithic (New Stone Age)
2000 BC	Beaker Folk (Bronze Age)
800 BC	Celts (Iron Age)
200 BC	Belgic tribes
AD 43	The Romans
AD 410	The Anglo-Saxons
8th and 9th centuries	The Scandinavians
AD 1066	The Norman Conquest

There are no realistic population figures for early Britain, but archaeological evidence suggests that the nomadic lifestyle of groups of up to 20 people gradually ceased and was replaced by more permanent settlements of up to a few hundred inhabitants. It is estimated that the English population during the Roman occupation was about 1 million. By the Norman period, the eleventh-century Domesday Book showed an increase to 2 million. The Domesday Book was the first systematic attempt to evaluate England's wealth and population, mainly for taxation purposes.

Growth and immigration to the twentieth century

Britain grew gradually to statehood after 1066, largely through the political unification of England, Wales, Ireland and Scotland under the English Crown. This process was accompanied by fierce and bloody conflicts between the four nations that resulted in lasting tensions and bitterness.

Immigration from abroad also continued over the centuries, due to factors such as religious and political persecution, trade, business and employment. Immigrants have had a significant impact on British society. They have contributed to financial institutions, commerce, industry and agriculture, and influenced artistic, cultural and political developments. But immigrant activity and success have resulted in jealousy, discrimination and violence from the native population.

Britain's growth was conditioned by two major events: first, a series of agricultural changes, and second, a number of later industrial revolutions. Agricultural expansion started with the Saxons who cleared the forests, cultivated crops and introduced inventions and equipment that remained in use for centuries. Their open-field system of farming (with strips of land being worked haphazardly by local people) was later added to by widespread sheep herding and wool production. Finally, after 1760 the open fields were enclosed (divided up into hedged fields for cultivation by individual farmers).

Britain expanded as an agricultural and commercial nation from the eleventh century, and also developed manufacturing industries. Immigration was often characterized by financial and agricultural skills. Jewish money lenders entered Britain with the Norman Conquest, and their financial talents later passed to Lombard bankers from northern Italy. The Lombard connection is today commemorated in Lombard Street in the City of London. This commercial expertise helped to create greater wealth, and Britain's trade was influenced by the merchants of the mainly German Hansa League, who set up their trading posts in London and on the east coast of England. Around 1330, Dutch and Flemish weavers arrived. By the end of the fifteenth century, they helped to transform England into a major nation of sheep farmers, cloth producers and textile exporters. Immigration in the fourteenth century also introduced specialized knowledge in a variety of manufacturing trades.

Some immigrants stayed only for short periods. Others remained and adapted themselves to British society, while preserving their own cultural and ethnic identities. Newcomers were often encouraged to settle in Britain, and the policy of using immigrant expertise continued in later centuries. But foreign workers had no legal rights, and early immigrants, such as Jews and the Hansa merchants, could be summarily expelled.

Agricultural and commercial developments were reflected in changing population concentrations. From Saxon times to around 1800, Britain had an agriculturally based economy and some 80 per cent of the people lived in villages in the countryside. Settlement was mainly concentrated in the south and east of England, where the rich agricultural regions of East Anglia and Lincolnshire had the greatest population densities. During the fourteenth century, however, the steady increase of people was halted by a series of plagues, and numbers did not start to increase again for another 100 years.

As agricultural production moved into sheep farming and its associated clothing manufactures, larger numbers of people settled around woollen ports, such as Bristol on the west coast and coastal towns in East Anglia. Others moved to inland cloth producing areas in the West Country, the Cotswolds and East Anglia and contributed to the growth of market towns. The south midland and eastern English counties had the greatest densities of people, and the population at the end of the seventeenth century is estimated at 5.5 million for England and Wales and 1 million for Scotland.

Meanwhile, political and military attempts had long been made by England to unite Wales, Scotland and Ireland under the English Crown. English monarchs tried to conquer or ally themselves with these other countries as a protection against threats from within the British Isles and from continental Europe, as well as for increased power and possessions.

Ireland was attacked in the twelfth century. The later colonization and control of Ireland by the English became a source of hatred between the two countries, but it also led to Irish settlements in London and west-coast ports such as Liverpool. Ireland became part of the United Kingdom in 1801, but, after unrest and political agitation, was divided in 1921 into the two political units of the independent Republic of Ireland and Northern Ireland (which remains part of the UK).

Wales lost its independence in 1285 after years of bloody conflict with the English, and, apart from a period of freedom in 1402–7, was eventually integrated with England by a series of Acts of Union between 1536 and 1542.

The English also tried to conquer Scotland by military force, but were repulsed at the Battle of Bannockburn in 1314. Scotland was then to remain independent until the political union between the two countries in 1707, when the creation of Great Britain (England/Wales and Scotland) took place. However, Scotland and England had shared a common monarch since 1603 when James V of Scotland became James I of England.

England, Wales and Scotland had meanwhile become predominantly Protestant in religion as a result of the European Reformation. Ireland, however, remained Catholic and tried to distance itself from England, thus adding religion to colonialism as a foundation for future problems.

Britain therefore is not a single, culturally homogeneous country, but rather a recent and potentially unstable union of four old nations. The political entity called Great Britain is only slightly older than the United States of America, and the United Kingdom (1801) is younger. Nor did the political unions appreciably alter the relationships between the four nations. The English often treated their Celtic neighbours as colonial subjects rather than equal partners, and Englishness became a dominant strand in concepts of Britishness, because of the role that the English have played in the formation of Britain.

However, despite the tensions and bitterness between the four nations, there was a steady internal migration between them. This mainly involved movements of Irish, Welsh and Scottish people into England. Relatively few English emigrated to Wales and Scotland, although there was English and Scottish settlement in Ireland over the centuries.

Other newcomers continued to arrive from overseas, including gypsies, blacks (associated with the slave trade) and a further wave of Jews, who in 1655 created the first permanent Jewish community. In the sixteenth and seventeenth centuries, the country attracted a large number of refugees, such as Dutch Protestants and French Huguenots, who were driven from Europe by warfare, political and religious persecution and employment needs. This talented and urbanized immigration contributed considerably to the national economy, and added a new dimension to a largely agricultural population. But, from around 1700, there was to be no more large immigration into the country for the next 200 years. Britain was exporting more people than it received, mainly to North America and the expanding colonies worldwide.

A second central development in British history was a number of industrial revolutions in the eighteenth and nineteenth centuries. These transformed Britain from an agricultural economy into an industrial and manufacturing country. Processes based on steam power and the use of coal for generating steam were discovered and exploited. Factories and factory towns were needed to mass-produce new manufactured goods. Villages in the coalfields and industrial areas grew rapidly into manufacturing centres. A drift of population away from the countryside began in the late eighteenth century, as people sought work in mines and factories to escape from rural poverty and unemployment. They moved, for example, to textile mills in Lancashire and Yorkshire and to heavy industries and pottery factories in the West Midlands.

The earlier agricultural population changed radically in the nineteenth century into an industrialized workforce. The 1801 census, which is the first reliable modern measurement of population, gave figures of 9 million for England and Wales and 1.5 million for Scotland. But, between 1801 and 1901, the population of England and Wales trebled to 30 million. The numbers in Scotland increased less rapidly, due to emigration, but in Ireland the population was reduced from 8 to 6 million because of famine, deaths and emigration. The greatest concentrations of people were now in London and in the industrial areas of the Midlands, south Lancashire, Merseyside, Clydeside, Tyneside, Yorkshire and South Wales.

The industrial revolution reached its height during the early nineteenth century. It did not require foreign labour because there were enough skilled British workers and a ready supply of unskilled labourers from Wales, Scotland, Ireland and the English countryside. Welsh people from North Wales went to the Lancashire textile mills; Highland Scots travelled to the Lowland Clydeside industries; and Irishmen flocked to England and Scotland to work in the manual trades of the industrial infrastructure constructing roads, railways and canals.

Industrialization expanded commercial markets. These attracted new immigrants who had the business and financial skills to exploit the industrial wealth. Some newcomers joined City of London financial institutions and the import/export trades, to which they contributed their international connections. Other settlers were involved in a wide range of occupations and trades. Immigration to Britain might have been greater in the nineteenth century had it not been for the attraction of North America, which was receiving large numbers of newcomers from all over the world, including Britain.

By the end of the nineteenth century, Britain was the world's leading industrial nation and one of the richest. But it gradually lost its world lead in manufacturing industry, most of which was in native British hands. However, its position in international finance, some of which was under immigrant control, was retained into the twentieth century.

Immigration in the twentieth century

Immigrants historically had relatively free access to Britain, but they could be easily expelled, had no legal rights to protect them and had restrictions increasingly imposed upon them. The 1871 census showed that the number of people in Britain born outside the British Empire was only 157,000 out of a population of some 31.5 million.

Despite these low figures, immigration became a topic of public and political concern, which continued through the twentieth century. In the early years of the century, Jews and Poles escaped persecution in Eastern Europe and settled in the East End of London, which has been a traditional area of immigrant concentration. Public demands for immigration control grew, and an anti-foreigner feeling spread, increased by the nationalism and spy mania caused by the First World War (1914–18). But laws (like the Aliens Act of 1905) that were designed to curtail foreign entry proved ineffective. By 1911, the number of people in Britain born outside the empire was 428,000, or 1 per cent of the population.

Despite legal controls, and partly as a result of the 1930s world recession and the Second World War, refugees from Nazi-occupied Europe and other immigrants entered Britain. After the war, Poles, Latvians, Ukrainians and other nationalities chose to stay in Britain. Later in the twentieth century, political and economic refugees arrived, such as Hungarians, Czechs, Chileans, Libyans, East African Asians, Iranians and Vietnamese, in addition to other immigrants. Many of these groups today form sizeable communities and are scattered throughout the country. Such newcomers have often suffered from discrimination, some more than others, since racism is not a new phenomenon in Britain.

Public and political concern later turned to the issues of race and colour, which were to dominate the immigration debate. The focus of attention became non-white Commonwealth immigration. Before the Second World War, most Commonwealth immigrants to Britain came from the largely white Old Commonwealth countries of Canada, Australia and New Zealand, and from South Africa. All Commonwealth citizens were allowed free access and were not treated as aliens.

From the late 1940s, however, people from the non-white New Commonwealth nations of India, Pakistan and the West

Indies came to Britain (sometimes at the invitation of government agencies) to fill the vacant manual and lower-paid jobs of an expanding economy. West Indians worked in public transport, catering, the Health Service and manual trades in London, Birmingham and other large cities. Indians and Pakistanis later arrived to work in the textile and iron industries of Leeds, Bradford and Leicester. By the 1970s, non-white people became a familiar sight in other British cities too such as Glasgow, Sheffield, Bristol, Huddersfield, Manchester, Liverpool, Coventry and Nottingham. There was a considerable dispersal of such immigrants throughout Britain, although many did tend to settle in the central areas of industrial cities.

These non-white communities have now increased and are involved in a broad range of occupations. Some, particularly Asians and black Africans, have been relatively successful in economic and professional terms. Others have experienced considerable problems such as low-paid jobs, unemployment, educational disadvantage, decaying housing in the inner cities and racial discrimination. Some critics argue that Britain possesses a deep-rooted racism based on the legacy of empire and notions of racial superiority, which continues to manifest itself and has limited the integration of the non-white population into the larger society. Many young non-whites who have been born in Britain feel particularly bitter at their experiences and at their relative lack of educational and employment possibilities and advancement.

So many New Commonwealth immigrants were coming to Britain that, from 1962, governments followed a two-strand policy on immigration. This consisted, first, of Immigration Acts to restrict the number of immigrants entering the country and, second, of Race Relations Acts to protect the rights of those immigrants who are already settled in Britain. Eventually, most Commonwealth citizens were treated as aliens.

Race Relations Acts make it unlawful to discriminate against persons on grounds of racial, ethnic or national origin in areas like education, housing, employment, services and advertising. Those who suffer alleged discrimination can appeal to special Race

Relations Tribunals. Official bodies to deal with racial discrimination have also been established, culminating with the Commission for Racial Equality in 1976. This body, which has been relatively successful, supports Community Relations Councils that have been set up in areas of ethnic concentration. It works for the elimination of discrimination and the promotion of equality of opportunity.

There is still criticism of the immigration laws and race-relations organizations. Some people argue that one cannot legislate satisfactorily against discrimination, and others would have liked stricter controls. The concerns of the white population are made worse by racialist speeches, the growth of extreme nationalist parties, such as the National Front and the British National Party, and alleged racially inspired violence in some cities. Non-white citizens, on the other hand, often feel that they too easily and unfairly become scapegoats for any problems that arise. Some become alienated from British society and reject institutions such as the police, the legal system and the political structures. Government policies since the 1940s have not always helped to lessen either white or non-white anxieties.

Immigration and race remain problematic. They are complex matters and are frequently exploited for political purposes, by both the right and the left. It is easy to exaggerate the issues and to over-dramatize them. Many non-white immigrants and their British-born children have slowly adapted to the larger society, whilst still retaining their cultural identities. Britain does have a relatively stable diversity of cultures, but outbreaks of racial tension, violence and harassment do occur, and there are accusations that the police and the courts ignore or underplay race crimes.

The number of people in Britain in 1967–8 of non-white origin or descent was estimated at 1,087,000 or 2.2 per cent of the population. The 1991 census classified 94.5 per cent of the population as white, whilst 5.5 per cent (3 million people) described themselves as belonging to non-white groups and 46 per cent were born in Britain. Indians are the largest non-white group, followed by West Indians (Afro-Caribbeans), Pakistanis, black Africans, Bangladeshis and Chinese.

The non-white population was earlier largely composed of immigrant families, single people or the head of a family. But this structure has changed as more dependants join settled immigrants and as British-born non-whites develop their own family organizations. The term 'immigrant' has now lost much of its earlier significance and the emphasis has switched to debates about what constitutes a 'multicultural society'.

Apart from a few categories of people who have a right of abode in Britain and who are not subject to immigration control, virtually all others require either entry clearance or permission to enter and remain. Generally speaking, such newcomers (apart from short-term visitors) need a work permit and the promise of a guaranteed job if they hope to stay in the country for longer periods of time. But dependants of immigrants already settled in Britain may be granted the right of entry and permanent settlement.

Immigration into Britain from Ireland continues. The Irish have historically been the largest immigrant group, and there are some 800,000 people of Irish descent. Movement from the Old Commonwealth countries has declined, while that of other Commonwealth citizens has dropped following entry restrictions. There has been an increase in immigrants from European Union and European Economic Area countries, who have the right to seek work and reside in Britain, with sizeable immigration from the USA and the Middle East.

Official figures show that 55,000 people were accepted for permanent settlement in 1995; 20 per cent were from New Commonwealth countries; and many were dependants joining settled immigrants. Such statistics reveal that a significant immigration into Britain continues, despite restrictive legislation, though governments have tightened the rules for the admission of asylum seekers, following suspicions that many were not genuinely in humanitarian need. Opinion polls suggest that race relations, immigrants and immigration are of less concern for British people now than they were from the 1960s to the 1980s. A MORI poll in 1995 found that 78 per cent of respondents said that they were not at all prejudiced against people of other races.

However, acceptance for settlement does not mean automatic citizenship. Naturalization occurs only when certain requirements have been fulfilled, together with a period of residence. New conditions for naturalization and redefinitions of British citizenship are contained in the Nationality Act of 1981. This Act has been criticized by some who have seen it as providing further restrictions on immigration procedures.

It is important that emigration from Britain should also be considered if the immigration and race debate is to be kept in perspective. Historically, there has usually been a balance of migration, which means that emigration has cancelled out immigration in real terms. But there have been periods of high emigration. Groups left England and Scotland in the sixteenth and seventeenth centuries to become settlers and colonists in Ireland and North America. Millions in the nineteenth and twentieth centuries emigrated to New Zealand, Australia, South Africa, Canada, other colonies and the USA. But in 1994, there was a net gain to the population as more people entered the country than left.

Population movements in the twentieth century

Industrial areas with heavy population densities were created in the nineteenth century. But considerable population shifts have occurred in the twentieth century that have been mainly due to economic and employment changes.

There was a drift of people away from industrial Tyneside and South Wales during the 1920s and 1930s trade depressions, as coal production, steel manufacture and other heavy industries were badly affected. Since the 1950s, there has been little increase in population in industrial areas of the Central Lowlands of Scotland, Tyneside, Merseyside, West Yorkshire and South Wales, which have seen a rundown in traditional industries and substantial rises in unemployment.

Instead, people moved away from these regions, first to the English Midlands, with their more diversified industries, and then to London and south-east England, where employment opportunities and affluence were greater. But the English Midlands have also suffered economically in recent years, and southern England experienced increased unemployment in the 1988–93 economic recession.

The reduction of the rural population and the expansion of urban centres continued into the twentieth century. But, by the middle of the century, there was a movement of people away from the centres of big cities such as London, Manchester, Liverpool, Birmingham and Leeds. This was due to bomb damage during the Second World War, slum clearance and the need to use inner-city land for shops, offices, warehouses and transport utilities. New Towns in rural areas and council housing estates outside the inner-cities were specifically created to accommodate the displanted population. Road systems were built with motorways and bypasses to avoid congested areas, and rural locations around some cities were designated as Green Belts, in which no building was permitted.

Many people choose to live some distance from their workplaces, often in a city's suburbs, neighbouring towns (commuter towns) or rural areas. This has contributed to the decline of the inner-city populations, and one in five British people now live in the countryside with the rest in towns and cities. Densities are highest in Greater London and in south-east England and lowest in rural regions of northern Scotland, the Lake District, Wales and Northern Ireland. The latest figures suggest an increasing movement of people to rural areas, particularly by retired people. This has been accompanied by population losses in and company relocations from large cities, particularly London.

In 1995, the population of the United Kingdom was 58,395,000, which consisted of England with 48,708,000, Wales with 2,913,000, Scotland with 5,132,000 and Northern Ireland with 1,642,000. These figures give a population density for the United Kingdom of some 600 persons per square mile (242 per sq. km), which is well above the European Union average. England has an average density of some 930 persons per square mile (373 per sq. km), and this average does not reveal the even higher

PLATE 2.1 A female crowd *(Joanne O'Brien/Format)*

densities in some areas of the country, such as parts of the south-east. Within Europe, only The Netherlands has a higher population density than England.

The British population grew by only 0.3 per cent between 1971 and 1978, which gave it one of the lowest increases in Western Europe. A similarly low growth rate is forecast into the twenty-first century, with the population expected to be some 59.4 million in the year 2011. It is also estimated that the counties of southern and central England will have the highest population

TABLE 2.2 Populations of major British cities, 1994

Greater London	6,900,000	Liverpool	471,000
Birmingham	1,009,000	Edinburgh	444,000
Leeds	725,000	Manchester	431,000
Glasgow	623,000	Bristol	399,000
Sheffield	530,000	Cardiff	300,000
Bradford	480,000	Belfast	289,000

growth and that the heaviest population losses will occur on Tyneside and Merseyside.

ATTITUDES

Attitudes to Britishness and national identity

Immigrants have historically been seen by some people as a threat to British moral, social and cultural values, whose presence would radically change the society. This view ignores the difficulty of defining what is meant by such norms at specific times in history. The British Isles have always been culturally and ethnically diverse. There are many differences between the four nations of England, Wales, Scotland and Ireland, and distinctive ways of life within each country. This situation, and the presence of immigrant communities, raise questions about the meaning of contemporary 'Britishness'.

The history of the British Isles before the eighteenth century is not about a single British identity or political entity. It is about four different nations and their peoples, who have often been hostile towards one another. 'Britishness' since the 1707 union between England/Wales and Scotland has been largely identified with centralized state institutions, such as monarchy, Parliament and church. It was only in the nineteenth century that concepts of Britishness were increasingly used, and these were tied to the Victorian monarchy and Britain's imperial position in the world.

Political terms like 'British' and 'Britain' can thus seem artificial to many of the peoples who comprise the present United Kingdom population and who have retained their individual cultural and national identities. Foreigners often call all British people 'English' and sometimes have difficulties in appreciating the distinctions, or the annoyance of the non-English population at such labelling. The Scots, Welsh and Northern Irish are largely Celtic peoples, while the English are mainly Anglo-Saxon in origin.

It is often argued that the contemporary 'British' do not have a strong sense of a 'British' identity. In this view, there needs to be a rethink of what it means to be British in the contexts of a multinational, multiracial UK and a changing Europe. But some critics suggest that the emphasis should be not so much on examinations of multiculturalism and separate ethnic identities as on a crosscultural perspective, with influences flowing between different parts of the society.

There has obviously been racial and cultural intermixture in Britain over the centuries, which resulted from adaptation by immigrant groups and internal migration between the four nations. Social, political and institutional standardization and a British awareness have been established. However, the British identification is often equated with English norms because political unification occurred under the English Crown, state power is concentrated in London, the English dominate numerically, and because of England's historical role.

English nationalism is arguably the most potent of the four nationalisms, and the English have had no real problem with the dual national role. The Scots and Welsh have always been more aware of the difference between their nationalism and Britishness; resent the English dominance; see themselves as very different to the English; and regard their nationalist and cultural feelings as crucial. Their sense of identity is conditioned by the tension between their own distinctive histories and centralized government from London.

National identifications have, until recently, been largely cultural, and the British political union was generally accepted in the four nations, except by some people in the minority Catholic population of Northern Ireland. However, political nationalism increased in the 1960s and 1970s in Scotland and Wales. Today it seems that calls for independence in these two nations are not strong, except from the Scottish National Party (SNP) and the Welsh National Party (Plaid Cymru). But the devolution of greater powers of self-government to Scotland and Wales may fuel a movement towards full independence in the two countries, and this goal is held by some 30 per cent of Scottish people.

Some commentators argue that Scottish and Welsh devolution may spark a resurgence in English nationalism, and arguably this is already occurring among English teenagers. A *Sunday Times* poll in 1997 found that 66 per cent regarded themselves as English rather than British; 72 per cent regarded their English nationality as important; 71 per cent were opposed to regional government in England; and 59 per cent thought that Britain would be divided into separate nations (England, Scotland and Wales) within 20 years. They thought that the following defined their sense of Englishness: the national football team (36 per cent); the national anthem (30); television soap operas such as *Eastenders* and *Coronation Street* (17); the royal family (14); Britpop (2); and the Houses of Parliament (1). National identification among the young is therefore no longer tied to traditional institutional features.

There are also differences to be found within the four nations. The English react against London influences, and there are some demands for decentralized political autonomy. Since the English are a relatively mixed people, their customs, accents and behaviour vary considerably, and local identification is still strong. The Cornish, for example, see themselves as a distinctive cultural element in English society and have an affinity with Celtic and similar racial groups in Britain and Europe. The northern English have often regarded themselves as superior to the southern English, and vice versa. English county, regional and local community loyalties are still maintained and may be demonstrated in sports, politics, competitions, cultural activities or a specific way of life.

In Wales, there are cultural and political differences between the industrial south (which supports the Labour

Party) and the rest of the mainly rural country; between Welsh-speaking Wales in the west and centre (which supports Plaid Cymru) and English-influenced Wales in the east and south-west (where the Conservative Party has some support, despite losing all its Welsh seats in the 1997 general election).

Yet Welsh people generally are very conscious of their differences from the English. Their national and cultural identity is grounded in their history, literature, the Welsh language (actively spoken by 19 per cent of the population), sport (such as rugby football), and festivals like the National Eisteddfod (with its Welsh poetry competitions, dancing and music). It is also echoed in close-knit industrial and agricultural communities and in a tradition of social, political and religious dissent from English norms. Today, many Welsh people feel that they are struggling for their national identity against political power in London and the erosion of their culture and language by English institutions.

Similarly, the Scots generally unite in defence of their national identity and distinctiveness because of historical reactions to the English. They are conscious of their traditions, which are reflected in cultural festivals and different legal, religious and educational systems. There is resentment against the centralization of political power in London and the alleged economic neglect of Scotland (although the British government provides greater economic subsidies per head of population to Scotland and Wales than to England).

Scots are, however, divided by three languages (Gaelic, Scots and English, with the former being spoken by 1.5 per cent of the Scottish population or 70,000 people), different religions, prejudices and regionalisms. Cultural differences separate Lowlanders and Highlanders, and deep rivalries exist between the two major cities of Edinburgh and Glasgow.

In Northern Ireland, the social, cultural and political differences between Roman Catholics and Protestants have long been evident and today are often reflected in geographical ghettos. Sizeable groups in both communities feel

PLATE 2.2 A Scottish fling *(The Hutchison Library)*

frustration with the English and hostility towards the British government in London, but the Protestant Unionists regard themselves as British and wish to continue the union with Britain, whilst many Catholic Nationalists feel Irish and would prefer to be united with the Republic of Ireland. On both sides there is a general interest in the distinctive Northern Irish local culture.

These features suggest that the contemporary British are a very diverse people, particularly when original settlement has been added to by centuries of later immigration. It is consequently as difficult, if not impossible, to find a typical English, Welsh, Scottish or Irish person who conforms to all or even some of the assumed national stereotypes, as it is to find a typical Briton.

Foreigners often have either specific notions of what they think the British are like or, in desperation, seek a unified picture of national character, based sometimes upon quaint traditions or theme-park and tourist views of Britain. The emphasis in this search should perhaps be more upon an examination of diversity in British life.

Sometimes, however, the four nations do employ national stereotypes. The English might like to see themselves as calm, reasonable, patient and commonsensical people, who should be distinguished from the excitable, romantic and impulsive Celts. The Celts, on the other hand, may consider the English to be arrogant, patronizing and cold, and themselves as having all the virtues. The English, and sometimes the British as a whole, are often thought of as restrained, reserved, unemotional, private and independent individuals, with a respect for the amateur and the eccentric. Underlying all, there is supposed to be a dry sense of humour that specializes in understatement, irony, self-deprecation and an enjoyment in using the language in very flexible ways. Such qualities may be offset by a certain aggressiveness, stubbornness and lack of cooperation. The British have often been characterized as tolerant and somewhat lazy, with a happy-go-lucky attitude to life. These

PLATE 2.3 Pearly people *(Timothy Beddow/The Hutchison Library)*

ATTITUDES

stereotypes may have some limited value, but cannot be taken to represent the whole truth about the four nations, Britain, or individuals.

EXERCISES

- **Explain and examine the following terms:**

nomads	bypass	Anglo-Saxon	industrialization
Neolithic	East End	Hansa	National Front
density	Celtic	devolution	Hastings
Merseyside	Domesday Book	immigrant	naturalization
racism	Britishness	Iberian	discrimination
census	emigration	Huguenots	Green Belt

- **Write short essays on the following topics:**

1 Describe in outline the history of settlement and immigration in Britain.

2 Examine the changing patterns of population distribution in Britain.

3 Is it correct to describe contemporary Britain as a 'multiracial' and 'multinational' society? If so, why?

Chapter 3

Political institutions

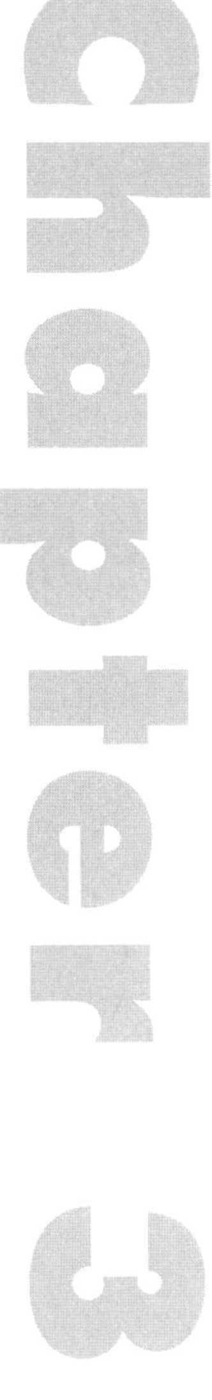

THE POLITICAL HISTORY OF THE BRITISH ISLES (particularly that of England) over the past 800 years has been largely one of reducing the power of the monarchy and transferring authority to a London-based Parliament as the sovereign legislative body for all of Britain. It has also involved the growth of political parties and campaigns for the extension of the vote to all adults. These developments have resulted in political, social and religious conflicts, as well as evolving governmental and constitutional institutions. The original structures were monarchical, aristocratic and non-democratic, but they have been slowly adapted to changing social conditions, parliamentary democracy and a mass franchise.

The roles of the political structures are still vigorously debated in contemporary Britain. Governments (based on Whitehall in London) are accused of being too secretive, too centralized, too party-political and insufficiently responsive to the needs and interests of the diverse peoples of the United Kingdom. It is also argued that Parliament has lost its controlling influence over the government and that political power has increasingly shifted to the Prime Minister and unelected executive agencies. Critics maintain that the political system at central, regional and local levels must be fundamentally reformed in order to make it more efficient, accountable and adaptable to modern needs.

In an attempt to devolve (decentralize) political power, the Labour government intends to create in 1999–2000 (after referendums in 1997) an elected Parliament with legislative and tax varying powers in Scotland and a non-legislative, non-tax raising elected Assembly in Wales. Devolution will allow the two countries to decide more of their own affairs, except for national matters such as defence, foreign policy, social security and economic policy.

This does not mean independence for Scotland and Wales (desired by the Scottish and Welsh National Parties) or a federal or regional system (advocated by Liberal Democrats). The Labour government insists that sovereignty will continue to be centralized in the London Parliament at Westminster. In this sense, Britain will still have a unitary political system rather than a federal one, and will remain a union of the United Kingdom (England, Scotland, Wales and Northern Ireland).

It is feared by some that devolution may lead to independence for Scotland and Wales and regionalism or decentralization (semi-federalism) throughout Britain. A National Opinion Poll in 1997 found that 43 per cent of those interviewed believed that devolution will lead to the eventual breakup of the United Kingdom, and only 23 per cent accept the government position that it will strengthen the union.

English political history

The early political history of the British Isles is the story of four independent nations (England, Wales, Scotland and Ireland) but a dominant English political and military expansionism over the centuries resulted in a united country. English systems were adopted in many areas of society after the seizing of Ireland in the twelfth century, the 1536–42 Acts of Union uniting England and Wales, the 1707 Act of Union between England/Wales and Scotland and the 1801 Act of Union joining Great Britain and Ireland as the United Kingdom.

Decline of monarchy and the rise of Parliament

Early English monarchs had considerable power, but generally accepted advice and some limitations on their authority. However, later kings, such as King John (1199–1216), often ignored these restrictions, and powerful French-Norman barons opposed John's dictatorial rule by forcing him to sign the Magna Carta in 1215. This document protected the feudal aristocracy rather than the ordinary citizen, but it came to be regarded as a cornerstone of British liberties. It restricted the monarch's powers; forced him to take advice; increased the influence of the aristocracy; and stipulated that no citizen could be punished or kept in prison without a fair trial.

Such developments encouraged the establishment of parliamentary structures. In 1265, Simon de Montfort called nobles and non-aristocrats to form a Council or Parliament. This initiative was followed in 1295 by the Model Parliament of Edward 1 (1272–1307), which was the first representative English Parliament. Its two sections consisted of the Lords/Bishops and the Commons (comprising male commoners).

However, the Parliament was too large to rule the country effectively. A Privy Council, comprising the monarch and court advisers, developed. This was the royal government outside Parliament, until it lost power to parliamentary structures in the late eighteenth and early nineteenth centuries.

Although Parliament now had some limited powers against the monarch, there was a return to royal dominance in Tudor England from 1485. The nobility had been weakened by wars and internal conflicts (such as the Wars of the Roses between Yorkists and Lancastrians), and monarchs chose landed gentry as members of their Privy Councils, which made them dependent upon royal patronage. Monarchs controlled Parliament and summoned it only when they needed to raise money.

Parliament showed more resistance to royal rule under the Stuart monarchy from 1603 by using its weapon of financial control. It was influenced by the gentry, who had now become more independent of the Crown and had a majority in the House of Commons. Parliament began to refuse royal requests for money. It forced Charles I to sign the Petition of Rights in 1628, which further restricted the monarch's powers and prevented him from raising taxes without Parliament's consent. Charles ignored these political developments, until he was obliged to summon Parliament for finance. Parliament refused the request. Realizing that he could not control Parliament, Charles next attempted to arrest parliamentary leaders in the House of Commons itself. His failure to do so meant that the monarch was in future prohibited from entering the Commons.

Charles's rejection of parliamentary ideals and belief in his right to rule without opposition provoked anger against the Crown, and a Civil War broke out in 1642. The Protestant Parliamentarians under Oliver Cromwell won the military struggle against the Catholic Royalists. Charles was beheaded in 1649 and the monarchy was abolished. England was ruled under a Protectorate by Cromwell and his son Richard (1649–60), and Parliament effectively comprised only the House of Commons.

However, Cromwell's Protectorate was harsh and unpopular, and most people wanted the restoration of the monarchy. The two Houses of Parliament were re-established, and in 1660 they restored the Stuart Charles II to the throne. Initially, Charles cooperated with Parliament, but his financial needs, belief in royal authority and support of the Catholic cause lost him popular and parliamentary backing. Parliament ended his expensive wars and imposed further restrictions, such as the Habeas Corpus Act in 1679, which stipulated that no citizen could be imprisoned without a fair and speedy trial.

The growth of political parties and constitutional structures

The growing power of Parliament against the monarch in the seventeenth century was reflected in the development of more organized political parties. These derived largely from the ideological and religious conflicts of the Civil War. Two groups (Whigs and Tories) became dominant, and this feature was to characterize future British two-party politics, in which political power has shifted between two main parties. The Whigs were mainly Cromwellian Protestants and gentry, who did not accept the Catholic sympathizer James II as successor to Charles II and wanted religious freedom for all Protestants. The Tories generally supported royalist beliefs, and helped Charles II to secure James's right to succeed him.

James's behaviour caused a reduction in royal influence. He attempted to rule without Parliament and ignored its laws. His manipulations forced the Tories to join the Whigs in inviting the Protestant William of Orange to intervene. William arrived in

England in 1688, James fled to France, and William succeeded to the throne as England's first constitutional monarch. Since no force was involved, this event is called the Bloodless or Glorious Revolution. Royal powers were further restricted under the Declaration of Rights (1689), which strengthened Parliament and provided some civil liberties. It was thus difficult for future monarchs to reign or act without Parliament's consent, and the Act of Settlement (1701) gave religious freedom to all Protestants.

The Glorious Revolution did affect the constitution and politics. It created a division of powers between an executive branch (the monarch through the government of the Privy Council), a parliamentary legislative branch (the House of Commons, the House of Lords and formally the monarch), and the judiciary (a legal body of senior judges independent of monarch and Parliament).

Parliamentary power grew in the early eighteenth century, because the German-born George I lacked interest in English politics. He distrusted the Tories with their Catholic sympathies and appointed Whigs such as Robert Walpole to his Privy Council. Walpole became Chief Minister in 1721 and led the Whig majority in the House of Commons, which now comprised wealthy land and property owners. Walpole's political power enabled him to increase parliamentary influence, and he has been called Britain's first Prime Minister.

Parliamentary authority was not absolute, however, and later monarchs tried to restore royal power. However, George III lost much of his authority after the loss of the American colonies in 1776. He was obliged to appoint William Pitt the Younger as his Tory Chief Minister, and it was under Pitt that the office of Prime Minister really developed.

The expansion of voting rights

Although parliamentary control continued to grow in the late eighteenth and early nineteenth centuries, there was still no widespread democracy in Britain. Political authority was in the hands of land owners, merchants and aristocrats in Parliament, and most people did not possess the vote. Bribery and corruption were common, with the buying of those votes that did exist and the giving away or sale of public offices.

The Tories were against electoral reform, as were the Whigs initially. But the country was rapidly increasing its population and developing industrially and economically. Pressures for political reform became irresistible. The Whigs extended voting rights to the expanding middle class in the First Reform Act of 1832. The Tory Disraeli later gave the vote to men with property and a certain income. However, the majority of the working class had no votes and were unrepresented in Parliament. It was only in 1884 that the Whig Gladstone gave the franchise to all male adults.

Women had to wait until 1928 for the full franchise to be established in Britain. Previously, only women over 30 had achieved political rights, and for centuries wives and their property had been the legal possessions of their husbands. The traditional role of women of all classes had been confined to that of mother in the home, although some found employment in home industries and factories or as domestic servants, teachers and governesses.

Women's social and political position became marginally better towards the end of the nineteenth century. Elementary education for all was established, and a few institutions of higher education began to admit women in restricted numbers. Some women's organizations had been founded in the mid-nineteenth century to press for greater political, employment and social rights. But the most famous suffragette movement was that of the Pankhursts in 1903. Their Women's Social and Political Union campaigned for the women's vote and an increased female role in society. However, some critics argue that a substantial change in women's status in the twentieth century occurred largely because of a recognition of the essential work that they performed during the two World Wars.

The growth of governmental structures

The elements of modern government developed haphazardly in the eighteenth and nineteenth centuries. Government ministers were generally members of the House of Commons. They became responsible to the Commons rather than the monarch, shared a collective responsibility for the policies and acts of government, and had an individual responsibility to Parliament for their own ministries. The prime ministership developed from the monarch's Chief Minister to 'first among equals' and finally to the leadership of all ministers. The central force of government became the parliamentary Cabinet of senior ministers, which grew out of the Privy Council. The government was formed from the majority party in the House of Commons. The largest minority party became the Official Opposition, which attempted through its policies to become the next government chosen by the people.

The nineteenth century also saw the growth of more organized political parties. These were conditioned by changing social and economic factors and reflected the modern struggle between opposing ideologies. The Tories, who became known as the Conservatives around 1830, had been a major force in British politics since the seventeenth century. They believed in established values and the preservation of traditions; supported business and commerce; had strong links with the Church of England and the professions; and were opposed to radical ideas.

The Whigs, however, were becoming a more progressive force, and wanted social reform and economic freedom without government restrictions. They gradually developed into the Liberal Party, which promoted enlightened policies in the late nineteenth and early twentieth centuries, but which declined after 1918.

The new Labour Party, established in its present form in 1906, became the main opposition party to the Conservatives and continued the traditional two-party system in British politics. It was supported by the trade unions, the working class and some middle-class voters. The first Labour government was formed in 1924 under Ramsay MacDonald, but it achieved majority power only in 1945 under Clement Attlee, when it embarked on radical programmes of social and economic reform, which laid the foundations for a corporate and welfare state.

Historically, the House of Commons gained power from both the monarch and the House of Lords and became the dominant element in the parliamentary system. Subsequent reforms, like the Parliament Acts of 1911 and 1949, affected the House of Lords and removed most of its political authority. Later Acts created non-hereditary titles (life peers), which supplement the old arrangement in which most peerages were hereditary. The Lords now has only delaying and amending power over parliamentary bills and cannot interfere with financial legislation. These changes demonstrated that political and taxation matters were to be decided by the members of the Commons as elected representatives of the people.

The constitutional and governmental framework

There have been few upheavals in the British constitutional system since 1688. Rather, existing constitutional principles have been pragmatically adapted to new conditions. Britain has no written constitution contained in any one document. Instead, the constitution consists of statute law (Acts of Parliament); common law (judge-made law); conventions (principles and practices of government that are not legally binding but have the force of law); some ancient documents like Magna Carta; and the new addition of European Union law.

These constitutional elements are said to be flexible enough to respond quickly to new conditions. National law and institutions can be created or changed by the Westminster Parliament through Acts of Parliament. The common law can be extended by the judges, and conventions can be altered, formed or abolished by general agreement.

The governmental model that operates in Britain today is a constitutional monarchy, or parliamentary system, and is divided into legislative, executive and judicial branches. The monarch is head of state and has a role on some executive and legislative levels. The Westminster Parliament or legislature (consisting of the House of Lords, House of Commons and formally the monarch) possesses supreme legislative power in most UK matters.

The executive national government of the day governs by passing its political policies through the Westminster Parliament in the form of Acts of Parliament. It operates through ministries or departments headed by Ministers or Secretaries of State. In future, a Scottish Executive will do a similar job in Scotland for devolved matters.

The judiciary is composed of the judges of the higher courts, who determine the common law and interpret Acts of Parliament and EU law. The judges are independent of the legislative and executive branches of government.

These branches of the governmental system, although distinguishable from each other, are not entirely separate. For example, the monarch is formally head of the executive, the legislature and the judiciary. A Member of Parliament (MP) in the House of Commons and a peer of the House of Lords may both be in the government of the day. A Law Lord in the House of Lords also serves that House as the highest appeal court.

The correct constitutional title of Parliament is the 'Queen-in-Parliament', and all state and governmental business is carried out in the name of the monarch by the politicians and officials of the system. But the Crown is sovereign only by the will of Parliament and acceptance by the people. In constitutional theory, the people, although subjects of the Crown, hold the political sovereignty to choose their government, while Parliament, consisting partly of their elected representatives in the Commons, has legal supremacy to make laws and is the focus of national sovereignty.

Challenges to traditional notions of parliamentary sovereignty have arisen, however, and the Westminster Parliament is no longer the sole legislative body in Britain. British membership of the European Union (1973) means that EU law is now superior to British national law in certain areas, and British courts must give it precedence in cases of conflict between the two systems. EU law has thus been added to, and coexists with, Acts of Parliament as part of the British constitution. In future, a Scottish Parliament will have power to legislate for devolved matters in Scotland in which Westminster has no say. But the London Parliament still has the constitutional right to abolish the Scottish Parliament and the Welsh Assembly and to withdraw from the EU.

Criticisms of the constitutional system

The British system, which is largely dependent upon conventions and observing the rules of the game, has been admired in the past. It combined stability and adaptability, so that a balance of authority and toleration was achieved. Most British governments tended to govern pragmatically when in power. The emphasis was on whether a particular policy worked and was generally acceptable. Governments were conscious of how far they could go before displeasing their own followers and the electorate, to whom they were accountable at the next general election. From a basis in the two-party system, the combination of Cabinet government and party discipline in the Commons seemed to provide a balance between efficient government and public accountability.

This system has, however, been increasingly criticized. Governments have become more radical in their policies and are able to implement them because of big majorities in the Commons. This means that there are few effective parliamentary restraints upon a strong government. There has also been concern at the absence of constitutional safeguards for individual citizens against state power, especially since there are few legal definitions of civil liberties in Britain.

These features have been seen as potentially dangerous, particularly when governments and their administrative bodies have a reputation for being too secretive. Government secrecy is a widely discussed issue, with critics arguing that Britain is ruled by a system of powerful small groups at the heart of government and unelected executive agencies. There have consequently been campaigns for more open government and more effective civil protection in the forms of a Bill of Rights (to safeguard individual liberties); a written constitution (to define and limit the powers of Parliament and government); greater judicial scrutiny of parliamentary legislation; a Freedom of Information Act (to allow the public to examine official documents); and the incorporation of the European Convention on Human Rights into British domestic law (allowing British citizens to pursue legal claims in Britain rather than having to go through the European Court of Human Rights).

Whilst there is still opposition to such proposals, the Labour government will legislate for a Freedom of Information Act and for the incorporation of the European Convention into British law. The role of the judiciary is queried in the latter case, particularly if Acts of Parliament conflict with the human rights legislation. But it is argued that both developments will improve the civil rights of British people.

Fifty per cent of respondents to a MORI poll in 1997 thought that the British system of government was out of date, 79 per cent said that a written constitution was needed, 79 per cent supported a Bill of Rights and 81 per cent wanted a Freedom of Information Act. Critics claim that the political system no longer works satisfactorily. They maintain that it has become too centralized and that the traditional bases are inadequate for the organization of a complex society. It is felt that political policies have become too conditioned by party politics at the expense of consensus; that government is too removed from popular and regional concerns; and that national programmes lack a democratic and representative basis. It is argued that there must be a fundamental reform of the existing political institutions if they are to reflect a contemporary diversity. However, changes are occasionally made to the present apparatus, such as devolution for Scotland and Wales, and the old evolutionary principles may be successfully adapted to new demands and conditions.

The monarchy

The English monarchy is the oldest secular institution in Britain and there is automatic hereditary succession to the throne, but only for Protestants. The eldest son of a monarch has priority over older daughters, although this may change in the future. The monarchy's continuity has been interrupted only by Cromwellian rule (1649–60), although there have been different lines of descent, such as the Tudors and Stuarts.

Royal executive power has disappeared, but the monarch still has formal constitutional roles and serves as head of state, head of the executive, judiciary and legislature, 'supreme governor' of the Church of England and commander-in-chief of the armed forces. In holding these positions, the monarch personifies the British state and is a symbol of national unity. Government ministers and officials are the monarch's servants, and Members of Parliament, judges, military officers, peers and bishops of the Church of England swear allegiance to the Crown. The monarchy is thus a permanent fixture in the British system, unlike temporary politicians. It still has a practical and constitutional role to play in the operation of government. There are provisions for the appointment of counsellors of state (or a regent in exceptional cases) to perform royal duties, should the monarch be absent from Britain or unable to carry out public tasks.

The monarch is expected to be politically neutral and is supposed to reign but not rule. In addition, he or she cannot make laws, impose taxes, spend public money or act unilaterally. The monarch acts only on the advice of political ministers, which cannot be ignored, and contemporary Britain is therefore governed by Her Majesty's Government in the name of the Queen.

The monarch does, however, still perform important duties, such as the opening (usually in autumn each year) and dissolving of Parliament; giving the Royal Assent (or signature) to bills that have been passed by both Houses of Parliament; appointing government ministers and other public figures; granting honours; leading proceedings of the Privy Council; and fulfilling international duties as head of state. In practice, these functions are performed by the monarch on the advice of the Prime Minister or other ministers.

A central power still possessed by the monarch is the choice and appointment of the Prime Minister. By convention, this person is normally the leader of the political party that has a majority in the House of Commons. However, if there is no clear majority or if the political situation is unclear, the monarch could in theory make a free choice. In practice, advice is given by royal advisers and leading politicians in order to present an acceptable candidate.

Constitutionally, the monarch has the right to be informed of all aspects of national life by receiving government documents and meeting regularly with the Prime Minister. The monarch also has the right to encourage, warn and advise ministers. It is difficult to evaluate the impact of monarchical advice on formal and informal levels, although critics suggest that it could be substantial. This raises questions about whether such influence should be held by an unelected, non-democratic figure who could potentially either support or undermine political leaders.

Much of the cost of the royal family's official duties is met from the Civil List (public funds that are approved by Parliament). Following concern over expense, the Civil List has now been reduced to a few members of the immediate royal family. Other costs incurred by the monarch as a private individual or as sovereign come either from the Privy Purse (finance received from the revenues of some royal estates) or from the Crown's own resources, which are very considerable and on which the monarch now pays income tax.

Critics of the monarchy argue that it lacks adaptability and is out-of-date, non-democratic, too expensive, too much associated with aristocratic privilege and establishment thinking and too closely identified with an English rather than a British role. It is argued that the monarchy's aloofness from ordinary life sustains class divisions and hierarchy in society. It is also suggested that, if the monarch's functions today are merely ceremonial and lack power, it would be more rational and democratic to abolish the office and replace it with a cheaper, non-executive presidency.

Critics who favour the monarchy argue that it is popular and has developed and adapted to modern requirements. It serves as a personification of the state; shows stability and continuity; has more prestige than politicians; is not subject to political manipulations; plays a worthwhile role in national institutions; possesses neutrality; and performs important ambassadorial functions overseas. The monarchy was also said in the past to reflect family values and has a certain glamour about it, which is attractive to many people.

The British public have often shown affection for the royal family beyond its representative role. But its behaviour and the role of the monarchy itself in recent years have attracted considerable criticism. An ICM poll in August 1997 showed that support for the monarchy had fallen to 48 per cent, the first time that figures had been less than 50 per cent. A majority felt that the monarchy would be replaced in the next 50 years unless it adapted further to changes in society. Republican feeling has also grown. But it seems likely that the institution of monarchy will continue.

Traditionalists fear that a modernized monarchy would lose that aura of detachment that is described as its main strength. It would then be associated with change rather than the preservation of existing values. At present, it balances uncomfortably between tradition and modernizing trends.

The Privy Council

The Privy Council developed historically from a small group of royal advisers into the executive branch of the monarch's government. But its powerful position declined in the eighteenth and nineteenth centuries as its functions were transferred to a parliamentary Cabinet and new ministries, which were needed to cope with a rapidly changing society.

Today it advises the monarch on matters such as the approval of Orders in Council (mainly government business that does not need to pass through Parliament) and the granting of Royal Charters to public bodies such as universities. Its members may be appointed to advisory and problem solving committees and it can be influential.

Cabinet ministers automatically become members on taking government office. Life membership is also granted by the monarch, on the advice of the Prime Minister, to eminent people in Britain and some Commonwealth countries. There are about 400 Privy Councillors at present, but the body works mostly through small groups or committees. A full council is usually summoned only on the death of a monarch and the accession of a new one, when there are serious constitutional issues at stake, or when a monarch plans to marry. Should the monarch be indisposed, counsellors of state or an appointed regent would work partly through the Privy Council.

Apart from its practical duties and its role as a constitutional forum, the most important tasks of the Privy Council today are performed by its Judicial Committee. This is the final court of appeal from some Commonwealth countries and the remaining dependencies. It may also be used as an arbiter for some courts and committees in Britain and overseas, and its rulings can be influential. The Committee (comprising five Law Lords from the House of Lords) will also rule in future on conflicts between Westminster and the Scottish Parliament.

Parliament

Parliament, also known as 'Westminster' and housed in the Palace of Westminster in London, is the supreme legislative authority in Britain. It has legal sovereignty in all matters and can create, abolish or amend laws and institutions for all or any part(s) of Britain. But Britain and Parliament are now subject to some European Union law, and a future Scottish Parliament will legislate in Scotland on devolved matters. Opinions differ as to how these developments affect parliamentary sovereignty. Constitutionally, and ultimately, Westminster has the legal power to abolish the Scottish Parliament and withdraw Britain from the European Union.

The Westminster Parliament's main functions are to pass laws; vote on financial bills so that the national government can carry on its legitimate business; examine government policies and administration; scrutinize European Union legislation; and debate important political issues.

Despite its absolute power, Parliament is supposed to legislate according to the rule of law, precedent and tradition. Politicians are generally sensitive to such conventions and to public opinion. Formal and informal checks and balances, such as party discipline, the Official Opposition, public reaction and pressure groups, normally ensure that Parliament legislates according to its legal responsibilities. But critics argue that parliamentary programmes may not reflect the will of the people.

Parliament comprises the House of Lords, the House of Commons and the monarch. It gathers as a unified body only on ceremonial occasions, like the State Opening of Parliament by the monarch (usually each autumn) in the House of Lords. Here it listens to the monarch's speech from the throne, which outlines the government's forthcoming legislative programme.

All three parts of Parliament must normally pass a bill before it can become an Act of Parliament and therefore law. A correctly created Act cannot be challenged in the law courts. However, the courts can now rule on British law to see whether or not it is compatible with European Union law in some areas. EU law exists side by side with domestic law, and the former takes precedence over the latter when there is a conflict.

A Parliament has a maximum duration of five years, but it is often dissolved and a general election called before this. The maximum has sometimes been prolonged by special legislation in emergency situations like the two World Wars. Each Parliament is divided into annual sessions, running normally from one October to the next, with a long recess from July to October. A dissolution of Parliament and the issue of writs for a general election are ordered by the monarch on the advice of the Prime Minister. If an individual MP dies, resigns or is given a peerage, a by-election is called only for that member's seat, and Parliament as a whole is not dissolved.

The *House of Lords* consists of Lords Temporal and Lords Spiritual. Lords Spiritual are the Archbishops of York and Canterbury and 24 senior bishops of the Church of England. The Lords Temporal comprise (1) some 760 peers and peeresses with hereditary titles; (2) about 380 life peers and peeresses, who have been created by political parties; and (3) the Lords of Appeal (Law Lords), who become life peers on their judicial appointments. The latter serve the House of Lords as the ultimate court of appeal for most purposes from most parts of Britain. This court consists not of the whole House, but only nine Law Lords who have held senior judicial office, who are under the chairmanship

of the Lord Chancellor and who form a quorum of three to five when they hear appeal cases.

Daily attendance varies from a handful to a few hundred. Peers receive no salary for parliamentary work, but may claim attendance and travelling expenses. The House collectively controls its own procedure, but is often guided by the Lord Chancellor, who is a political appointee of the government and who sits on the Woolsack (or stuffed woollen sofa).

There are demands that the unrepresentative, unelected House of Lords should be replaced. The problem consists of which alternative model to adopt. An elected second chamber could threaten the constitutional powers of the House of Commons and might result in conflict between the two. An appointed House would consist of unelected members chosen by political parties. Until a model is agreed, the Labour government is committed to abolishing the sitting and voting rights of hereditary peers. This means that the House would then consist of politically appointed life peers.

The House of Lords does its job well as an experienced and less partisan forum than the House of Commons. It has an important revising, amending and delaying function, which may be used to block government legislation for up to one year or to persuade governments to have a second look at bills. It is a safeguard against over-hasty legislation by the Commons, and plays a considerable constitutional role as an antidote to powerful governments. This is possible because the Lords are more independently minded than MPs in the Commons and do not suffer rigid party discipline. The House has a number of crossbenchers (or Independents sitting across the back of the chamber) who do not belong to any political party. Although there is a nominal Conservative majority in the total membership, Conservative governments cannot automatically count on this support. The House of Lords is an anachronism in many ways, but it works. It also takes a substantial legislative and administrative burden from the Commons.

PLATE 3.1 The Houses of Parliament *(Maggie Murray/Format)*

The *House of Commons* comprises 659 Members of Parliament (MPs), who are elected by adult voters and represent citizens in Parliament. Although 117 of them are women (double the figure in the 1992 general election), women still face problems in being selected as parliamentary candidates and winning seats in the Commons. There are 540 parliamentary seats for England, 40 for Wales, 61 for Scotland and 18 for Northern Ireland. The number of Scottish MPs will be reduced once Scotland has its own Parliament. MPs are paid expenses and a salary that, at about twice the average national wage, is low in international and domestic terms for comparable jobs.

PLATE 3.2 Tony Blair and female politicians *(Mils Jorgensen/Rex)*

The Westminster parliamentary electoral system (general elections)

Britain is divided for Westminster parliamentary electoral purposes into 659 constituencies (geographical areas of the country containing about 66,000 voters). Each returns one MP to the House of Commons at a general election. Constituencies are adjusted by Boundary Commissioners in order to ensure fair representation and to reflect population movements.

General elections are by secret ballot, but voting is not compulsory. British, Commonwealth and Irish Republic citizens may vote if they are resident in Britain, included on a constituency register of voters, aged 18 or over and not subject to any disqualification. Expatriate Britons may also vote under special conditions. People not entitled to vote include members of the House of Lords, mentally ill patients who are detained in hospital or prison, and persons who have been convicted of corrupt or illegal election practices.

1	**BROWN** James Edward Brown, 42 Spinney Road, Upton, Northshire **Labour**	
2	**SMITH** Frederick Alistair Smith, The Hut, Peasants' Row, Upton, Northshire **Conservative**	
3	**JONES** Gertrude Mary Jones 15 Lavender Crescent, Upton, Northshire **Liberal Democrat**	

FIGURE 3.1 Ballot paper

Each elector casts one vote at a polling station, set up on election day in their constituency, by making a cross on a ballot paper against the name of the candidate for whom the vote is cast. Those who are unable to vote in person in their local constituency can register postal or proxy votes.

The turnout of voters is over 70 per cent at general elections out of an electorate of some 42 million people. The candidate who wins the most votes in a constituency is elected MP for that area. This system is known as the simple majority or the 'first past the post' system. There has historically been no voting by proportional representation (PR), except for local and EU Parliament elections in Northern Ireland.

Many see the British electoral system as undemocratic and unfair to smaller parties. Campaigns continue, particularly by the Liberal Democrats, for some form of PR, which would create a wider selection of parties in the House of Commons and cater for minority political interests. The two big parties (Labour and Conservative) have preferred the existing system, since it gives them a greater chance of achieving power. However, the Labour government may introduce a different voting system, following a report on the electoral system and a referendum, and it will use partial forms of PR for European Parliament elections in 1999 and for elections to the Scottish Parliament and Welsh Assembly.

It is argued that the British people prefer the stronger government that can result from the 'first past the post' system. PR systems are alleged to have weaknesses, such as resulting coalition or minority government, frequent breakdown, a lack of firm policies, power bargaining between different parties in order to achieve government status, and tension afterwards. But weak and small-majority government can also result from the current British system.

The party-political system

The electoral structure depends upon the party-political system, which has existed since the seventeenth century. Political parties present their policies in the form of manifestos to the electorate for consideration during the intensive few weeks of campaigning before General Election Day. A party candidate (chosen by a specific party) in a constituency is elected to the Westminster Parliament on a combination of election manifesto, the personality of the candidate and the attraction of the national party. But party activity continues outside the election period itself, as the politicians battle for power and the ears of the electorate.

Since 1945, there have been seven Labour and eight Conservative governments in Britain. Some have had large majorities in the House of Commons, while others have had small ones. Some, like the Labour government in the late 1970s, had to rely

TABLE 3.1 British governments and Prime Ministers since 1945

Date	*Government*	*Prime Minister*
1945–51	Labour	Clement Attlee
1951–5	Conservative	Winston Churchill
1955–9	Conservative	Anthony Eden (1955–7)
		Harold Macmillan (1957–9)
1959–64	Conservative	Harold Macmillan (1959–63)
		Alec Douglas-Home (1963–4)
1964–6	Labour	Harold Wilson
1966–70	Labour	Harold Wilson
1970–4	Conservative	Edward Heath
1974 (Feb.)	Labour	Harold Wilson
1974 (Oct.)	Labour	Harold Wilson
1974–9	Labour	Harold Wilson (1974–6)
		James Callaghan (1976–9)
1979–83	Conservative	Margaret Thatcher
1983–7	Conservative	Margaret Thatcher
1987–92	Conservative	Margaret Thatcher (1987–90)
		John Major (1990–2)
1992–7	Conservative	John Major
1997–	Labour	Tony Blair

on the support of smaller parties, such as the Liberals and nationalist parties, in order to remain in power.

The great majority of the MPs in the House of Commons belong to either the Conservative or the Labour Party, which are the largest political parties. This division continues the traditional two-party system in British politics, in which power has alternated between two major parties.

The Labour Party has historically been a left-of-centre party with its own right and left wings. It emphasized social justice, equality of opportunity, economic planning and the state ownership of industries and services. It was supported by the trade unions (who had been influential in the party's policy development), the working class and some of the middle class. Its electoral strongholds have been in Scotland, South Wales and the Midland and northern English industrial cities.

Class-based support has changed, however, with more social and job mobility. In recent years, the Labour Party embarked on policy reviews in order to broaden its appeal to middle-class voters in southern England, take account of changing economic and social conditions and remain a force in British politics. Its leader (and the current Prime Minister), Tony Blair, has modernized the party by moving to the centre ground, capturing some voters from the Conservative Party and distancing itself from the trade unions and its doctrinaire past.

The Conservative Party is a right-of-centre party that also has right- and left-wing sections. It regards itself as a national party and appeals to people across class barriers. It emphasizes personal, social and economic freedom, individual ownership of property and shares, and the importance of law and order. The Conservatives also became more radical in their eighteen years of government power (1979–97), although splits in the party on policy directions (particularly Europe) deepened.

The party's support comes mainly from business interests and the middle and upper classes, but a sizeable number of skilled male workers and working-class women vote Conservative. The party's strongholds are in southern England, with scattered support elsewhere in the country. However, it lost all its seats in

Scotland and Wales as well as support in southern England at the 1997 general election. The party's defeat in this election persuaded its new leader, William Hague, to reorganize the party, strive for unity and develop policies and an image that are more attractive to voters.

The Liberal Democratics were formed in 1988 when the old Liberal Party and the Social Democratic Party (formed in 1981) merged into one party. Under their present leader, Paddy Ashdown, they see themselves as an alternative political force to the Conservative and Labour Parties, based on the centre or centre-left of British politics.

They are relatively strong in south-west England, Wales and Scotland, and doubled the number of their MPs at the 1997 general election. But they suffer from the lack of a clearly separate identity from the Labour Party, particularly as Labour has moved to the centre ground. The Liberal Democrats have won some dramatic by-elections and achieved considerable success in local government elections, but they have not made a huge breakthrough into the House of Commons or the EU Parliament. They hope that electoral reform to a pure form of PR might increase the number of their MPs.

Smaller political parties are also represented in the House of Commons, such as the Scottish National Party; Plaid Cymru (the Welsh National Party); the Ulster Unionists and the Democratic Unionists (Protestant Northern Irish parties); the Social Democratic and Labour Party (moderate Roman Catholic Northern Irish party); and Sinn Fein (Republican Northern Irish party). Other small parties, like the Greens and publicity seeking fringe groups, may also contest a general election. But a party that does not achieve a certain number of votes in the election loses its deposit (the sum paid when a party registers to fight an election).

Social class and class loyalty used to be important factors in British voting behaviour. But these have now been replaced by property, employment, share owning and other considerations. A more volatile political situation exists as voters switch between Labour, Conservative and Liberal Democrat, and employ 'tactical voting' in constituencies to prevent specific party candidates from being elected. The changing character of the electorate has moved political parties to the centre ground and forced them to adopt policies that are more representative of people's wishes and needs.

The party that wins most seats in the House of Commons at a general election usually forms the new government, even though it has not obtained a majority of the popular vote. A party will generally have to gather more than 33 per cent of the popular vote before winning a substantial number of seats, and nearly 40 per cent in order to expand that representation and have a chance of forming a government with an overall majority (a majority over all the other parties counted together). This overall majority enables it to carry out its election manifesto policies (the mandate theory).

Election success often depends on whether support is concentrated in geographical areas, for a party gains seats by its local strength. Smaller parties, which do not reach the percentages above and whose support is scattered, do not gain many seats in the Commons. It is this system of representation that PR supporters wish to change, in order to reflect the popular vote and the appeal of minority parties.

The situation may be illustrated by the 1997 general election results (see table 3.2), which showed a 10 per cent swing to the Labour Party from the Conservatives on a 71.3 per cent turnout of voters. Labour became the government with 44.4 per cent of the popular vote, while the opposition parties together obtained 55.6 per cent. Labour gained 418 seats with its share of the popular vote, the Conservatives received 165 seats with 31.4 per cent, while the Liberal Democrats with 17.2 per cent received 46 seats. Labour thus had a very large 177 seat overall majority in the House of Commons. Looked at in a different way, Labour had nearly two-thirds of the seats in the Commons with 44.4 per cent of the popular vote; the Conservatives received 31.4 per cent of the vote, but only 25 per cent of the seats, and the Liberal Democrats got 17.2 per cent of the vote but only 7 per cent of the seats. The main reasons for this result were the 'first past the post' system, the fact that the Liberal Democrats' popular support is spread widely (and thinly) over the country, resulting

TABLE 3.2 General election results, 1997

Party	*Popular vote (%)*	*Members elected*
Labour	44.4	418
Conservative	31.4	165
Liberal Democrat	17.2	46
Ulster Unionists		10
Democratic Unionists		2
Social Democratic and Labour		3
Sinn Fein	7	2
United Kingdom Unionists		1
Plaid Cymru		4
Scottish National		6
Independent (Martin Bell)		1
Speaker elected unopposed		1
Total	100	659

Swing from Conservative to Labour: 10%
Turnout of voters: 71.3%
Overall Labour majority: 177
Non-Labour vote: 55.6%

in them coming second in many constituencies, and the traditional concentration of Labour and Conservative Party votes in specific geographical areas.

The result of a general election may be a 'hung Parliament', where no one party has an overall majority. A minority or coalition government would then have to be formed, in which the largest party would be able to govern only by relying on the support of smaller parties in the Commons.

In most cases, however, the largest minority party becomes the Official Opposition, with its own leader and 'shadow government'. It plays an important role in the parliamentary system, which is based on adversarial politics and the two-party tradition of government. The seating arrangements in the House of Commons reflect this system, since leaders of the government and opposition parties sit on facing 'front benches', with their supporting MPs, or 'backbenchers', sitting behind them. The effectiveness of parliamentary democracy is supposed to rest on the relationship between the government and opposition parties and the observance of procedural conventions. Some parties, such as the Liberal Democrats, dislike this confrontational tradition and advocate more consensus politics. It seems as though the Labour government will encourage this by allowing Liberal Democrat membership of some Cabinet committees.

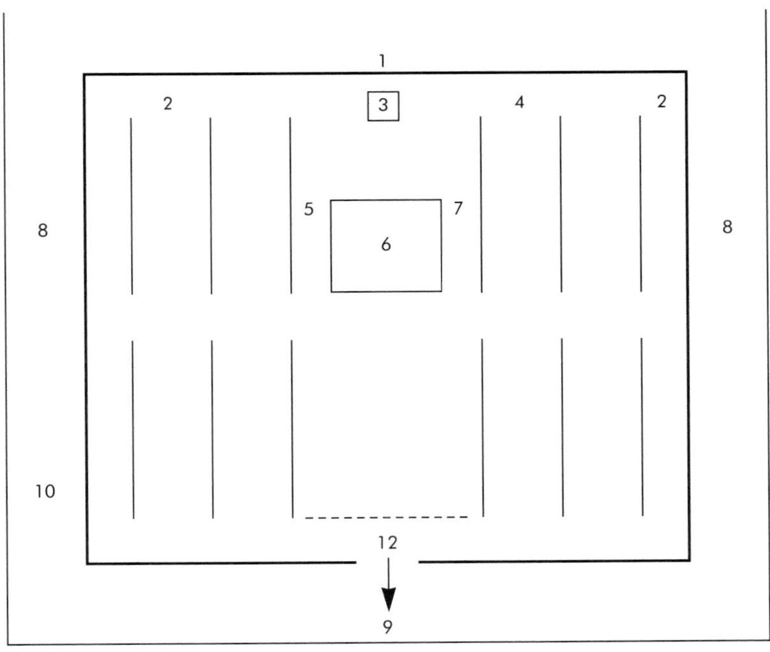

1 Press gallery
2 Voting lobbies
3 Speaker's chair
4 Civil servants
5 Government front bench
6 Dispatch box
7 Opposition front bench
8 Galleries for MPs
9 Public gallery
10 VIP gallery
11 Bar of House
12 House of Lords

FIGURE 3.2 The House of Commons

The opposition parties may try to overthrow the government by defeating it on a 'vote of no confidence' or a 'vote of censure'. These techniques are not usually successful if the government has a comfortable majority and can count on the support of its MPs. The opposition parties consequently attempt to influence the formation of national policies by their criticism of pending legislation, by trying to obtain concessions on bills by proposing amendments to them, and by striving to increase support for their performance and policies inside and outside the Commons. They take advantage of any publicity and opportunity that might improve their chances at the next general election.

Inside Parliament, party discipline rests with the Whips, who are chosen from party MPs by the party leaders and who are under the direction of a Chief Whip. Their duties include informing members of forthcoming parliamentary business, and maintaining the party's voting strength in the Commons by seeing that their members attend all important debates or are 'paired' with the opposition (agreed matching numbers so that MPs need not be present in the House on all occasions). MPs receive notice from the Whips' office of how important a particular vote is, and the information will be underlined up to three times. A 'three-line whip' signifies a crucial vote, and failure to attend or comply with party instructions is regarded as a revolt against the party's policy.

The Whips also convey backbench opinion to the party leadership. This is important if rebellion and disquiet are to be avoided. Party discipline is very strong in the Commons, though less so in the Lords, and in both Houses it is essential to the smooth operation of party politics. A government with a large majority should not become complacent or antagonize its backbenchers. If it does so, a successful rebellion against the government or abstention from voting by its own side may destroy the majority and the party's policy.

Outside Parliament, control rests with the national and local party organizations, which can be influential. They promote the party at every opportunity, but especially at election time, when constituencies select the party candidates and are in charge of electioneering on behalf of their party.

Parliamentary procedure and legislation

Parliamentary procedure in both Houses of Parliament is based on custom, convention, precedent and detailed rules (standing orders). The House of Commons normally meets every weekday afternoon and sits until 10.30 pm, although business can continue beyond midnight. On Fridays it sits from 9.30 am until 3 pm, after which MPs may spend the weekend in their constituencies attending to business. The organization and procedures of the Commons have been criticized. It is felt that the number of hours spent in the House should be reduced and that pay and resources should be improved.

The Speaker (currently Betty Boothroyd, the first woman to hold the position) is the chief officer of the House of Commons and is chosen by MPs. The Speaker is an elected MP who, on election to the Speaker's chair, ceases to be a political representative and becomes a neutral official whose role is to interpret the rules of the House with the assistance of three deputy speakers.

The Speaker protects the House against any abuse of procedure; may curtail debate so that a matter can be voted on; can adjourn the House to a later time; may suspend a sitting; controls the voting system; and announces the final result. Where there is a tied result, the Speaker has the casting vote, but must exercise this choice so that it reflects established conventions. The Speaker is important for the orderly running of the House. MPs can be very combative and often unruly, so that the Speaker is sometimes forced to dismiss or suspend a member from the House.

Debates in both Houses of Parliament usually begin with a motion (or proposal) that is then debated. The matter is decided by a simple majority vote at the end of discussion. In the Commons, MPs enter either the 'Yes' or 'No' lobbies (corridors running alongside the Commons chamber) to record their vote, but they may also abstain from voting.

The proceedings of both Houses are open to the public and may be viewed from the public and visitors' galleries. The transactions are published daily in *Hansard* (the parliamentary 'newspaper'); debates are televised; and radio broadcasts may be in live or recorded form. This exposure to public scrutiny has increased interest in the parliamentary process, although negative comments are made about low attendance in both Houses and the behaviour of MPs in the Commons.

Legislative proceedings

The creation of new national law and changes to existing law are the responsibility of the Westminster Parliament. In practice, this means the implementation of the government's policies, but it can also cover non-party matters and responses to European Union law. In future, the Scottish Parliament will legislate for devolved matters in Scotland.

A government will usually issue certain documents before the parliamentary law making process commences. A Green Paper is a consultative document that allows interested parties to state their case before a bill is introduced into Parliament. A White Paper is not normally consultative, but is a preliminary document that details prospective legislation.

A draft law is drawn up by parliamentary civil servants and takes the form of a bill. Most bills are 'public' because they involve state business and are introduced in either House of Parliament by the government. Other bills may be 'private' because they relate to matters such as local government issues, while some are 'private members' bills' introduced by MPs in their personal or private capacity. These latter bills are on a topic of interest to MPs, but are normally defeated for lack of parliamentary time or support. However, some important private members' bills concerning homosexuality, abortion and sexual offences have survived the obstacles and become law. Bills must pass through both Houses and receive the Royal Assent before they can become law.

The Commons is normally the first step in this process. A bill will receive a formal first reading when it is introduced into the Commons by the government. The bill is later given its second reading following a debate on its general principles, after which it usually passes to a standing committee for detailed discussion and amendment. This stage is followed by the report stage, during which further amendments to the bill are possible. The third reading of the bill considers it in its final form, usually on a purely formal basis. However, debate is still possible if demanded by at least six MPs. This delaying tactic may sometimes be used by the opposition parties to hold up the passage of a bill. But the government, in its turn, can introduce a 'guillotine motion' that cuts off further debate.

After the third reading, a Commons bill will be sent to the House of Lords. It will then go through broadly the same stages again. The Lords can delay a non-financial bill for one session, or roughly one year. It can also propose amendments, and, if amended, the bill goes back to the Commons for further consideration. This amending function is an important power and has been frequently used in recent years. But the Lords' role today is to act as a forum for revision, rather than as a rival to the elected Commons. In practice, the Lords' amendments can sometimes lead to the acceptance of changes by the government, or even a withdrawal of the bill.

When the bill has eventually passed through the Lords, it is sent to the monarch for the Royal Assent (or signature), which has not been refused since the eighteenth century. After this, the bill becomes an Act of Parliament and enters the statute-book as representing the law of the land at that time.

This process from bill to Act may appear unduly drawn out, but it does normally avoid the dangers of hasty legislation and ensures that the bill is discussed at all levels. It also allows the opposition parties to join in the legislative process, either by carrying amendments or sometimes by voting down a bill with the help of smaller parties and disaffected members of the government party.

The government

The British government is mainly centred on Whitehall in London, where its ministries and the Prime Minister's official residence (10 Downing Street) are located. It consists of about a hundred

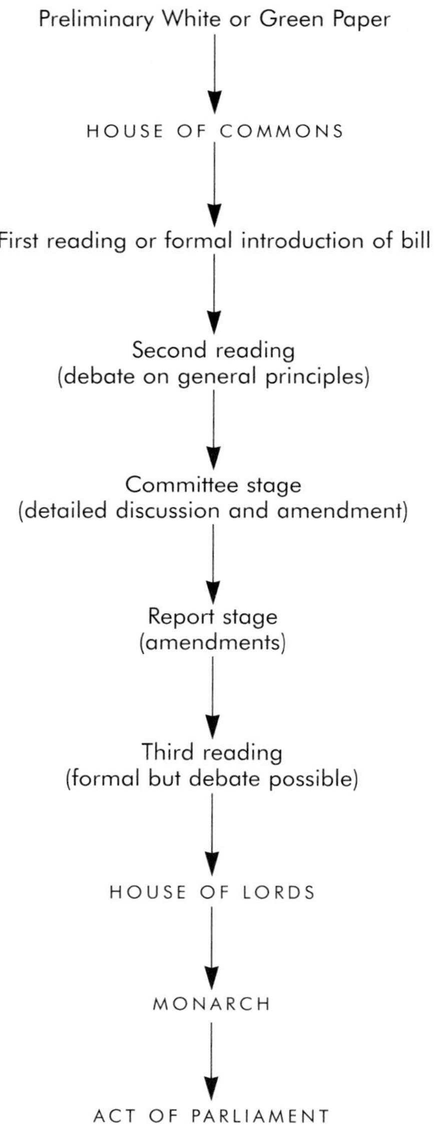

FIGURE 3.3 From bill to Act of Parliament

ministers and other officials who can be chosen from both Houses of Parliament and who are appointed by the monarch on the advice of the Prime Minister. They belong to the party that forms the majority in the Commons, from which they derive their authority and are collectively responsible for the administration of national affairs. The composition of the government can vary in the number of ministers and ministries established by the Prime Minister. In future, Scotland will have its own Executive and First Minister to deal with devolved matters in Scotland.

The *Prime Minister* is appointed by the monarch and is normally the leader of the majority party in the Commons. His or her power stems from majority support in Parliament; the authority to choose and dismiss ministers; the leadership of the party in the country; and control over policy making. The Prime Minister usually sits in the Commons, as do most of the ministers, where they may be questioned and held accountable for government actions and decisions. The Prime Minister was historically the connection between the monarch and parliamentary government, and this convention continues today in the weekly audience with the monarch, at which the policies and business of the government are discussed.

The Prime Minister consequently has great power within the British system of government, and it is suggested that the office has become like an all-powerful executive presidency. But there are considerable checks on this power, inside and outside the party and Parliament, that make the analogy less than accurate. However, there is a greater emphasis upon prime ministerial government today, rather than the traditional constitutional notions of Cabinet government.

The *Cabinet* is a small executive body within the government and usually comprises 21 senior ministers, who are chosen and presided over by the Prime Minister. Examples are the Chancellor of the Exchequer (Finance Minister), the Foreign Secretary, the Home Secretary, the Minister of Defence, the Secretary of State for Education and Employment and the Secretary of State for Trade and Industry. The Cabinet originated historically in meetings that the monarch had with ministers in a royal Cabinet or

Privy Council committee. As the monarch gradually withdrew from active politics because of the growth of parliamentary government and party politics, the royal Cabinet developed into a parliamentary body.

Constitutional theory has traditionally argued that government rule is Cabinet rule, because the Cabinet collectively initiates and decides government policy at its weekly meetings in 10 Downing Street. But this notion has weakened. Since the Prime Minister is responsible for Cabinet agendas and controls Cabinet proceedings, the Cabinet can become a 'rubber-stamp' to policies that have already been decided by the Prime Minister or smaller groups.

Much depends upon the personality of Prime Ministers in this situation and the way in which they avoid potential Cabinet friction and tension. Some are strong and like to take the lead, whilst others give the impression of working within the Cabinet structure, allowing ministers to exercise responsibility within their own ministerial fields. Much of our information about the operation of the Cabinet comes from 'leaks' or information divulged by Cabinet ministers. Although the Cabinet meets in private and its discussions are meant to be secret, the public is usually and reliably informed of Cabinet deliberations and disputes by the media.

The mass and complexity of government business, and the fact that ministers are very busy with their own departments, suggest that full debate in Cabinet on every issue is impossible. But it is felt that the broad outlines of policy should be more vigorously debated. The present system arguably concentrates too much power in the hands of the Prime Minister; overloads ministers with work; allows too many crucial decisions to be taken outside the Cabinet; and consequently reduces the notion of collective responsibility.

Collective responsibility is that which all ministers, but mainly those in the Cabinet, share for government actions and policy. All must support a government decision in public, even though some may oppose it during private deliberations. If a minister cannot do this, he or she may feel obliged to resign.

Some Cabinet ministers have resigned in recent years because they could not accept government policies.

A minister also has an individual responsibility for the work of his or her government department. This means that the minister is answerable for any mistakes, wrongdoing or bad administration that may occur, whether personally responsible for them or not. In such cases, the minister may resign, although this is not as common today as it was in the past. This also enables Parliament to maintain some control over executive actions because the minister is answerable to Parliament.

Government departments (or *ministries*) are mainly centred in London and are the chief instruments by which central government implements its policy. A change of government does not necessarily alter the number or functions of departments. Examples of government departments are the Foreign Office, the Ministry of Defence, the Home Office and the Treasury (of which the Chancellor of the Exchequer is head).

Government departments are staffed by the *Civil Service*, which consists of career administrators. Civil servants are employed by central government in London and throughout the country and are involved in a wide range of government activities. They are responsible to the minister in whose department they work for the implementation of government policies. A change of minister or government does not require a change of civil servants, since they are expected to be politically neutral and to serve the government impartially. Restrictions on political activities and publication are consequently imposed upon them in order to ensure neutrality.

There are some 500,000 civil servants in Britain today. Nearly half of these are women, but few of them achieve top ranks in the service. Many aspects of departmental work have now been transferred to executive agencies in London and throughout the country, which have administrative rather than policy making roles, such as the Driver and Vehicle Licensing Agency (DVLA) in Cardiff and social security offices.

The heart of the Civil Service is the Cabinet Office, whose Secretary is the head of the Civil Service. The Secretary organizes

Cabinet business and coordinates high-level policy. In each ministry or department, the senior official (Permament Secretary) and his or her assistants are responsible for assisting their minister in the implementation of government policy.

There have been frequent accusations about the efficiency and effectiveness of the Civil Service, and civil servants do not have a good public image. There have been attempts to make the Civil Service respond to the demands of efficient administration in a cost-effective manner, and to allow a wider category of applicants than the traditional entry of Oxbridge-dominated university graduates. Numbers in the Service have been reduced, departments have been broken down into executive agencies, and posts are being advertised in order to attract older people from industry, commerce and the professions.

It is alleged that the Civil Service imposes a certain mentality upon its members that affects implementation of government policies and which ministers are unable to combat. There is supposed to be a Civil Service way of doing things and a bias towards the status quo. But much depends upon ministers and the manner in which they manage departments. There may be some areas of concern, but the stereotyped image of civil servants is not reflected in the many who serve their political masters and work with ministers for departmental interests. The Civil Service is also highly regarded in other countries for its efficiency and impartiality.

Parliamentary control of government

Constitutional theory suggests that Parliament should control the executive government. But unless there is small-majority government, rebellion by government MPs or widespread public protest, a government with an overall majority in the Commons can carry its policies through Parliament, irrespective of Parliament's attempts to restrain it. This is particularly the case with the Labour government's very large overall majority of 177 seats following the 1997 general election. Critics argue for stronger parliamentary control over the executive, which has been described as an elective dictatorship. But there seems little chance of this without, for example, moving to a PR electoral system and more consensus politics.

Opposition parties can oppose in Parliament only in the hope of persuading the electorate to dismiss the government at the next general election. Formal devices such as votes of censure and no confidence, as well as amendment motions, are normally inadequate when confronting a government with a large majority in the Commons. Even rebellious government MPs will usually rally round the party on such occasions, out of both a self-interested desire to preserve their jobs and a need to prevent the collapse of the government.

Examinations of government programmes can be employed at Question Time in the Commons, when the Prime Minister (30 minutes on Wednesdays) and other ministers are subjected to oral and written questions from MPs. But the government can prevaricate in its answers to written questions and, while reputations can be made and lost at oral Question Time, it is a rhetorical and political occasion rather than an opportunity for in-depth analysis of government policy. However, it does have a function in holding the executive's performance up to public scrutiny. The opposition parties can also choose their own topics for debate on a limited number of days each session, which can be used to attack the government.

A 1967 attempt to restrain the executive was the creation of the Parliamentary Commissioner for Administration, who can investigate alleged bad administration by ministers and civil servants. But the office does not have the powers of Ombudsmen in other countries and the public have no direct access to it. It is limited as a watchdog over executive behaviour, although its existence does serve as a warning.

In an attempt to improve the situation, parliamentary committees have been established. Standing committees of MPs in the Commons examine bills during procedural stages. Such committees generally have little influence on actual policy. But in 1979 a new select committee system was created that now has fourteen committees. They comprise MPs from most parties, who monitor the administration and policy of the main government departments and investigate proposed legislation. MPs previously had problems in scrutinizing government activity adequately, and party discipline made it difficult for them to act independently of party policy.

It is often argued that the real work of the House and parliamentary control of the executive is done in the select committees. Their members are now proving to be more independent in questioning civil servants and ministers who are called to give evidence before them. Select committees can be very effective in examining proposed legislation and expenditure, and their reports can be very damaging to a government's reputation. Although opinions differ about their role, it does seem that they have in practice strengthened Parliament's authority against government. Nevertheless, although parliamentary scrutiny is important, it should also be remembered that under the mandate system a government is elected to carry out its declared policies.

ATTITUDES

Attitudes to politics and politicians

Polls reveal that British politicians, political parties and Parliament rate very low in people's esteem. After recent allegations of sleaze, corruption and unethical behaviour, there are now stricter controls on politicians and their interests outside their political jobs. A National Opinion Poll (NOP) before the 1997 general election found that politicians were the least admired group. A MORI poll in May 1997 showed an increase in political apathy, particularly among the young, and a distrust in politicians to rectify social ills. Politicians are regularly criticized and heavily satirized in magazines, the press and on radio and television.

Nevertheless, the NOP poll also revealed that people thought general elections were important: 60 per cent were interested in the 1997 election; some 75 per cent believed that the election result would change Britain; and over 60 per cent said that they usually or sometimes watched party political broadcasts and political discussion programmes on television. People appeared to be more interested in the political process than is popularly assumed. But the actual turnout of voters at the 1997 general election decreased by 7 per cent from the 1992 election.

The public's attitudes are volatile, and poll findings can be confusing since they are conditioned by biases towards particular political parties and policies. The electorate clearly holds political views that are reflected in its voting behaviour. But its reactions to government programmes may be heavily dependent upon the current economic climate, national issues and personal situations.

None of the political parties, in spite of their frequent drifts to the centre ground, individually encompasses the diversity of views represented by the people, who may vary between egalitarian economic views and authoritarian social and moral positions. People appear to be looking for a political party and society that would more adequately reflect their sense of contemporary reality. They desire economic freedom and personal liberty, but also want state interventionist policies in some social areas. The division of the popular vote in general elections, the abstention rate, political volatility and tactical voting reflect a wide diversity of opinion in the electorate about politicians and the British political system.

EXERCISES

■ Explain and examine the following terms:

Whigs	executive	'three-line whip'
constitution	minister	life peers
Cabinet	manifesto	Oliver Cromwell
Magna Carta	conventions	Question Time
civil servant	secret ballot	backbenchers
Lords Spiritual	Tories	constitutional monarchy
the Speaker	legislature	'hung Parliament'
Whitehall	sovereignty	select committees

■ Write short essays on the following topics:

1 Describe what is meant by the 'two-party system', and comment upon its effectiveness.

2 Does Britain have an adequate parliamentary electoral system? If not, why not?

3 Critically examine the role of the Prime Minister.

4 Discuss the position and powers of the monarch in the British constitution.

Chapter 4

Local government

LOCAL GOVERNMENT CONSISTS OF various types of elected councils throughout the country that have historically provided public services like law and order, schools, sanitation, libraries, transport, fire brigades, social services and housing for their local areas. Britain's unitary political system means that central government in London has responsibility for major national matters and that the structures and powers of local government derive from Acts of Parliament.

Devolution (with Scotland and Wales managing more of their own affairs in 1999–2000) will not, at least initially, affect this unitary structure. The Westminster Parliament will create the Edinburgh Parliament and Cardiff Assembly and the two countries will also retain their existing lower tiers of local government. But Edinburgh and Cardiff will clearly influence their own local government areas.

Local government structures are complicated and have been further reformed since 1996. To simplify matters, this chapter mainly examines local government in England. But the English model and changes have also been reflected in Wales, Scotland and Northern Ireland. These three countries each have a minister in the London government who is responsible for their organization, although the Scottish and Welsh ministerial roles will decline as a result of devolution. The main links between English local authorities and central government are the Environment, Health and Education Departments and the Home Office.

English local government has been created by Acts of Parliament since the nineteenth century. These define the duties and powers that exist between local and central government and between different units at the local level. This means that the central government, through the Westminster Parliament, has considerable control over local government. It can and does intervene in local affairs and specifies the services that must be available at the local level. It can change, increase or abolish the powers and structures of local government. Regulations and by-laws can be introduced by local councils to implement facilities in their areas, but often only with central government approval.

However, local authorities do have a certain autonomy and discretion as to how they prioritize and organize their services to the public within central government guidelines. This system combines the efficiency of knowing what is most suitable for an area with the democratic right of local people to organize their own affairs. It implies a sense of community and liberty outside the restraints of central government.

Central government now provides 80 per cent of the money spent by local authorities on their services, and because of this there is sometimes political and financial friction between the two levels. Local councils can incline to particular political lines or prioritize certain services, which may result in policies and budgets that are not acceptable to the community as a whole or to central government.

Central government has not historically exercised detailed supervision in local activities, but governments have increasingly intervened in policy and financial matters. The Conservatives (1979–97) tightly controlled local authorities by introducing reforms and competitive considerations into their organization, and were accused of centralizing political power in Westminster. Local government, in return, tried to retain its traditional powers and freedom of operation.

The notion that local government should itself provide all services has changed. Many local councils now act as enabling authorities; that is, they enable external providers to supply local services. The Labour government and the Liberal Democrats support the strengthening of local government. However, it remains to be seen which model (traditional, enabling or any alternative) will develop in future. Meanwhile, 'localism' and 'centralism' continue as competing forces in British life.

Ultimately, central government does have the duty to maintain financial stability in local government and has the power to demand national uniformity in the provision and standard of local services. The problems of local government are thus significant aspects of life in contemporary Britain. They raise questions about the nature of local autonomy and democracy and the power of central government to intervene in local affairs in the national interest. Devolution is often seen as an attempt to break London's centralizing tendencies, but local government in Scotland and Wales may also suffer from centralized control in Edinburgh and Cardiff.

English local government history

Early attempts to divide England up into smaller areas for the purpose of more efficient administration occurred in Saxon times. The main units of local government gradually became the parish, the borough and the county (or shire). Before the nineteenth century, boroughs and counties were organized on behalf of the central government by local civil officials.

The *parish* is still the smallest unit of local government. It was centred on the churches, which were built after England was converted to Christianity in AD 596–7. The parish was granted civil functions in later centuries, which allowed it to provide for the welfare of the poor and the maintenance of roads and buildings in its area. Today, rural parishes still elect councils, which have some limited duties in local government, but urban parishes have now lost all their civil functions and serve only as church units.

The next largest local government entity was the *borough*. From Norman times until recently, the status of borough was granted to large towns or areas by the monarch. This gave the new borough independence to organize its local government services. It had its own law courts, by-laws and agricultural markets and was able to send representatives to Parliament. In addition, some towns were given the special title of 'city' because of their size, economic importance or roles as cathedral centres. Today English cities and towns vary considerably in size and population, but some now have their own separate local government status as unitary authorities.

The *county* has generally been the most important and largest unit of local government devoted to large-scale policies in its area. The physical outlines of English counties have not altered much over the centuries, although there have been amalgamations of some of them, abolition of others and new creations in the twentieth century. But their population sizes have varied considerably over time and have reflected demographic, social and economic changes.

The English population increased rapidly during the nineteenth century industrial revolutions. Large manufacturing towns developed and the countryside was progressively depopulated. Demand grew in both urban and rural areas for basic public services, such as sanitation, education, housing, health facilities and transport, which could be controlled by elected local councils. The development of modern local government on a nationally planned basis was begun in the nineteenth century in response to these needs.

The Municipal Corporations Act of 1835 created a council system of councillors and aldermen in the boroughs, who were elected by local rate payers (owners who paid taxes on their property). As urban areas expanded in the 1880s, larger towns were given a new independent status as county boroughs and functioned separately within their geographical counties.

Similar changes also affected the counties. Local Government Acts gave administrative duties to county councils, which consisted of councillors who were elected by borough rate payers. Later in the nineteenth century, each county was divided into urban and rural districts. The county councils were mainly responsible for large-scale functions in their areas and for overall policy making. The urban and district councils were concerned with more local duties and the implementation of county programmes.

This complicated system of local government continued into the twentieth century. It had to provide for further population increases, the growth of towns and the demands of the new welfare state. But the system became increasingly unsatisfactory as towns expanded their suburbs into rural areas. This development was particularly severe in the conurbations (large areas of dense population around the major cities such as Birmingham, London, Manchester and Liverpool). Rural areas included urban and suburban components and the distinction between town and countryside was lost in an 'urban sprawl'. Planning programmes, policy implementation and provision of services became more difficult and uncoordinated.

The system required radical reform, but attempts before the 1960s to change local structures provoked resistance from groups with community pride or vested interests. However, substantial alterations did occur in the 1960s and 1970s, although accompanied by much controversy and bitter debate. They were intended to make local government more efficient, more representative and more suitable to the needs and complexity of contemporary society.

The London reforms

Local government in London was the first to be altered in 1963, because population growth had resulted in most people living outside the old County of London limits. The London Government Act created a new County of London ('Greater London'), which contained some 8 million people, 3 million of whom lived within the old county boundaries or 'Inner London'. But the new London population and its size of 610 square miles (1,580 sq. km) were too large for effective unified supervision by one body. Greater London was therefore divided up into 32 boroughs, each with about 250,000 inhabitants. Local services were organized by elected councils in these boroughs, and the large-scale policy and planning functions rested with an elected Greater London Council (GLC).

The GLC was the object of bitter political battles in the early 1980s, as it fought for its survival against central government. But the Conservative government abolished the GLC in 1986 and transferred its functions to the 32 boroughs and joint authorities. The abolition battle was controversial. Critics argued that the government was interfering politically in the running of a Labour-controlled authority and was concerned to centralize its power in Westminster. The government considered the GLC to be too large, inefficient and given to overspending on dubious policies and causes.

Critics (and polls) have suggested that London should have its own elected council. The Labour government (following a referendum in 1998) intends to create an authority with overall strategic responsibility for the capital and an elected mayor (or chief executive) of London. The boroughs would continue as units within the new authority.

The ancient City of London, which covers 1 square mile (1.6 sq. km), was not affected by the London reforms and is a separate unit of local government within Greater London. It is a commercial, banking, legal and financial centre with few public services and permanent inhabitants, although property developments like the Barbican have encouraged more people to live there. The annually elected Lord Mayor of London is the chief official of the City (not of London). This office is largely ceremonial, but is important for fund raising and public relations. It is likely that the Labour government will reform the City's electoral system and representation.

Reforms outside London

The Local Government Reorganization Act of 1972 simplified the local government system outside London and reduced the number of councils. Essentially, two main tiers of local authority were created, consisting of counties and smaller districts.

England remained divided into counties. But some new counties were formed and others were amalgamated or disappeared, albeit in the face of strong local opposition. Elected county councils were responsible for overall planning policies and large-scale services in their areas, such as the police, education, fire brigades, libraries and social services. The counties were subdivided into elected district councils, which attended to items such as housing and sanitation, environmental health and the implementation of county programmes in their areas.

PLATE 4.1 Manchester town hall *(COI)*

The 1972 Act also established six metropolitan county councils to serve the overall needs of large conurbations with heavy population densities in the Midlands and the north. These councils contained 36 metropolitan district councils, which were responsible for more local services. But the Conservative government abolished the metropolitan county councils in 1986, arguing that they were too large, remote, inefficient and financially wasteful. Their powers were given to the metropolitan district councils and joint authorities.

Similar changes in the rest of Britain were also made. In Wales, the counties were reduced from 13 to eight and subdivided into 37 district councils; some new counties were also created. Scotland was divided into nine regions with subdivisions into 53 districts, together with authorities for the Orkneys, the Shetlands and the Western Isles. Northern Ireland was divided into 26 district councils.

These changes in local government structures were controversial, difficult and expensive. They were confusing to local citizens and often seen as an affront to community pride and identity. The decrease in the number of local councils resulted in fewer elected councillors and a corresponding reduction in local representation. Jurisdictional conflicts grew between county and district authorities. Critics argue that, while the local government reforms introduced some rationalization and economic sense, they lacked any real discussion of how local democracy could best be served.

Contemporary changes in local government structure

English local government became more complicated from 1992, when the Conservative government appointed a Commission to consider whether, following local consultation, the two-tier structure (of county and district councils) should be replaced by single-tier unitary authorities. Unexpectedly, the existing system of county councils and district councils has largely remained, except for some 14 areas in counties that became unitary authorities by April 1996. More followed in 1997 and there may be new creations in the future. These structures now handle all the local government functions in their area and authority is undivided. Figure 4.1 shows where some unitary authorities were created by June 1996, but other areas within counties (like big cities) also become unitary authorities.

From 1996 in Scotland, 29 new unitary councils replaced the system of nine regional and 53 district councils, but with three continuing Islands councils. In Wales, from 1996, 22 unitary authorities replaced the eight county councils and 37 district councils. In Northern Ireland, the existing 26 district councils remain.

There was tension between the Commission and the Conservative government over these changes, and controversy at local level by people who opposed them. Critics argued that the

FIGURE 4.1 English counties and unitary authorities, 1996
Local Government Chronicle

exercise was a Conservative attempt to centralize power and control smaller local government units. But the new unitary authorities welcome the opportunity for undivided control over their areas.

The functions of local government

Counties, districts and unitary authorities have their own councils, which are elected by the adult population of the area. The number of councillors elected depends on population size. Elections are staggered, but most take place every four years and most councillors hold office for four years. They are elected by the 'first past the post' system in most parts of Britain (except Northern Ireland, where PR operates). Public interest in local elections is small, unless there are pressing or controversial issues at stake, with less than 30 per cent of the electorate voting in many areas.

Councillors are not paid for their council work, thus continuing the amateur, part-time tradition of local government. But they may receive attendance and expense allowances for performing their duties. They decide policy for their local area and come from a broad cross-section of society, such as industrial workers, teachers, business people, academics, trade unionists and housewives.

Their reasons for serving may be from a sense of public duty, notions of prestige or a desire for political power. Councillors may gain some indirect personal benefit from their positions. But standards of honesty and integrity are generally high, although occasional cases of fraud and corruption are reported. Nevertheless, councillors do devote a considerable amount of time and energy to their duties, without which local government would collapse.

Councils have a presiding officer who is chosen by the council members to preside over council meetings and who usually holds office for one year. These officers have other formal duties, since they are the official representatives of their areas. In a borough, they may have the ancient title of Mayor and in some large cities that of Lord Mayor. In Scottish towns, the equivalent titles are Provost and Lord Provost.

Local politics was once run partly on non-party lines, and there were many 'Independent' or non-party councillors. Today, local government is dominated by national political parties. They try to achieve power bases in the regions, which will solidify their national position, and local government often serves as a training ground for potential Westminster politicians. Labour, Conservatives and Liberal Democrats fight each other for control of the councils. A council may be controlled by one of these parties if it wins a majority of the seats at the election. But a minority party may hold the balance of power if no other party has an overall majority and can influence policy making. Critics argue that the participation of national parties in, and the disappearance of Independents from, local government have affected local democracy and made it an aspect of national politics.

PLATE 4.2 Britain's first Asian mayor: Rabindara Pathak at Ealing Town Hall, London, 1987 *(Brenda Prince/Format)*

Local elections have increasingly been seen as an indication of how the electorate is responding to the current central government. The public may demonstrate disapproval of government policy by its voting patterns in local elections, to such an extent that the planning of a general election can in part depend upon local results. In recent years, the Conservatives have performed very badly, losing many seats and control of local councils; the Labour Party has capitalized on Conservative unpopularity by substantially gaining seats and council control; and the Liberal Democrats have also strengthened their position.

The work of local government is onerous and must be shared out, rather than being dealt with by the councillors in the full council. Most councils therefore operate through committees, which usually represent one main aspect of the council's work, such as education or housing. They consist of elected councillors, with the different parties represented proportionally to party strength. But, normally, important issues and policy matters are decided by the full council, to which individual committees can make recommendations. In most cases, all the meetings, reports, minutes and papers of the council are now open to the public in the interests of greater freedom of information and official accountability.

Councillors and their committees are serviced by permanent professional staff. These function similarly to civil servants in central government and are expected to be neutral in carrying out the policies of the council. While they are essential to the operation of local government, critics argue that they have increased bureaucracy and inefficiency, as well as distancing elected representatives from their constituents. As more work is devolved to unelected officials, there is a potential danger of the further professionalization and remoteness of a system that was initially intended to provide citizen self-government.

Local government employs some 1.4 million people (one tenth of the national workforce). These include professional and technical administrators, teachers (who form half the number), firemen, manual workers, social services staff and the police. Conservative governments tried to reduce public spending in these areas by financial restrictions and by encouraging greater competition, such as tendering contracts for local services to the private sector, with councils becoming 'enabling authorities'. Its policies on public housing ('right to buy') and state schools ('opting out') also limited local authority spending and control (see chapters 8 and 9). But the cost of local government still amounts to some 25 per cent of total central government expenditure.

Councils need finance in order to pay for services. In Britain there is no income tax paid directly by local people to their councils. Local government finance comes mainly from central government grants (52 per cent); business rates charged on commercial properties throughout Britain (28 per cent), which is redistributed by central government to local government (except in future in Scotland); and the council tax (20 per cent), which is determined by the local council. This tax, payable by every homeowner in the area, is based on the value of domestic property (divided into eight price bands, depending upon market value) and a personal element (of at least two two adult people occupying a property). Rebates from the tax are given to low-income groups and single-occupancy properties.

Further finance may be raised by council borrowing and the rent from council houses and flats (public housing let usually to low-income groups). The proceeds of the sale of such housing under the 'right to buy' policy (sitting tenants purchasing their rented property) goes to central government. But the Labour government intends to release this money to local government so that it can provide more council housing.

The central government therefore makes substantial grants of 80 per cent to local councils. These come from national tax revenues and provide finance, without which local government would be unable to implement its policies or services. Grants vary in amount because of disparities in wealth between different parts of the country and because of different needs for services. However, the government can alter or withhold (capping) its grants to those councils that set excessive budgets, and this may lead to a reduction in local services.

Such policies have been seen by critics as financial and political interference in local affairs by central government, and the Labour government intends to abolish capping. Local councillors maintain their right to set appropriate budgets in order to provide the services for which they were elected. Under the Conservatives

(1979–97), the situation resulted in battles between the two levels of government. Central government involved itself in local government to a greater extent than in the past, and was perceived to be increasing central control, both politically and financially. Educational and housing reforms, privatization measures, pressures on central government grants and compulsory tendering of services led to a reduction in the traditional areas of local autonomy. But the Labour government intends to redress this situation by giving local government more freedom from central control.

The problems of local government might be solved by more satisfactory local structures in which councils have powers to promote their own legislation and raise income tax directly from their constituents. This would give more genuine autonomy over local affairs and allow local government to decide which services it would provide itself and which could be contracted out to external agencies. But central government has been loath to give up its powers and to decentralize authority. There is consequently a widespread feeling that the twentieth-century reforms of local government have been inadequate.

ATTITUDES

Attitudes to local government

Polls consistently reveal that local government and its services (particularly the council tax, housing, schools and the social services) are a source of concern for British people. They still seem to feel that certain basic services should be provided by local government rather than external services. But while some are dissatisfied with their local councillors (particularly in London), others seem to be reasonably content and feel that officials are not as faceless as they are sometimes assumed to be. Attitudes differ in different parts of the country, and may depend upon the commitment and input of local political parties.

ATTITUDES

However, critics argue that low turn-outs for local elections indicate that people feel that local government is unimportant, or that it is too remote and party-based to respond effectively to their needs. But local inhabitants still count on council services, which are often essential to their daily lives, and can react to community issues.

The supporters of local government emphasize its democratic political role as a safeguard against an over-centralized state. Opponents argue that it has become inefficient and irrelevant to the needs of contemporary society. The middle way searches for an appropriate structure, role and identity for local government after a period when its traditional functions have been eroded.

EXERCISES

- **Explain and examine the following terms:**

by-laws	Provost	council tax	Inner London
district	Mayor	councillors	urban sprawl
borough	county	conurbation	unitary authority
GLC	parish	'Independent'	decentralization
capping	tendering	business rate	enabling authority

- **Write short essays on the following topics:**

1 How is local government finance raised, and of what does it consist?

2 Is the system of English local government satisfactory? If not, suggest alternatives.

3 What is the role of central government in English local government?

Chapter 5

International relations

BRITAIN'S HISTORICAL POSITION as a major colonial, economic and political power was in relative decline by the early decades of the twentieth century. Some large colonies had already achieved self-governing status, and the growth of nationalism in African and Asian nations later persuaded Britain to decolonize further. The effects of global industrial competition, two World Wars, the emergence of superpower Cold War politics (dominated by the USA and Soviet Union) and domestic economic and social problems gradually forced Britain to recognize its reduced international status. It sought slowly and with difficulty to find a new identity and to establish different priorities. Some of the previous overseas links continue in altered form, while other relationships are new. But, in spite of these fundamental changes, Britain still experiences uncertainties about its potential influence and appropriate role on the world stage.

Foreign policy and defence

Britain's international position today is that of a medium-sized country that is dwarfed economically by Germany, the USA and Japan. Yet some of its leaders still believe that it can have international influence and a global role. For example, the Labour government is developing a 'moral foreign policy' with human rights as its basis. This could be applied to Britain's dealings with other countries, particularly in terms of arms sales, human rights issues and nationalist conflicts.

Critics, on the other hand, argue that Britain's foreign policy and national self-image do not reflect the reality of its world position and conflict with its domestic interests. Although it has progressively reduced its defence and overseas commitments, the current expenditure in these areas might arguably be directed more profitably to internal problems.

Nevertheless, Britain's foreign and defence policies continue to reflect its traditional position as a major trading nation. It is therefore self-interestedly concerned to maintain stable economic and political conditions through global cooperation. Although its manufacturing base has declined, international commercial activities are still very important, and Britain maintains its position as a world finance centre. Its exports of goods and services accounted for 28 per cent of its gross domestic product in 1995. It has substantial overseas investments (30 per cent of its overseas earnings) and a range of international activities, and it imports 9 per cent of its food and 4 per cent of its basic manufacturing requirements. Britain is therefore dependent upon maintaining its global connections, even though it is increasingly committed to Europe.

Britain's *foreign policy* and membership of international organizations is based on the notion that overseas objectives can be best attained by cooperation with other nations on a regional or global basis. The imperial days of unilateral action are now largely past, although Britain did take such action in the 1982 Falklands War. But its foreign policy can reflect particular biases, with support for one country outweighing that for another. The USA has been Britain's closest ally in recent years and it has often been considered, rightly or wrongly, that a 'special relationship' exists between the two. Indeed, 63 per cent of Americans in 1997 (according to a Harris poll) regarded Britain as a close ally of the USA, second only to Canada. But this association varies according to circumstances, although Britain is concerned to maintain the American military presence in Europe and NATO.

However, polls reveal that British people feel that the USA is now of less importance to Britain than Europe. Britain's membership of the European Union means that it is to some extent dependent upon common EU foreign policy. But, although the EU is moving to more unified policies, the member states do sometimes have conflicting interests, and Britain is determined to follow its own foreign policy when necessary.

Britain also has diplomatic relations with over 160 nations and is a member of some 120 international organizations, ranging from bodies for economic cooperation to the United Nations (UN). Support for the UN and the principles of its charter has been part of British foreign policy since 1945, although there has sometimes been a scepticism about its effectiveness as a practical body. As a permanent member of the UN Security Council, however, Britain has a vested interest in supporting the UN. It sees a strong UN as a necessary framework for achieving many of its own foreign policy objectives, such as the peaceful resolution of conflict, arms control, disarmament, peace keeping operations and the protection of human rights. UN agencies also provide important forums for discussing issues in which Britain is involved, such as disaster relief, the use of the sea-bed, terrorism, the environment, energy development and world resources. Yet Britain, like other nations, is ready to ignore the UN when it sees its own vital interests challenged.

Britain's major *defence* alliance is with the North Atlantic Treaty Organization (NATO). This comprises Belgium, Canada, Denmark, Iceland, Italy, Luxembourg, The Netherlands, Norway, Spain, Portugal, Britain, the USA, Greece, Turkey and Germany (expanded to include Poland, Hungary and the Czech Republic in 1997, with Russia having a representative role). The original justification for NATO was that it provided its members with greater security than any could achieve individually, and was a deterrent against aggression by the now-defunct Warsaw Pact countries.

All the major British political parties are in favour of retaining the NATO link and, according to opinion polls, the public would not support any party that tried to take Britain out of the alliance. Membership of NATO also allows Britain to operate militarily on the international stage. Its defence policy is based on NATO strategies, and it assigns most of its armed forces and defence budget to the organization.

Despite changes in Eastern Europe since 1989 and moves to transform NATO into a more flexible military association, the British government has taken such developments cautiously and is concerned to maintain its military defence with both conventional and nuclear forces. This position is due to fears of European instability and the risk to its own security if it was to reduce its armed defences substantially.

However, some countries in the European Union would like to see the EU develop its own defence and foreign policies outside the NATO alliance, possibly through the vehicle of the Western European Union (WEU). Britain is opposed to such a development and wishes to maintain both its own defence capability and the NATO structure.

The British government has cut its defence budgets considerably in the 1990s by reductions in the number of the armed forces, ships, aircraft and equipment. It will in future depend on leaner, more flexible forces, although there have been strenuous objections to these policies from the military. Britain's defence expenditure remains a considerable proportion of its gross domestic product (with a planned reduction to 2.7 per cent by 1998–9). The primary objectives of defence policy are to ensure the country's security and the NATO commitment and to allow British forces to engage in high-intensity war as well as in peace keeping roles. However, defence spending is still higher than in other European countries.

Nuclear weapons, which account for a large part of the defence budget, continue to be fiercely debated. Britain's independent nuclear deterrent consists mainly of long-range American-built Trident missiles carried by a fleet of four submarines. Successive governments have committed themselves to upgrading nuclear weapons. Critics want cheaper alternatives, or the cancellation of the nuclear system. But, even with recent changes in Eastern Europe, it seems that the British nuclear strategy will continue. All the major political parties are now multilateralist (keeping nuclear weapons until they can be abolished on a global basis).

Britain is also able to operate militarily outside the NATO and European area, although this capacity is becoming increasingly expensive and limited. Military garrisons are stationed in Brunei, Cyprus, the Far and Middle East, the Falkland Islands and Gibraltar. The 1982 Falklands War and the 1991 Gulf War showed that Britain was able to respond to challenges outside the NATO area, although the operations did draw attention to defects and problems in such commitments.

The total strength of the armed forces, which are now all volunteer following the abolition of conscription in 1960, was 161,008 in 1997. This was made up of 45,506 in the Royal Navy and Royal Marines, 109,500 in the Army and 60,302 in the Royal Air Force. Women personnel in the Army, Navy and Air Force are integral parts of the armed services. They were previously confined to support roles, but may now be employed in more front-line military activities. Reserve and auxiliary forces support the regular professional forces, such as the Territorial Army (TA), which reinforces NATO ground troops and helps to maintain security in Britain. However, the TA may be downgraded in future.

The Commonwealth

The British Empire was built up over several centuries. It began initially with the internal domination of the British Isles by the English, and was followed by trading activities and colonization in North and South America. Parts of Africa, Asia and the West Indies were also exploited commercially over time and many became colonies. Emigrants from Britain settled in countries such as Australia, South Africa and New Zealand. By the nineteenth century, British imperial rule and possessions embraced a quarter of the world's population.

The Empire developed into the British Empire and Commonwealth in the late nineteenth and early twentieth centuries when Canada, Australia, New Zealand and South Africa became self-governing dominions and achieved independence. Many of their people were descendants of those settlers who had emigrated from Britain in earlier centuries. They regarded Britain as the mother country and preserved the values of a shared kinship. But this relationship has changed considerably as national identities have become more firmly established.

PLATE 5.1 The Foreign and Commonwealth Office, Whitehall, London *(COI)*

In the mid-twentieth century, the British Empire and Commonwealth became the British Commonwealth, as British governments granted independence to other colonies. India and Pakistan became independent in 1947, followed by African territories in the 1950s and 1960s, and later many islands of the West Indies. The British Commonwealth then developed into the Commonwealth of Nations, as most of the remaining colonies became independent. They could choose whether they wanted to break all connections with the colonial past or remain within the Commonwealth as independent nations. Most of them decided to stay in the Commonwealth. Only a few small British colonies, dependencies and protectorates now remain, and are scattered widely, such as the Falklands and Gibraltar.

The present Commonwealth is a voluntary and flexible association of some 53 independent states (including Britain). It does not have written laws, an elected Parliament, or one political ruler. There is evidence of colonial rule in many of the countries, such as their educational and legal systems, but few have kept the British form of parliamentary government. Some have adapted it to their own needs, while others are one-party states or have constitutions based on a wide variety of models, with varying records on civil and democratic rights.

The Commonwealth has nearly a quarter of the world's population and comprises peoples of different religions, races and nationalities, who share a history of struggles for independence from colonialism. The Commonwealth is sometimes described as a family of nations, and, despite occasional wars, tensions and quarrels between these family members, it can operate as a worthwhile organization.

The British monarch is its non-political head and has varying constitutional roles in different countries, depending on whether they are separate kingdoms or republics. The monarch is a focal point of identification and has an important unifying and symbolic function that has often kept the Commonwealth together in times of crisis and conflict.

The Prime Ministers, or heads of state, in Commonwealth countries meet every two years under the auspices of the monarch for Commonwealth Conferences in different parts of the world. Common problems are discussed and sometimes settled, although there seem to have been more arguments than agreements in recent years, with Britain having a minority position on some issues (such as opposing trade sanctions against the former apartheid regime in South Africa).

There is a Commonwealth Secretariat in London which coordinates policy for the Commonwealth, in addition to many Commonwealth societies, institutes, libraries, professional associations and university exchange programmes. Commonwealth

PLATE 5.2 The Queen and Heads of State at the Commonwealth Conference in the Bahamas, 1985 *(Rex Features, London)*

citizens still travel to Britain as immigrants, students and visitors, while British emigration to Commonwealth countries continues in reduced amounts. English in its many varieties remains the common language of the Commonwealth, and the Commonwealth Games are held every four years. There are many joint British/Commonwealth programmes on both official and voluntary levels in agriculture, engineering, health and education, in which some vestiges of the old relationship between Britain and the Commonwealth are still apparent.

Doubts are, however, raised as to whether the Commonwealth has an effective and influential voice in world affairs.

Arguably, there is no longer the traditional sense of Commonwealth solidarity and purpose, and Britain has little in common with some Commonwealth nations. Critics argue that unless member countries feel that there are valid reasons for continuing an association that represents historical accident rather than common purpose, the long-term future of the Commonwealth must be in doubt. Indeed, successive British governments have been moving closer to Europe and distancing themselves from the Commonwealth. Opinion polls reveal that Europe is now more important for British people than the Commonwealth.

Britain had preferential trading arrangements with the Commonwealth before it joined the European Union in 1973, and the Commonwealth question formed part of the debate on membership. EU entry was seen as ending the relationship between Britain and the Commonwealth, but trading between the two has continued, although Britain has a declining share of this market and its economic priorities are now more with the European Union and other world partners. Nevertheless, Britain still contributes some 56 per cent of its overseas aid to developing countries in the Commonwealth.

The European Union (EU)

The ideal of a united Europe, strong in economic and political institutions, became increasingly attractive to European statesmen after the Second World War (1939–45). There was a desire to create a peaceful and prosperous Europe after the destruction of two World Wars and after centuries of antagonism and mutual distrust between the European powers.

The foundations for a more integrated Europe were established in 1957, when six countries (West Germany, France, Belgium, The Netherlands, Luxembourg and Italy) signed the Treaty of Rome and formed the European Economic Community (EEC). Britain did not join, but instead helped to create the European Free Trade Association (EFTA) in 1959, together with Sweden, Norway, Austria, Denmark, Portugal and Switzerland.

Britain distanced itself from closer European connections in the 1950s and saw its future in the trading patterns of the Commonwealth and an assumed 'special relationship' with the USA. It regarded itself as a commercial power and did not wish to be restricted by European relationships. An ancient suspicion of Europe also caused many British people to shrink from membership of a European organization, which they thought might result in the loss of their identity and independence.

A European commitment grew among sections of British society in the 1960s, but attempts by Britain to join the EEC were vetoed by the French President, Charles de Gaulle. He was critical of Britain's relationship with the USA (particularly on nuclear weapons policies), queried the extent of British commitment to Europe, and arguably did not want Britain as a potential rival for the leadership of the EEC.

De Gaulle resigned from the French presidency in 1969, and new British negotiations on membership began in 1970 under the pro-European Conservative Prime Minister, Edward Heath. In 1972, Parliament voted in favour of entry, despite widespread doubts and the strong opposition of a politically diverse group of interests among the British people. Britain, together with Denmark and the Irish Republic, formally joined the EEC on 1 January 1973, having left EFTA in 1972.

A new Labour government (1974) under Harold Wilson was, however, committed to giving the British people a referendum on continued membership. After further renegotiations of the terms of entry, the referendum was held in 1975, the first in British political history. The pro-marketeers won by a margin of two to one (67.2 per cent in favour, 32.8 per cent against).

The EEC was based initially on economic concerns, and instituted harmonization programmes, like Common Agricultural and fisheries policies, abolition of trade tariffs between member states, and development aid to depressed areas within its borders. Britain's poorer regions have benefited considerably from regional funds. In 1986, the member states formed an internal or Single European Market, in which goods, services, people and capital could move freely across national frontiers within what was then called the European Community. Today, 60 per cent of British exports go to the EU, and Britain receives 57 per cent of its imports from EU countries.

Some politicians had always hoped that increased economic integration would lead to political initiatives and result in a federal Europe. The Maastrict Treaty (1992) was a step in this process, as a result of which the European Community became the European Union (EU). The Treaty provides for the introduction of a common European currency (the Euro), a European Bank and common defence, foreign and social policies.

The Conservative government, however, was opposed to more integration or federalism. It opted out of Maastricht's monetary provisions and also the Social Chapter (which gives social and employment benefits to EU workers and which the Labour government has now joined in 1997). It also withdrew in 1992 from the Exchange Rate Mechanism (ERM) of the European Monetary System (EMS), which is intended to promote currency stability by drawing European currencies closer together. Some British politicians want full economic and political integration on federal lines, while others see the EU as a free-trade area in which national legal rights and interests are firmly retained.

There are now 15 EU members (Britain, Denmark, Germany, Greece, Spain, Belgium, Ireland, Luxembourg, The Netherlands, France, Italy, Portugal, Sweden, Finland and Austria) with a total population of 360 million people. Since 1994, most of the EU single market measures have also been extended to Iceland, Norway and Liechtenstein, through the creation of the European Economic Area (EEA). The actual and potential growth of the EU (to include Eastern European nations) has been seen as providing an important political voice in world affairs and a powerful trading area in global economic matters. Today, EEA member states comprise the world's largest trading bloc and account for 40 per cent of world trade.

The institutions involved in the running of the EU are the European Council, Council of Ministers, European Commission, European Parliament and European Court of Justice.

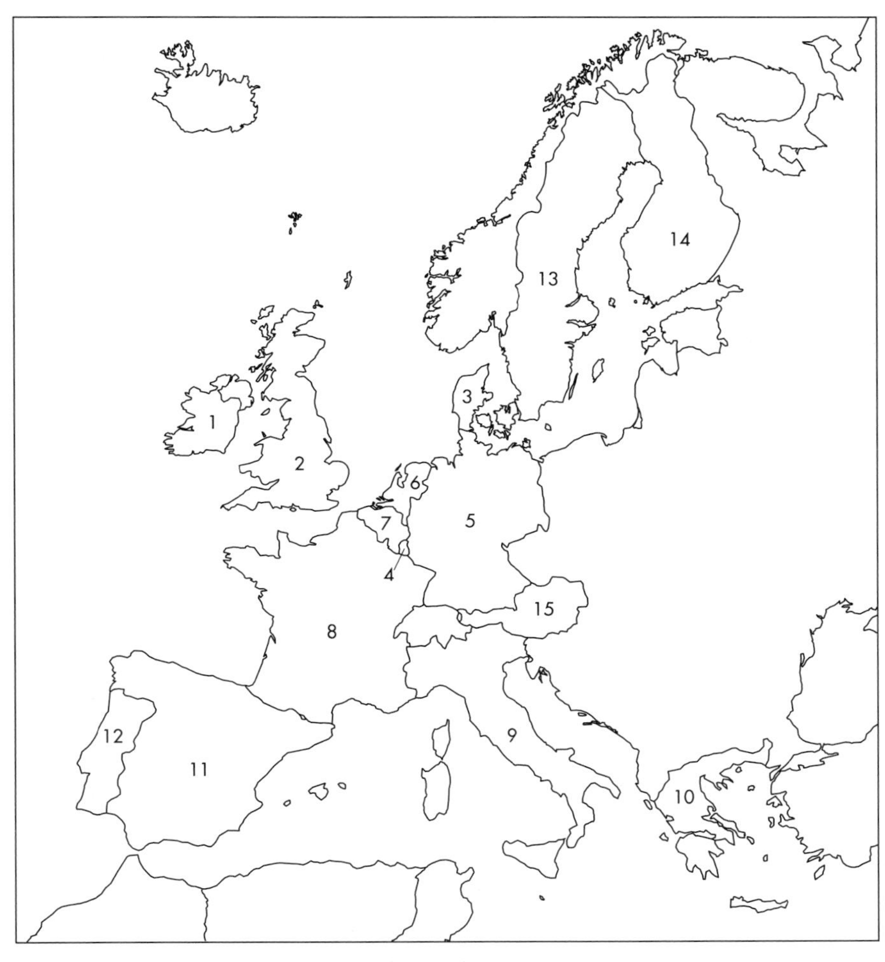

1 Irish Republic
2 Britain
3 Denmark
4 Luxembourg
5 Germany
6 The Netherlands
7 Belgium
8 France
9 Italy
10 Greece
11 Spain
12 Portugal
13 Sweden
14 Finland
15 Austria

FIGURE 5.1 The European Union, 1997

The European Council consists of government leaders who meet several times a year to discuss and agree on broad areas of policy. The Council of Ministers is the principal policy implementing body and is normally composed of Foreign Ministers (or their equivalents) from the member states.

The Commission (under an appointed President) is the central administrative force of the EU, proposing programmes and policy to the Council of Ministers. It comprises commissioners (with two from Britain) chosen from member states to hold certain portfolios, such as agriculture or competition policy, for a renewable five-year period. Their interests then become those of the EU and not of their national governments.

The European Parliament (in which Britain has 87 seats – see table 5.1) is directly elected for a five-year term on a party-political basis from the EU-wide electorate. Its functions are to advise the Council of Ministers on Commission proposals, to determine the EU budget and to exert some political control over the Council and the Commission. Its powers of veto over EU policy have now been extended by the Maastricht Treaty. In the 1994 British EU Parliament elections, the Conservatives did very badly compared with the Labour Party, while the Liberal Democrats suffered because of the 'first past the post' system. The next British EU Parliament election in 1999 will take place under a partial PR arrangement with party lists.

The Court of Justice comprises judges from the member states. It settles disputes concerning EU law and is a very influential factor because it also determines the application of EU law in the domestic systems of the member states.

Critics argue that the Council of Ministers and the Commission should be more democratically accountable and that the Parliament, as the only elected body, should have more power. But it will take time before EU institutions achieve their final shape and before the member states agree as to what that shape should be.

British membership of the EU has been a difficult one. It has complained about its contribution to the EU budget; objected to the workings of Common Agricultural and fisheries policies;

TABLE 5.1 European Union Parliament: election results (Britain), 1994

Party	*Seats*	*Vote (%)*
Conservative	18	26.9
Labour	62	42.7
Liberal Democrats	2	16.1
Scottish National Party	2	3.1
Northern Irish parties	3	7.1

and opposed movements towards greater political and economic integration. Critics argue that Britain's sovereignty and independence are threatened by EU developments. But all the major political parties are pro-European, although there are opposition groups (Eurosceptics) in the Labour and (particularly) the Conservative parties. The country is now so closely tied to Europe in economic and institutional ways that withdrawal would be difficult in practical terms, although it is possible constitutionally. But there are divided views about the pace and direction of future developments. For example, the Labour government will not take Britain into the first wave of the common currency in 1999. It will wait until Britain's economy is in line with other members, and will see how the measure develops before putting the issue to a referendum. In 1997, European Commission polls suggested that 65 per cent of Britons were against joining a common currency.

British support for the EU peaked in the early 1980s but has since eroded. A 1997 MORI poll found that, for the first time, the public is evenly divided on whether Britain should stay in or get out of the EU: 40 per cent are now on each side, with the rest as 'don't knows'. These figures coincide with a 1997 Eurobarometer poll that found that barely 38 per cent of British respondents felt that EU membership was a good thing. Only Sweden and Austria were more sceptical. Public support for the EU tends therefore to be lukewarm and indifferent. The turn-out for British EU Parliament elections is the lowest in Europe, and there is ignorance about the EU and its institutions. But polls show that Europe is considered to be more important to Britain than the USA and the Commonwealth, and Europeanism seems to be more easily and naturally accepted by younger people.

Eire and Northern Ireland

Northern Ireland (also known as 'the six counties', or Ulster after the ancient kingdom in the north-east of the island) is constitutionally a part of the United Kingdom, but its history is inseparable from that of the Republic of Ireland (Ireland or Eire). Historically, mainland Britain has been unable to accommodate itself successfully to its next-door neighbours. During the twentieth century, as Britain has detached itself from empire and entered the European Union, its relationship with Northern Ireland and Eire has been problematic.

A basic knowledge of the island's long and troubled history is essential in order to understand the present situation in Northern Ireland, for any solution to the problems there cannot be simplistic. Ireland was first attacked by England in the twelfth century. Since then there have been continuous rebellions by the native Irish against English colonial, political and military rule.

The situation worsened in the sixteenth century, when Catholic Ireland refused to accept the Protestant Reformation, despite much religious persecution. The two seeds of future hatred, colonialism and religion, were thus early sown in Irish history. A hundred years later, Oliver Cromwell crushed rebellions in Ireland and continued the earlier 'plantation policy', by which English and Scottish settlers were given land and rights over the native Irish. These colonists also served as a police force to put down any Irish revolts. The descendants of the Protestant settlers became a powerful political minority in Ireland as a whole and a majority in Ulster. In 1690, the Protestant William III (William of Orange) crushed Catholic uprisings at the Battle of the Boyne and secured Protestant dominance in Northern Ireland.

Ireland was then mainly an agricultural country, dependent upon its farming produce. Crop failures were frequent, however, and famine in the middle of the nineteenth century caused death and emigration, with the result that the Irish population was reduced by a quarter. The people who remained demanded more Irish autonomy over their own affairs. Irish MPs in the Westminster Parliament called persistently for 'home rule' for Ireland (control of internal matters by the Irish through an assembly in Dublin). The home rule question dominated late nineteenth- and early twentieth-century British politics and led to periodic outbreaks of violence, as the Northern Irish Protestant majority feared that an independent and united Ireland would be dominated by the Catholics.

Eventually, in 1921, Ireland was divided (or partitioned) into two parts as a result of uprisings, violence and eventual political agreement. This attempted solution of the historical problems has been at the root of the troubles ever since. The 26 counties of southern Ireland became the Irish Free State and a dominion in the Commonwealth. It later developed into the Republic of Ireland (Eire), remained neutral in the Second World War and left the Commonwealth in 1949. The six counties in the north became known as Northern Ireland and remained constitutionally part of the United Kingdom. They had their own Protestant-dominated Parliament (at Stormont outside Belfast), which was responsible for governing the province.

After the Second World War, Northern Ireland developed agriculturally and industrially. Urban centres expanded and more specifically Catholic districts developed in the towns. But the Protestants, through their ruling party (the Ulster Unionists) in Parliament, maintained an exclusive hold on all areas of life in the province, including employment, the police force, local councils and public services. The minority Catholics suffered systematic discrimination in these areas.

The present troubles in Northern Ireland began in 1968–9. Marches were held to demonstrate for civil liberties and were initially non-sectarian. But the situation deteriorated, fighting erupted between Protestants and Catholics, and violence escalated. The

Northern Ireland government asked for the British Army to be sent in to restore order. The Army was initially welcomed, but was soon attacked by both sides. Relations between Catholics and Protestants worsened and political attitudes became polarized. Violence has continued since 1968; the political situation is unresolved and outrages have come from both sides of the sectarian divide.

On one side of the violence is the Provisional wing of the Irish Republican Army (IRA), which is supported by some republicans and Catholics. The IRA is illegal in both Eire and Northern Ireland and is committed to the unification of Ireland, as is its legal political wing, Provisional Sinn Fein. The IRA fights to remove the British political and military presence from Northern Ireland by a campaign of bombings, shootings and murders.

Protestant paramilitary groups and Unionist Parties, like the Democratic Unionists under the leadership of Ian Paisley, are equally committed to their own views. They are loyal to the British Crown and insist that they remain part of the United Kingdom. Protestant politicians have refused to accept reforms that would give Catholics genuine participation in Northern Ireland's political life. Protestant paramilitaries, partly in retaliation for IRA activities and partly to emphasize their demands, have also carried out sectarian murders and terrorist acts. British troops and the Royal Ulster Constabulary (the police force in Northern Ireland) are supposed to control the two populations and to curb terrorism, but they are also targets for bullets and bombs, and have even been accused of perpetrating atrocities themselves.

At present, responsibility for Northern Ireland lies with the British government in London (direct rule), because the Northern Ireland Parliament was dissolved in 1972. Since then, there have been various assemblies and executives in Northern Ireland, which were attempts to give the Catholic minority political representation in cooperation with the Protestant majority (power sharing). But these efforts have failed, largely because of Protestant intransigence, although most injustices to Catholic civil liberties have been removed.

The Anglo-Irish Agreement of 1985 was another attempt to resolve the troubled situation. It was hoped that the Dublin and

London governments would discuss common problems to a greater extent than in the past. The agreement aimed to solve difficulties (such as border security and extradition arrangements) in order to achieve a devolved power sharing government for Northern Ireland. The Republic of Ireland had to make some political concessions as the price for the agreement, but now has a significant role to play in the resolution of the Northern Irish situation. However, the Republic's cooperation with Britain was seen by Northern Irish Protestants as the first step to reunification of the island, and they have opposed the agreement. The Republic now sees unification as a long-term aim. The British government, for its part, states that no change in Northern Ireland will take place unless a majority of the inhabitants there agree (consent). The 1997 population of Northern Ireland consisted of 1 million Protestants and 600,000 Catholics.

The level of violence in the province has fluctuated since 1968, but emergency legislation and the reduction of legal rights for suspected terrorists continue. Moderates of all political persuasions, who were squeezed out as political polarization grew, are appalled by the outrages and the historical injustices. Outsiders often feel that a rational solution should be possible, but this is to underestimate the deep emotions on both sides, the historical dimension and the extremist elements. Part of the problem is that there is little agreement over its cause, with views including ethnic, national, religious and economic reasons.

British governments have periodically launched initiatives to persuade Northern Irish political parties to meet in order to discuss the realistic possibilities of power sharing in Northern Ireland. The Downing Street Declaration of 1993 by the Irish and British governments largely restated existing positions, but was also a further attempt to halt the violence and bring all parties to the conference table in order to discuss the future of the whole of the country. But these initiatives did not initially produce any real change in attitudes.

However, building on a Protestant paramilitary ceasefire, the Labour government in 1997 set out conditions and a schedule for peace talks between all the political parties. An IRA ceasefire was called, which allowed Sinn Fein into the peace process that began in September 1997. But profound difficulties remain in the path of progress. The Protestant Unionists want to remain part of the United Kingdom, oppose union with the Republic of Ireland, insist upon the decommissioning of all terrorist weapons and argue that any future solution for Northern Ireland must lie in consent by a majority of the people living there. Sinn Fein and the IRA, however, are committed to a united Ireland, disagree about the decommissioning of terrorist weapons and argue that a majority of all people (Northern Ireland and the Republic) must consent to any eventual proposed solution.

Opinion polls in recent years indicate a weariness by the mainland British population with both sides in Northern Ireland and a desire to be rid of the problem. A majority of people seem to be in favour of the unification of Ireland, rather than Northern Ireland continuing to be part of the United Kingdom; support the withdrawal of British troops; and do not accept the British government's strategy of withdrawal only with the consent of the majority in Northern Ireland.

EXERCISES

■ Explain and examine the following terms:

Commonwealth	Falklands	Treaty of Rome
decolonization	Boyne	NATO
direct rule	Stormont	referendum
power sharing	Trident	'special relationship'
Sinn Fein	Maastricht	European Commission
EFTA	IRA	pro-marketeer
Euro	Unionists	EEA

■ Write short essays on the following topics:

1. What solution(s) would you suggest to the present situation in Northern Ireland? Give your reasons.
2. Does the Commonwealth still have a role to play today?
3. Discuss possible future developments of the European Union.

Chapter 6

The legal system

BRITAIN DOES NOT HAVE A common legal system. Instead, there are three separate elements – those of England and Wales (with which this chapter is mainly concerned), Scotland, and Northern Ireland. They differ from each other in their procedures, legal professions and courts. Some laws are peculiar to only one of the nations, although much Westminster legislation applies to all of Britain. But from the year 2000, a Scottish Parliament will legislate for Scotland in devolved matters.

British court cases are divided into civil and criminal law. Civil law mainly involves private rights and settles disputes between individuals or organizations. It deals with claims for compensation (financial or otherwise) by a person (the plaintiff) who has suffered loss or damage (like a breach of contract or a negligent act) at the hands of another (the defendant). Civil cases may be decided by settlement before trial or by a judge (and sometimes a jury) after trial.

Criminal law protects society by punishing those (the accused or defendants) who commit crimes against the state, such as theft or murder. The state usually prosecutes an individual or group at a trial in order to establish guilt. The result may be a fine or imprisonment. Such punishment is supposed to act as a deterrent to potential offenders, as well as stating society's attitudes on a range of matters.

The legal system is one of the oldest and most traditional British institutions. Its authority and influence are due to its independence from the executive and legislative branches of government. It is supposed to serve citizens; control unlawful activities against them and the state; protect civil liberties; and support legitimate government.

It has, however, historically been accused of harshness; supporting vested and political interests; favouring property rather than human rights; maintaining the isolation and mystique of the law; encouraging the delay and expense of legal actions; and showing a bias against the poor and disadvantaged. It has been criticized for its resistance to reform and the maintenance of professional privileges that may conflict with the public interest.

Critics feel that the law has still not adapted to changing conditions, or understood the needs of contemporary society. Recent miscarriages of justice have embarrassed the police, government and judiciary and increased public concern about the quality of criminal justice. Similar misgivings are also felt about the expense and operation of the civil law.

The legal system has changed over the centuries. Today, consumer demands, professional pressures and government reforms are forcing it to develop, sometimes rapidly and sometimes slowly. Most people in the past were ignorant of the law. It now affects citizens more directly and to a greater practical extent than before. Increased demands are made upon it by individuals, the state and corporate bodies. Concern about crime has emphasized the control role of the criminal law, while increased divorce, family breakdown and other factors have led to a heavier workload for the civil law.

English legal history

English legal history has been conditioned by two basic concerns: first, that the law should be administered by the state in national courts, and second, that judges should be independent of royal and political control.

State centralization of the law meant that the same laws should be applicable to the whole of England. This aim was realized by Norman rulers in the twelfth century. The early courts were centred mainly in London, where they dealt with canon (or church), criminal, civil and commercial law.

There was increasingly a need for courts in local areas outside London to apply the national law, and so by the end of the twelfth century, London judges were travelling the country and deciding cases locally. In 1327, Edward III appointed magistrates (Justices of the Peace) in each county who could hold alleged criminals in gaol until their later trial by a London judge. The powers of the magistrates were gradually extended, and they ran a system of local criminal courts with the London judges. But there was no adequate provision for local civil courts. These were not established until 1846, and a fully integrated apparatus of local civil and criminal law was only gradually established nationwide after this date.

Through the centuries, a growing population, an expanding volume of legal work and an increasing social and economic complexity necessitated more courts and specialization. But the number of local and London courts in this haphazard historical development resulted in an overlapping of functions and diversity of procedures, which hindered implementation of the law. The two periods of major reform to alleviate this situation were in 1873–5, when the Judicature Acts carried out a complete court revision, and in 1970–1, when further changes produced the present court system in England and Wales.

The second concern was that the judiciary should be independent of the executive and legislative branches of government. The monarch had been largely responsible for the administration of the law in earlier centuries, and later interfered in the legal process, as well as dismissing unsympathetic judges. Judicial independence was achieved only in 1701, when the Act of Settlement made judges irremovable from office, except by an appeal to the monarch from both Houses of Parliament. This principle has now been relaxed for junior judges, who may be dismissed in certain cases, and all judges who commit criminal offences are expected to resign.

Sources of contemporary English law

The three main sources of English law today are the common law, statute law and European Union law.

The oldest source is the *common law*, which is based on the customs of successive settlers and invaders from Europe. After the Norman Conquest, it became a uniform body of rules and principles that were decided and written down by judges in court cases (case law). These judgments were recognized as the law of the land and were applied by common law courts. Today, the same rules guide judges in their interpretation of statutes and in the expansion of the common law itself.

Common law decisions form precedents from which later judges can deduce the principles of law that may be applied to new cases. Precedents are strong in English law and the judges of the lower courts must generally follow them. Normally, the power to create new precedents is reserved to the House of Lords, as the supreme court of appeal. Its rulings represent the current state of the law to be applied by all courts. The tradition of following precedent maintains consistency and continuity. But it can also make the law conservative and fail to take account of changing social conditions.

Statute law was originally created by the monarch, but by the thirteenth century was gradually made through royal orders in response to petitions from Parliament. Parliament itself later became the legislating authority because of its growing power against the monarch. Modern statutes are a nineteenth- and twentieth-century development and arose because new rules were required to meet the needs of a rapidly changing society.

Statutes are Acts of Parliament, created after a bill has passed through Parliament. Parliament makes new laws, which have usually been initiated by the government. Acts are supreme over all other forms of law (except for some European Union law). From 2000, the Privy Council will resolve any conflicts between Westminster Acts and Scottish Parliament Acts. Much British law (criminal and civil) is now in statute form and shows the influence of the state in citizens' lives.

European Union law became part of English (British) law following Britain's entry into the European Economic Community in 1973. EU law takes precedence over British domestic law in certain areas, and judges must apply EU law when there is a conflict with Acts of Parliament. EU law and British domestic law now coexist, and Britain plays its part in creating EU law.

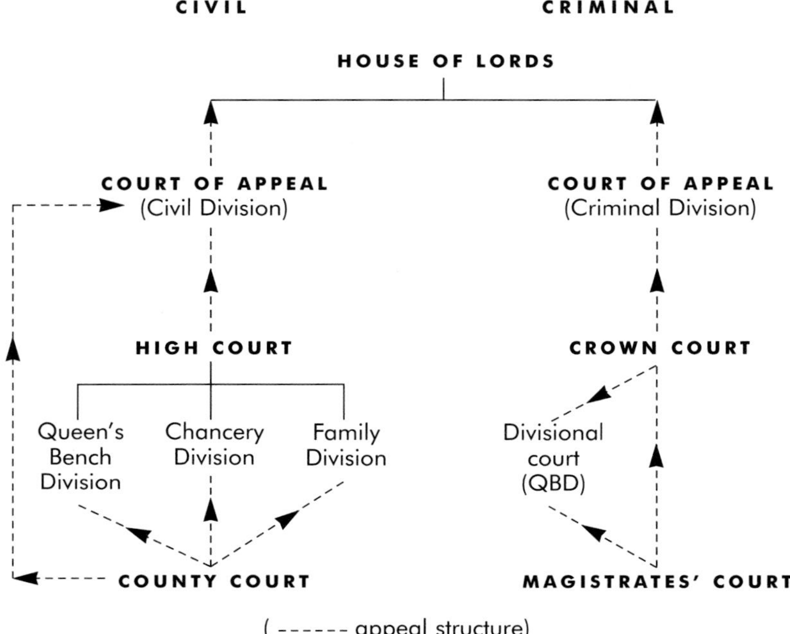

FIGURE 6.1 Civil and criminal courts

The court system in England and Wales

The formal court system is divided into criminal and civil courts at various levels (see figure 6.1).

Criminal courts

There are two levels of criminal courts. The lower and busiest is the magistrates' court, which deals with summary (less serious) cases and handles over 95 per cent of all criminal matters. The more serious (indictable) criminal offences, such as murder, are tried by the higher court, the crown court.

Magistrates' courts serve urban and rural local areas in England and Wales. Two types of magistrates sit in the courts: Justices of the Peace (JPs) and stipendiary magistrates.

PLATE 6.1 Inside the magistrates' court *(Priscilla Coleman)*

Most magistrates' courts are presided over by 30,000 lay magistrates (JPs). They are part-time judicial officials chosen from the general public, who hear cases without a jury, receive no salary for their services (only expenses) and who have some legal training before they sit in court. Magistrates may be motivated by the desire to perform a public service or by the supposed prestige of the position. They sit daily in big cities and less frequently in rural areas. They date from 1327 and illustrate a legal system in which the ordinary person is judged by other citizens, rather than by professionals.

Magistrates are appointed by the Crown on the advice of the Lord Chancellor, who receives suitable names from local committees in each county. This procedure has been criticized for its secrecy and exclusivity. Magistrates in the past were white middle- or upper-class males who were prominent in the local community, such as land owners, doctors, retired military officers and businessmen. In recent years, the committees have recruited magistrates of both sexes from wider and more representative social, ethnic and gender backgrounds.

The magistrates' court has an average of three JPs when hearing cases, composed usually of men and women. They decide a case on the facts and the punishment (if any). They are advised on points of law by their clerk, who is a legally qualified, full-time official, and a professional element in the system. The clerk is restricted to an advisory role and must not be involved in the magistrates' decision making. But, in order to avoid delays and improve cost-efficiency, it is proposed to upgrade the clerks' role by making them 'trial managers'. They would handle some duties of magistrates, such as decisions about trial by jury, extending bail (see below) and discontinuing cases. Magistrates oppose such developments, arguing that they will give the clerks a judicial role.

Everyone accused of a criminal offence (defendant) must usually appear first before a magistrates' court. The court can try summary offences and some indictable/summary offences ('either-way offences'). The defendant must consent to the latter, but also has the right (which may be abolished in future for some offences) to choose jury trial in the crown court. However, the magistrates may decide that an offence is more suitable for the crown court, and the defendant has no choice in the matter. The magistrates will then (and with other indictable offences) hold committal proceedings to decide whether evidence of the alleged crime is strong enough for committal (sending on) to the crown court for trial.

Magistrates have limited powers of punishment. They may impose fines up to £5,000 for each offence, or send people to prison for six months on each offence up to a maximum of one year. They prefer not to imprison if a fine or other punishment is sufficient and the majority of penalties are fines.

There is a need for uniform punishments in magistrates' courts, but sentences vary in different parts of the country. This factor, in addition to alleged bias and the amateur status of JPs, has led to criticism of the system. There have been proposals to replace magistrates with lawyers or other experts and to centralize the system. But these suggestions are criticized by those who oppose the professionalization of the legal process and who argue that such changes would not necessarily result in greater competence or justice.

An important function of magistrates is to decide criminal cases involving young persons under the age of 18 in Youth Courts. Media reports of these cases must not normally identify the accused, and there is a range of punishments for those who are found guilty. Youth Courts have a central role to play, particularly at a time when most crimes are committed by young people. The Labour government proposes tougher treatment for young offenders and to make parents responsible for their children. It may also restrict magistrates to guilty pleas and give not-guilty pleas to stipendiary magistrates.

Magistrates' courts also handle limited civil matters involving family problems and divorce, road traffic violations, and licence applications for public amenities such as restaurants, clubs, public houses (pubs) and betting shops.

Stipendiary magistrates are qualified lawyers and full-time officials who are paid by the state. They usually sit alone to hear and decide cases and work mainly in the large cities. Since the magistrates' system is divided between JPs and professional stipendiaries, it is sometimes argued that the latter should be used to replace the amateurs on a national basis. But this proposal has been resisted by those who wish to retain the civilian element in the magistrates' courts.

The higher *crown courts*, such as the Central Criminal Court in London (popularly known as the Old Bailey), are situated in about 90 cities in England and Wales and are administered by the Lord Chancellor's Department in London.

The crown court has jurisdiction over all indictable criminal offences, and innocence or guilt after a trial is decided by a jury of 12 citizens. After the court has reached its decision on the facts of the case, sentence is passed by the judge who is in charge of proceedings throughout the trial.

DEFEND·THE·CHILDREN·OF·THE·
POOR·&·PVNISH·THE·WRONGDOER·

In Scotland, minor criminal cases are tried summarily in District Courts but mainly in Sheriffs' Courts. The sheriff sits alone to hear summary offences and has the help of a jury (15 members) for indictable cases. Serious cases are handled by the High Court of Justiciary. Northern Irish criminal courts generally follow the system in England and Wales.

Criminal appeal courts in England and Wales

The appeal structure (see figure 6.1) is supposed to be a safeguard against mistakes and miscarriages of justice. But the number of such cases has increased, resulting in much publicity and concern. They have been caused by police tampering with or withholding evidence; police pressure to induce confessions; and the unreliability of forensic evidence. Appeal courts are criticized for their handling of some appeals, and an independent authority (the Criminal Cases Review Commission) was created in 1995. It reviews alleged miscarriages of justice and now receives many applications.

Appeals to a higher court can be expensive and difficult, and permission must usually have been granted by a lower court. Appeals may be made against conviction or sentence and can be brought on grounds of fact and law. If successful, the higher court may quash the conviction, reduce the sentence or order a new trial. The prosecution can also appeal against a lenient punishment and a heavier sentence may be substituted.

The crown courts are appeal courts from the magistrates' courts, and both may appeal on matters of law to a divisional court of the Queen's Bench Division. Appeals from the crown court are made to the Criminal Division of the Court of Appeal and heard by two judges. Appeals may then go to the House of Lords as the highest court in England and Wales, but permission for this is granted only if a point of law of public importance is involved. Up to five Law Lords hear the case and their decisions represent the current state of the law.

PLATE 6.2 The Old Bailey, London *(Tony Parry/Barnaby)*

PLATE 6.3 Inside the Old Bailey, London *(Priscilla Coleman)*

In Scotland, the High Court of Justiciary in Edinburgh tries criminal cases and also hears criminal appeals. Northern Ireland has its own appeal courts, but the Court of Appeal and the House of Lords in London may also be used.

Civil courts in England and Wales

Civil law proceedings can be brought either in the county court or in the High Court (see figure 6.1). The main difference between the two is that actions up to a value of £50,000 can be dealt with in the county court, whereas more expensive and complicated cases are decided in the High Court.

England and Wales are divided into 250 districts, with a *county court* for each district, and a county court or circuit judge has responsibility for a number of courts. The judge usually sits alone when hearing cases.

PLATE 6.4 The Royal Courts of Justice, London *(John Oakland)*

The county court handles a range of money, property, contract, divorce and family matters. It is much busier than the High Court and is equivalent to the magistrates' court. In Scotland, the sheriff court deals with most civil actions, because its jurisdiction is not financially limited, although the higher Court of Session may also be used for some cases.

The *High Court of Justice* has its main centre in London, with branches throughout England and Wales. It is divided into three divisions which specialize in specific matters. The *Queen's Bench Division* has a wide jurisdiction, including contract and negligence cases; the *Chancery Court Division* is concerned with commercial, financial and succession matters; and the *Family Division* deals with domestic issues such as marriage, divorce, property and the custody of children.

Civil appeal courts in England and Wales

The High Court hears appeals from magistrates' courts and county courts. But the main avenue of appeal is to the Court of Appeal (Civil Division), which deals with appeals from all lower civil courts on questions of law and fact. It can reverse or amend decisions, or sometimes order a new trial.

Appeals from the Court of Appeal may be made to the House of Lords. The appellant must normally have obtained permission from either the Court of Appeal or the House of Lords. Appeals are usually restricted to points of law where an important legal issue is at stake. In Scotland at present, civil appeals are made first to a sheriff-principal, then to the Court of Session and finally to the House of Lords in London.

Civil and criminal procedure in England and Wales

Civil procedure

A civil action in the county court or the High Court begins when the plaintiff serves documents (containing details of a claim) on the defendant. If the defendant defends the action, the court is informed; documents are prepared and circulated to all parties; and the case proceeds to trial and judgment. A decision in civil cases is reached on the balance of probabilities. The court also decides the expenses of the action, which may be considerable, and the loser usually pays both his own and his opponent's costs.

Civil litigation can be relatively cheap, quick and efficient in the county court, but it can be complicated, expensive and subject to delay in the High Court. It is often advisable that disputes be settled by negotiation out of court to avoid high costs and any uncertainty about a trial result.

Attempts are being made to reorganize civil law procedures because of concern about the lack of efficiency of the system, with its delays and expense. Much of the High Court's work has been transferred to the county court, and cheaper, quicker alternative forms of settlement have been implemented, particularly those dealing with smaller matters.

Criminal procedure

Crimes are offences against the laws of the state, and the state usually brings a person to trial. Prior to 1985, the police in England and Wales were responsible for prosecuting criminal cases, but a Crown Prosecution Service (CPS) now does this job. It is independent of the police, financed by the state and staffed by state lawyers. There is criticism of the performance of the CPS, which suffers from understaffing and underfunding. The CPS and its head (the Director of Public Prosecutions – DPP) have the final word in deciding whether to proceed with difficult cases. In Scotland, prosecution duties rest with the Crown Office and Procurator-Fiscal Service, and in Northern Ireland with the police and the DPP.

Arrests for most criminal offences are made by the police, although any citizen can make a 'citizen's arrest'. Arrests of suspects and searches of property can now be made by the police for certain arrestable offences without applying to the magistrates' court for arrest and search warrants, although in some cases they must still follow this procedure.

The police operate under codes of practice that lay down strict procedures for the protection of suspects. The police have no authority to question people or to detain them at a police station if they have not been arrested or charged. Once a person has been arrested and charged with an offence, he or she must be brought before a magistrates' court, normally within 24 hours. This period can be extended to up to 96 hours without charge in serious cases. After 96 hours, the police must release the suspect if no charges are brought. The police have been heavily criticized in recent years for their arrest, questioning and charging practices.

When a person appears before a magistrates' court prior to a trial, the magistrates can grant or refuse bail (freedom from custody). If bail is refused, a person will be kept in custody in a remand centre or in prison. If bail is granted, the individual is set free until his or her later court appearance. The court may require certain assurances from the accused about conduct while on bail, such as residence in a specific area and reporting to a police station.

Application for bail is a legal right, since the accused has not yet been found guilty of a crime, and there should be strong reasons for refusing it. There is concern that people who are refused bail are, at their later trial, either found not guilty or are punished only by a fine. The system thus holds alleged criminals (one-fifth of prison inmates) in custody to await trial and increases overcrowding in prisons. But there is also public concern about accused persons who commit further serious offences while free on bail.

Many people charged with minor offences, such as road traffic violations, are not arrested. They are summoned to appear in court to hear the charges against them. It is often suggested that the summons procedure could be used more widely in order to avoid bail problems and prison overcrowding.

Criminal trials in the magistrates' and crown courts are, with a few exceptions, open to the public. But the media can report only the court proceedings and must not comment upon them while the trial is in progress (the *sub judice* rule).

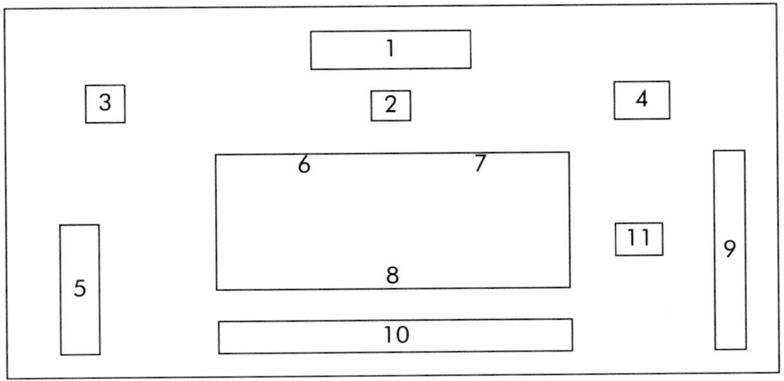

1 Magistrates
2 Clerk to the Justices
3 Defendant
4 Witness
5 Press seats
6 Defending lawyer
7 Prosecuting lawyer
8 Probation officers
9 Witnesses who gave evidence
10 The public seats
11 Court ushers

FIGURE 6.2 A typical magistrates' court in action

The accused enters the dock, the charge is read and he or she pleads 'guilty' or 'not guilty'. On a 'guilty' plea, the person is often sentenced after a short presentation of the facts by the prosecution. On a 'not guilty' plea, the trial proceeds in order to establish the person's innocence or guilt. An individual is innocent until proved guilty, and it is the responsibility of the prosecution to prove guilt beyond a reasonable doubt. If proof is not achieved, a 'not guilty' verdict is returned by magistrates in the magistrates' court or by the jury in the crown court. In Scotland, there is an additional possible verdict of 'not proven'.

The prosecution and defence of the accused are usually performed by solicitors in magistrates' courts and by barristers and solicitor-advocates in crown courts. But it is possible to defend oneself. An English trial is an adversarial contest between defence and prosecution. Both sides call witnesses in support of their case, who may be questioned by the other side. The rules of evidence and procedure in this contest are complicated and must be strictly observed. The accused may remain silent when arrested and charged and at the trial and need not give evidence. However, the right to silence has been abolished for terrorist trials in Northern Ireland and limited in all courts. This means that the police must warn arrestees that their silence may affect their later defence. The judge at the trial may comment on the defendant's silence and it may influence the decision of juries and magistrates.

Critics argue that the adversarial nature of criminal trials can result either in the conviction of innocent people or the guilty escaping conviction. They maintain that the inquisitorial system of other European countries would be better. This allows the prior

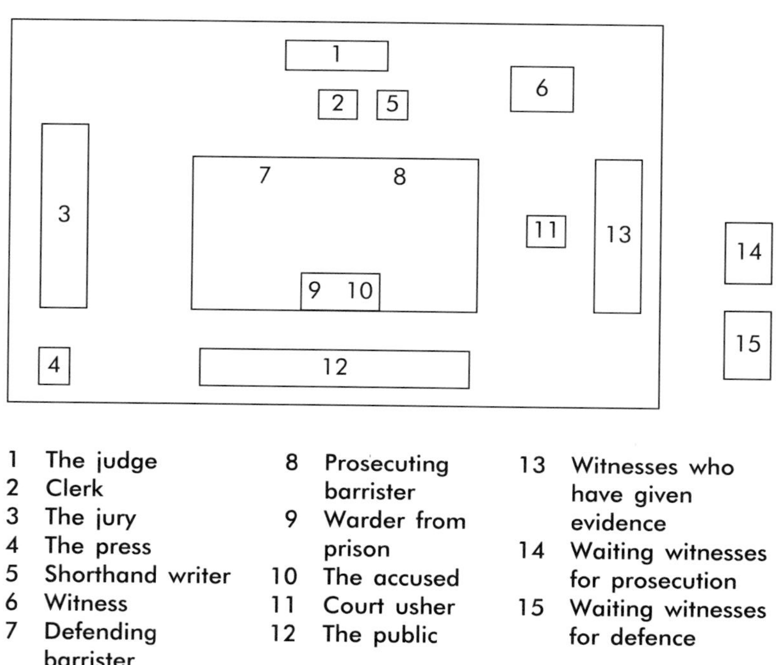

FIGURE 6.3 A typical crown court in action

questioning of suspects and establishing of facts to be carried out by professional impartial interrogators rather than the police.

The judge in the crown court and the magistrates in the magistrates' court are controlling influences in the battle between defence and prosecution. They apply the rules of the court and give directions on procedure and evidence. But they should not interfere too actively, or show bias. After the prosecution and the defence have concluded their cases, the magistrates decide both the verdict and sentence. In the crown court, the jury delivers the verdict after the judge has given a summing-up and the judge pronounces sentence. Details of other admitted crimes may be taken into account before sentence on a 'guilty' decision, and the defence may offer a plea of mitigation in an attempt to reduce the sentence.

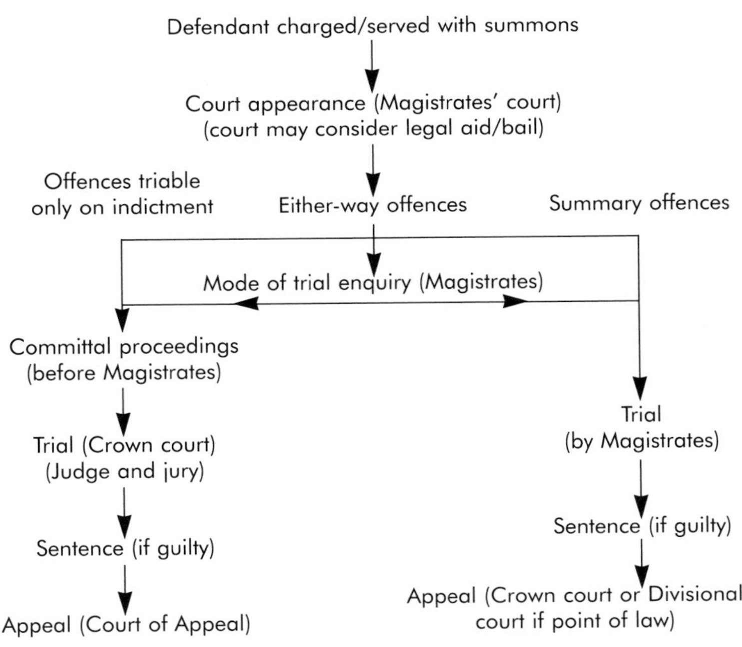

FIGURE 6.4 Criminal procedure

The jury

Trial by jury is an ancient and important feature of English justice. Although it has declined in civil cases (except for libel and fraud), it is the main element in criminal trials in the crown court. Most categories of British residents are obliged to undertake jury service when summoned.

Before the start of a criminal trial in the crown court, 12 jurors are chosen from a list of 30 names randomly selected from local electoral registers. They listen to the evidence at the trial and give their verdict on the facts, after having been isolated in a separate room for their deliberations. If a jury cannot reach a decision, it will be discharged and a new one sworn in. The accused can thus be tried twice for the same offence (as in appeals that order a new trial). Such results are an exception to the principle that a person can be tried only once for an offence. In most cases, the jury reaches a decision, and until 1967 the verdict had to be unanimous. But now the judge accepts a majority verdict after the jury has deliberated for more than two hours, provided that there are no more than two dissentients (that is 10 to two). The jury does not decide the punishment or sentence, except in some civil cases where it awards damages.

The jury system is the ordinary citizen's link with the legal process. It is supposed to safeguard individual liberty and justice, because a commonsense decision on the facts either to punish or acquit is taken by fellow citizens rather than by professionals. The system has, however, been criticized because of its high acquittal rates; allegedly unsuitable or subjective jurors; intimidation of jurors; and need to save time and expense. Some critics would like to replace the jury with panels of experts and reduce the right to jury-trial for some either-way offences like theft. But it seems that the jury will continue in its present form for most cases.

Legal aid

The legal aid fund was established in 1949. It enables those persons who are unable to afford legal representation and advice in criminal and civil matters to have their bills paid by the state. Applicants must prove that they have a suitable case and that their income falls below certain financial limits. Only those with very low incomes or who are receiving welfare benefits qualify. There are frequent demands to raise the income limits to include more people, but governments have, in fact, reduced the legal aid fund so that fewer people are eligible for help. This is seen as a serious development in the provision of justice, especially when demand is constantly rising. Given the high costs of legal actions, only the poor or the very rich can afford litigation costs without hardship.

A recent reform may ease the pressures on legal aid and on those people who wish to start civil actions but who cannot afford the cost. Clients can enter into conditional agreements with lawyers, in which payment of legal fees on a percentage basis is made only if the client wins. The Labour government intends to extend this scheme to most civil disputes that involve money or damages, and also to cap legal aid fees. But critics argue that 'no-win' work will appeal to lawyers only if there is a reasonable chance of winning, and that it will not solve the problem of insuring against the cost of losing.

Punishment and law enforcement

Crime and punishment

The overall cost of crime to Britain in 1997 (including the expense of the criminal justice system) was estimated by the Home Office to be £30 billion a year, or nearly 5 per cent of national income. Law and order in Britain are therefore serious issues that are of great concern to people and on which political parties base their claims for public support.

Problems in this area are the reliability of statistics, the non-reporting of offences such as burglary and rape, and the arguable findings by research organizations. Government figures show that there was a 10 per cent decrease in overall reported crime in 1996 and early 1997 in England and Wales, but a 9 per cent increase in violent crimes like assaults, robberies and sexual offences. This increase was mostly restricted to London, since reported violent crime in other parts of the country fell. But the number of unsolved crimes remains high, with a clear-up rate of 23 per cent, and it is estimated that only one in 50 crimes results in a conviction.

Disturbing aspects of these statistics are the greater use of firearms in criminal acts (leading to demands that the police should be armed), the increased amount of drug-related crime, and the number of offences committed by young people. Britain has a serious problem with young offenders: the peak age for committing crime is 15, and one in four criminal offences is committed by teenagers under 16.

The International Crime Victimization Survey (interviews with crime victims) suggested in 1997 that England and Wales had the worst crime record among 11 nations (USA, Canada, The Netherlands, France, Switzerland, Scotland, Sweden, Finland, Austria and Northern Ireland). Apparently, 4 per cent of the population suffered violent crime every year, compared with an international average of 2.5 per cent, and a third were victims of overall crime in 1996. However, such victim-based statistics can create a more frightening picture than actually exists. Nevertheless, a 1997 MORI poll showed that the number of crimes committed in England and Wales might be twice the figure recorded by the police, and 50 per cent of victims did not report incidents to the police because they had no confidence that the criminals would be caught. The Home Office itself admits that only 23 per cent of all crimes are recorded.

Interviewees in a 1990 MORI poll thought that the causes of crime in Britain (repeated in later polls) were: lack of parental discipline (75 per cent); drugs (71); alcohol (62); lenient sentencing (62); unemployment (61); lack of school discipline (51); poverty (40); television (27); poor policing (20); and national newspapers (10). The Labour government is trying to ease public concern by promising 'zero tolerance' for crime and by being 'tough on crime and the causes of crime'. Punishment will be stricter (particularly for young offenders), curfews and restrictions will be placed on persistent offenders, and greater protection will be given to the public. Privately owned handguns were banned in 1997, and replica handguns will be outlawed. But some gun owners have merely switched to higher calibre weapons, such as carbines.

A person found guilty of a first criminal offence may receive no punishment, or be placed on probation for a period under supervision of a probation officer. Other punishments for adults are usually fines or imprisonment (over 21), which vary according to the severity of the offence and any previous convictions. There have been attempts to avoid giving prison sentences because of overcrowded prisons. But stricter sentencing will lead to more prisoners, and 18 per cent of convicted persons are imprisoned, which is a higher rate than in other European countries. Britain had the largest prison population in Western Europe with 56,000 prisoners in 1997 (4 per cent women), and this figure is expected to rise to 75,000 by 2005. This increase will require the building of at least 30 new prisons.

Alternatives to prison are community service (serving the community in some capacity for a number of hours) and prison sentences that are suspended for a period, if no further offences are committed. Young people under 21 may be punished by being fined (under 17), taken into local authority care, confined in a young offenders' institution (17 to 20) or supervised in the community. Re-offending among young people after a custodial sentence is high, but supervision outside institutions reveals a decrease in re-offending. A further alternative to prison is the plan to extend 'tagging' (arm or leg bracelets connected electronically to local police stations), whereby non-violent offenders are confined to a specific area and have to observe a curfew. The tag is activated if these conditions are broken.

The death penalty by hanging for murder and some other crimes was abolished in 1969. The House of Commons has since voted on several occasions against its re-imposition. But polls, despite recent miscarriages of justice, consistently show that a majority of the public are in favour of the death penalty, especially for terrorist offences and the murder of policemen. The general public seem to support harsh treatment of criminal offenders and argue that more sympathy and aid should be given to the victims of crime. The government has tried to support such victims with financial compensation, but its programmes have not satisfied the critics or the victims.

Many British people feel that the penalties for criminal offences are inadequate as deterrents to prevent crime, despite the fact that most prisons are old and decayed, lack humane facilities, are unfitted for a modern penal system, are understaffed and their personnel overworked. Prison conditions have resulted in serious disorder and riots in recent years and low morale among prisoners and prison staff. Debates about punishment as opposed to the rehabilitation of offenders continue. But proposals to improve the situation usually encounter the problems of expense, although the government is building more courts and prisons. Some prisons and prison services (such as escorting prisoners to court) have now been privatized.

The majority of prisoners are not reformed by their sentences, nor does fear of prison or punishment act as a deterrent. Some critics maintain that institutions should be humanized and prisoners given a sense of purpose. Alternatives to custodial sentences, such as supervised housing, probation hostels and supervised work projects, are also advocated. But others argue that the main concern of the criminal system should be punishment and not rehabilitation.

Law enforcement and the police

The armed forces in Britain are subordinate to the civilian government and are used only for defence purposes. An exception has been the deployment of the army in Northern Ireland since 1969, where they support the police force (the Royal Ulster Constabulary).

The maintenance of law and order rests with the civilian police. The oldest police force is the Metropolitan Police, founded in 1829 by Sir Robert Peel to combat crime in London, and from which the modern forces have grown. Today there is no one national police force. Instead, there are 52 independent forces, which undertake law enforcement in local county or regional

PLATE 6.5 British police *(D. McNeelance/Rex Features, London)*

areas, with the Metropolitan Police being responsible for policing London. The regional forces are under the political control of police committees composed of local politicians, although their direct influence is small. Authority rests with the head of each regional force (Chief Constable), who has organizational independence and responsibility for the actions of the force. The Home Secretary is responsible for the Metropolitan Police, which is centred on Scotland Yard in London.

There are about 150,000 policemen and women in Britain, or one officer for every 380 people in the population. Only a disproportionately small number are from ethnic communities. Many of their members are hostile to or sceptical of the police, although there have been attempts to recruit more of them to the forces, with varying degrees of success.

The police are not allowed to join trade unions or to strike, but they do have staff associations to represent their interests. They are subject to the law, and can be sued or prosecuted for any wrongdoing in the course of their work. It is difficult to bring successful prosecutions against them, although individuals can appeal to the Police Complaints Authority. However, this body is largely composed of police representatives and lacks independence. Critics argue that complaints procedures are unsatisfactory and that democratic control of the police in practice does not exist.

The police, with their peculiar helmets and lack of firearms, are often regarded as a typical British institution. They embody a presence in the local community by 'walking the beat', and supposedly personify fairness, stolidity, friendliness, helpfulness and incorruptibility. These virtues still exist to a degree, and the traditional view is that the police should control the community by consent rather than force and that they should be visible in local areas.

In recent years, however, the police have been taken off foot patrols and put into cars to increase effectiveness and mobility; more are now armed and trained in riot-control programmes. They have been accused of racism, sexism, corruption, brutality, excessive use of force, perverting the cause of justice and tampering with evidence in criminal trials. Some of these accusations have been proved in a number of cases.

The police tread a thin line in community activities, strikes and demonstrations. They are in the middle of opposing forces, much is expected of them, and uncertain law sometimes hinders their effectiveness. The problems of violent crime, relations with ethnic communities and an increasingly complex society have made their job more difficult. The police are trying to find ways of adequately and fairly controlling a changing society. They are concerned about their image, but insist that their primary duty is to maintain law and order.

The legal profession in England and Wales

The legal profession in England and Wales is divided into two types of lawyer: barristers and solicitors. Each branch has its own vested interests and jurisdiction and fiercely protects its position against external opposition. This system has been criticized because of the duplication of services, delay in the legal process and expense. But reforms have occurred in the legal profession and legal services in order to benefit consumers and to promote easier access to the law.

There are some 83,000 *solicitors*, who practise mainly in private firms, but also in local and central government, legal centres and industry. Most are now organized by their self-regulating professional body, the Law Society. The solicitors' branch is a middle-class profession, but it is increasingly attracting members from a relatively wide spectrum of society.

Solicitors deal with general legal work, although many now specialize in one area of the law. Their firms (or partnerships) offer services such as conveyancing (the buying and selling of property); probate (wills and succession after death); family matters; criminal and civil litigation; commercial cases; and tax and financial affairs. Conveyancing, which used to be a monopoly for solicitors, may now be done by licensed conveyancers, banks and building societies. This reform has caused difficulty for some solicitors' firms that rely upon conveyancing fees as their chief source of finance.

Complaints by dissatisfied clients against solicitors, of which there are an increasing number (some 19,000 a year), are investigated by the Office for the Supervision of Solicitors. This body is supposed to provide an impartial investigation into complaints, but is criticized by consumers for its lack of powers and independence from the Law Society.

The client with a legal problem will first approach a solicitor, who can often deal with all aspects of the case. In the past, solicitors were able to appear (rights of audience) for their clients only in the lower courts (county and magistrates' courts), and if the case had to be heard in the higher courts, it then had to be handed to a barrister. This practice, which was criticized as expensive and inefficient, is being changed to allow solicitor-advocates to appear in higher courts.

In order to become a solicitor, it is now necessary to have a university degree, not necessarily in law. After passing additional professional examinations organized by the Law Society, the student serves a practical apprenticeship as a trainee solicitor with an established solicitor for some two years. After this total period of about six years' education and training, the new solicitor can practise law.

There are 8,000 *barristers* (known as advocates in Scotland) in private practice, who have the right to appear before any court in England and Wales. They belong to the Bar, which is an ancient legal institution controlled by the self-regulating Bar Council and four Inns of Court in London (Gray's Inn, Lincoln's Inn, Middle Temple and the Inner Temple). Barristers have two main functions: first, to give specialized advice on legal matters, and second, to act as advocates in the courts. Most of the general public cannot approach a barrister directly, but must be introduced by a solicitor.

In order to become a barrister, one must usually have a university degree, pass professional examinations and become a member of an Inn of Court. The student must dine in the Inn for a number of terms before being 'called to the Bar', or accepted as a barrister. He or she must then serve for a one-year period (pupillage) under a practising barrister. After this total training period of about five years, the new barrister can practise alone.

Barristers are self-employed individuals who practise the law from chambers (or offices), together with other barristers. The barrister's career starts as a 'junior' handling minor briefs (or cases). He or she may frequently have difficulty in earning a reasonable living or in becoming established in the early years of

PLATE 6.6 Barristers in full dress *(Rex Features, London)*

practice, with the result that many barristers drop out and enter other fields. However, should the barrister persist and build up a successful practice as a junior, he or she may then 'take silk' and become a Queen's Counsel (QC). A QC is a senior barrister who can charge higher fees for his or her work, but who is then excluded from appearing in lesser cases. Appointment as a QC may lead to a future position as a judge, and it is regarded as a necessary career step for the ambitious.

The *judges* constitute the judiciary, or independent third branch of the constitutional system. There are a relatively small number of judges at various levels of seniority, who are located in most large cities and in the higher courts in London. They are appointed from the ranks of senior barristers, although solicitors have now become eligible for some of the lower posts. The highest appointments are made by the Crown on the advice of the Prime Minister, and lower positions on the advice of the Lord Chancellor. This appointments procedure has been criticized because it rests with the Lord Chancellor and the senior judiciary, who consequently hold much power and patronage. But, in an attempt to combat 'elitism', more judgeships are now advertised for open competition, although proposals that lay people should in future assist in the choosing of new judges through a Judicial Appointments Commission have been dropped.

PLATE 6.7 Barristers' chambers, Gray's Inn, London
(John Oakland)

The Lord Chancellor is a political appointee of the sitting government; effective head of the legal system and profession; a member of the Cabinet; presiding officer (or Speaker) of the House of Lords; and a Law Lord. But other judgeships are supposedly made on non-political grounds. Once appointed, senior judges cannot be removed from office until the retiring age of 75, although junior judges can be dismissed by the Lord Chancellor for good reasons before retirement age at 72. There have been proposals that complaints against judges and their possible dismissal should be handled by a complaints board. It is argued that judges should be more easily removable from office. But the existing measures have been designed to ensure the independence of the judiciary and its freedom from political involvement.

Critics feel that judges are socially and educationally elitist and remote from ordinary life. They are usually people who will not cause embarrassment to the establishment, although there are exceptions to this rule. They generally tend to support the accepted wisdom and status quo, and are overwhelmingly male. Although over half of law students are female, there are few women judges, QCs or senior partners in solicitors' firms. While judges often appear to support the policies of the government, they are also capable of ruling against it. But British judges are not supposed to be political animals seeking to change the established order, and their freedom to speak out in public on a range of issues is restricted. However, the judiciary is gradually changing to admit more women, members of ethnic communities and people with lower-class and educationally diverse backgrounds.

The judiciary tends to be old in years because judgeships are normally awarded to senior practising lawyers and there is no career structure that people may join early in life. A lawyer's income will often be greatly reduced on accepting a judgeship, but the honour and added security are supposed to be some compensation. There are promotional steps within the judiciary from recorder to circuit judge to High Court judge, and thence to the Court of Appeal and the House of Lords.

ATTITUDES

Attitudes to the legal system and crime

Britain is not usually thought of as a litigious society. People avoid the difficulty and cost of legal actions if possible and regard the law and lawyers as a last resort. Indeed, a National Opinion Poll in 1997 showed that while the police were (surprisingly, perhaps) the most admired professional group after doctors and nurses, lawyers were the least admired group. But, in recent years, more Britons have been using the civil law to gain satisfaction and large damages for matters ranging from libel cases to complaints about the school and health systems.

Polls reveal that a majority of people are dissatisfied with the legal system. In a 1993 MORI poll, 54 per cent of interviewees disagreed with the statement that 'you can have confidence in the legal system' and 29 per cent agreed. There is support for reforms of the legal system and a desire to see more government action on the law's delays, risks and costs.

Crime, vandalism and violence are a main concern for many Britons. Prior to the 1997 general election, a MORI poll showed that, in a list of worries, 32 per cent of respondents worried about law and order. A NatWest survey in 1997 indicated that 70 per cent of respondents would accept tax rises if significant cuts in crime would result, and that nearly 50 per cent considered drugs and drug-related offences to be the biggest crime problems, far ahead of burglary and assault.

A British Social Attitudes survey (1995–6) showed public attitudes to crime. The following percentages said they felt unsafe walking alone after dark: ages 18–34 (men 11 per cent and women 59 per cent); ages 35–59 (men 13 and women 44); ages 60+ (men 29 and women 62). The percentage of those who felt that worries about crime affect their everyday life were: ages 18–34 (men 21 per cent and women 38 per cent); ages 35–59 (men 25 and women 30);

ATTITUDES

ages 60+ (men 25 and women 32). In a 1993 MORI poll, 59 per cent of interviewees were satisfied with the way their areas were policed, but by 1994, only 36 per cent gave the same response. The 1993 poll also showed that 81 per cent of respondents thought that the police were handicapped in the fight against crime by the criminal justice system.

EXERCISES

- **Explain and examine the following terms:**

civil law	plaintiff	conveyancing
barrister	legal aid	Crown Prosecution Service
indictable	Inns of Court	common law
solicitor	Lord Chancellor	Metropolitan Police
jury	crown court	county court
JP	statute law	bail
'tagging'	summary	stipendiary magistrate

- **Write short essays on the following topics:**

1. Describe and comment critically on the structure of the legal profession in England and Wales.
2. How is the courts system in England and Wales organized?
3. Discuss the role of the police in law enforcement.

Chapter 7

Economic and industrial institutions

HISTORICALLY, THE BRITISH ECONOMY has been influenced by agricultural and industrial revolutions; the growth and then reduction of manufacturing industry; government policies and intervention in the national economy; and a relative economic decline from the late nineteenth century. It has experienced considerable problems in the twentieth century but recovered from a 1988–93 recession and was buoyant in 1997.

Economic history

Britain was a largely rural country until the eighteenth century and its economy was based on products generated by successive agricultural revolutions. But there had also been industrial and manufacturing developments over the centuries, which were located in the larger towns. Financial and commercial institutions, such as banks, insurance houses and trading companies, were gradually founded to finance and service the expanding and increasingly diversified economy.

The growth of a colonial empire contributed to national wealth as Britain capitalized on its worldwide trading connections. Colonies supplied cheap raw materials, that were converted into manufactured goods in Britain and then exported. Overseas markets grew quickly because British merchants and traders were protected at home and abroad. They exploited the colonial markets and controlled foreign competition. By the nineteenth century, Britain had become an economic power. Its wealth was based on international trade and the payments that it received for its exported goods. Governments believed that a country increased its wealth if exports exceeded imports.

This trading system and its financial institutions benefited the industrial revolutions, which began in the late eighteenth century with new manufacturing inventions. A rich supply of domestic materials and energy sources, such as coal, iron, steam power and water, stimulated industrial production and the economy. Manufacturers, who had gained by foreign trade and demand for British goods abroad, invested in new industries and modern technology. Factories were built, industrial towns expanded, and a transport infrastructure of roads, railways and canals developed. Efficient manufacturing methods made British products competitively priced and attractive to foreign markets, and Britain was transformed into an urban and industrialized country.

Industrialization was, however, opposed by some people. The Luddites, for example, destroyed new machinery in an attempt to halt progress and preserve existing jobs. Industrial development had its negative effects, such as long working hours for low wages and bad conditions in mines and factories. It also resulted in the depopulation of rural areas and the decline of traditional home and cottage work. Industrial conditions caused social and moral problems in towns and the countryside, and mechanization was often regarded as exploitative and dehumanizing. The situation was worsened by the indifference of many manufacturers, employers and politicians to the human cost of industrialization.

However, the industrial changes did transform Britain into a rich and powerful nation, despite economic slumps, unemployment and resulting hardship in the nineteenth century. Manufacturing output was now the chief generator of wealth; production methods and technology advanced; and domestic competition improved the quality of goods and services. But this industrial leadership and dominance of world trade did not last long. They declined relatively by the end of the nineteenth century, as other countries like Germany and the USA industrialized and became more competitive. However, financial expertise in the City of London continued to be influential in global commercial dealings.

The modern economy: policies, structure and performance

Britain's economic performance and international standing further declined in the early decades of the twentieth century, although this downturn was disguised by an apparent prosperity. It was then affected by economic problems created by two World Wars; international recessions; global competition; structural changes in the domestic economy; a lack of competitiveness in industrial and commercial life; alternating government policies; and a series of 'boom and bust' cycles in which economic growth fluctuated greatly.

Economic policies

Since the 1940s, British governments have become more involved in economic planning, and the performance of the economy has been tied to their policies. Keynesian economic theory was the dominant school of thought in the mid-twentieth century. It was based on government management of the economy and the stimulation of demand and growth by the injection of money into the economic system. All British governments, to greater or lesser degrees, intervened in economic life.

The Conservative Party has traditionally advocated non-interference in the economy (*laissez-faire* or letting things take their own course). But this has been only partially achieved in practice. Government intervention was necessary as international competition grew and domestic demands became more complex. The Labour Party argued that the economy should be centrally planned and its essential sectors should be owned and managed by the state. Clause 4 of its constitution, which stated this policy, was dropped only in 1995.

Labour governments from 1945 consequently nationalized (transferred to state or public ownership) railways, road transport, water, gas and electricity, ship-building, coal-mining, iron and steel industries, airlines, the health service, post office and telecommunications. Public services and central industries were run by the state (through government-appointed boards) and were responsible to Parliament. They were subsidized by taxation for the benefit of the whole country, rather than for private owners or shareholders. They were expensive to run, and governments were expected to rescue any that had economic problems.

This policy was reversed by Conservative governments. They argued that public industries and services were too expensive and inefficient; had outdated technology and bad industrial relations; suffered from lack of investment in new equipment; were dependent upon tax subsidies; and were run as state services with too little attention paid to profit making, consumer demand or market forces. They denationalized some state industries and returned them to private ownership. Conservative denationalization was later (1979–97) called 'privatization' or 'deregulation'. Deregulation means removing restrictions on industries so that they can operate freely and competitively. For example, the stock market and public transport were deregulated, resulting in greater diversity in the City of London, and bus companies operated by local authorities competing with private bus firms for customers.

Conservative governments privatized state industries such as British Telecom, British Airways, British Petroleum, British Gas, water and electricity supplies, British Coal and British Rail. Ownership was transferred from the state to private owners mainly through the sale of shares. The industry is then run as a profit making concern and is regulated in the public interest by independent regulators, although the effectiveness of these is criticized.

Conservatives believe that privatization improves efficiency, reduces government spending, increases economic freedom and encourages share ownership. The public were eager to buy shares in the new private companies, and share owning increased, if largely by financial institutions. But there was concern about privatization. Private industries became virtual monopolies with little effective competition. There have been frequent complaints about their services, prices and products, although some of them are now profitable and many initial problems have been solved.

The Labour government (1997-) has accepted privatization and may partially privatize the London Tube and the Post Office. The major parties are now committed to 'market economics', and there may not be violent reversals of policy by future governments. The essential question is one of how to manage the deregulated 'market' economy effectively, while maintaining some public or state services.

Economic structure

Government policies have given Britain a mixed economy, divided into public and private sectors. The public sector includes the remaining state-run industries and public services, which now amount to under one-third of total goods and services. Over two-thirds of the economy is now in the private sector and will increase with further privatization.

Unlike public-sector concerns, which are owned and operated by the state, the private sector belongs to people who have a financial interest in a company. It consists of small businesses owned by individuals; companies whose shares are sold to the public through the Stock Exchange; and larger companies whose shares are not offered for sale to the public. The majority of companies in Britain are private and are small or medium-size. They are important to the national economy and generate 50 per cent of new jobs. Some 10 per cent of the economy is controlled by foreign corporations, which employ 10 per cent of the workforce. These percentages will grow as more overseas firms buy into the economy, since Britain is seen as an attractive, low-cost country for foreign investment.

The shareholders are the real owners of those companies in which they have invested their money. However, the daily organization of the business is left to a board of directors under a chairman(woman) or managing director. In practice, most shareholders are more interested in receiving profit dividends on their shares from a successful business than in being concerned with its running. But shareholder power is occasionally mobilized if the company is performing badly.

National and foreign companies are sometimes associated with takeovers and mergers in the private sector. A takeover occurs when a larger company takes over (or buys) a smaller, often loss making, firm. Mergers are amalgamations between companies of equal standing. Such battles for control can be fiercely fought and have resulted in sections of the economy, such as cars, hotels, media concerns and food products, being dominated by a relatively small number of major groups.

Takeovers and mergers can be a source of concern, particularly since the methods used are not always beneficial to the companies or workforces involved. An independent Monopolies and Mergers Commission is supposed to control this situation by preventing any one group forming a monopoly or creating unfair trading conditions. It examines the potential situation and reports to the Secretary of State for Trade and Industry, who may rule against the proposed takeover or merger. Some ministers have stopped undesirable developments, but others have allowed situations that amount to near-monopolies, and the role of the Commission is criticized.

Economic performance

Britain's economic problems since the Second World War have resulted in periods of recession and boom, relatively high unemployment and inflation, international trade weaknesses and fluctuations in the strength of the pound. These have been tied to structural changes in the national economy, which have seen considerable growth in service industries and a relative decline in industrial and manufacturing trades.

The location of British industry, which was dictated by the industrial revolutions, has been a factor in manufacturing and industrial decline. Industries were situated in areas where there was access to natural resources and transport systems and where there was often only one major industry. They could be easily damaged in a changing economic climate, unless they managed to diversify. But even regions that had diversified successfully in the past were affected by further deindustrialization and recession in the 1970s and 1980s.

Many manufacturing industries were unable to adapt to new markets and demands. They had not diversified or produced goods efficiently and cheaply enough to compete, and had often priced themselves out of the world market. This situation was not improved by the number of cheap imports flooding the traditional trades. In 1938, Britain still produced 22 per cent of the world's exports of manufactured goods. But this figure slumped to 6.5 per cent by 1989, due to world competition and the rundown of manufacturing industries.

Industrial decline badly affected northern England, the English Midlands, industrial Scotland and South Wales. Traditional industries such as textiles, steel, ship-building, iron and coal-mining were greatly reduced in the process of deindustrialization. Governments, helped by European Union grants, tried to revitalize depressed areas with financial aid and the creation of new industry, but these policies have only slowly had an effect, although there have been improvements in places like Liverpool, Glasgow, Newcastle and Birmingham.

However, Britain remains an important industrial and manufacturing country, and employs one-fifth of its workforce in these sectors. It is a major exporter of finished goods, despite its reduced share of the world market. Manufacturing production increased in the late 1980s, but then slumped and has only slowly recovered. Manufactured goods comprise 84 per cent of Britain's exports, even though they amount to 22 per cent of the gross domestic product. Engineering and transport machinery, electronic equipment, chemicals, food, drink and tobacco are the largest groups of manufactured goods.

Structural changes in industry, manufacturing and commerce forced the economy to adjust to different demands. The introduction of new technology and production methods resulted in a growth of specialized industries and the service sector (like banking, insurance, catering, leisure and financial services). The service and construction sector now accounts for some 69 per cent of the gross domestic product.

The discovery and exploitation of North Sea oil and gas since the mid-1970s have contributed greatly to the British economy, and made it less dependent upon imported energy. But this development has disguised the true state of the economy. Gas

PLATE 7.1 Textile factory, Inverness, Scotland
(The Hutchison Library)

PLATE 7.2 The Aston Martin car factory *(Rex Features, London)*

and oil are finite. Britain thus has problems in finding alternative energy sources when these diminish and must also fill the financial gap with new revenues. Critics argue that oil income has been unwisely spent on social targets, rather than being used more positively for investment in new industry and in creating a modern economic infrastructure.

Britain's trading patterns have changed and its chief partners are now the European Union (58 per cent), North America (13) and other countries (16). But it still has a balance of payments problem. The economy suffers when exports do not exceed imports because a trade deficit (gap between exports and imports) results, and Britain has had deficits since 1983. However, 'invisible exports' contribute greatly to the economy. These are financial services, insurance charges, tourism, shipping and aviation revenues, which are not calculated in the balance of payments equation.

The economy is also affected by fluctuations in the value of the pound, which is vulnerable to political instability and currency speculation. Devaluation (reduction of the pound's exchange value) was used by governments in the 1960s and 1970s to improve the economic situation. This encouraged exports by making them cheaper on the world market, but raised the cost of imports and dissuaded people from buying expensive foreign goods. However, direct devaluation has not been used recently as a formal economic weapon. Instead, the pound was allowed to 'float' from 1972 and find its own market value in competition with other currencies.

Economic performance since 1979

The economy was in poor shape in the late 1970s, due to a lack of competitiveness, high inflation and unemployment, global recessions, inadequate economic structures and industrial relations problems. Conservative governments (1979–97) tried to improve the situation, and opinions differ on their record, which staggered between 'boom' and 'bust'.

They initially attempted to reduce inflation by controlling the amount of money circulating in the economic system. This involved cutting government and public spending. Industry and commerce were left to fend for themselves under market forces. They were supposed to restructure themselves; increase their growth rates and productivity; cut down overmanning in the workforce; and become more efficient.

Such deflationary measures, combined with a continuing world recession, resulted in the 1980 British economy falling to very low levels. Inflation was 22 per cent and interest rates were high, so that companies could not borrow money to re-equip or modernize. The exchange rate of the pound fluctuated, and British goods were expensive on the world market. Many businesses went bankrupt, while others had to cut back drastically on their workforces and production in order to survive. By 1982, some 3 million people were unemployed (12 per cent of the workforce). But public spending had fallen somewhat, and inflation had been reduced to 6 per cent.

Government policy and the depressed state of the economy provoked fierce arguments through the mid-1980s. There were calls for reflationary programmes to boost the economy. Yet, by the end of 1986, things started to improve, and economic performance throughout 1987 and early 1988 was positive. Unemployment and interest rates were reduced; there was increased investment in industry; manufacturing productivity improved; inflation fell; and the economy grew at a high rate.

However, the economy overheated from mid-1988. Under a consumer boom, the balance of payments assumed record deficits, inflation increased and the pound was under attack. The government raised interest rates to reduce inflation. This did not help industry and business, which need low interest rates for expansion. Consequently, in 1989–93, and due to domestic and international factors, Britain experienced its worst recession since the 1930s world depression.

In an attempt to improve the economy, Britain joined the European Exchange Rate Mechanism (ERM) in 1990 which, by linking European monies, is supposed to stabilize currencies. This move was expected to cut interest rates, reduce inflation and boost the national economy. But, following heavy speculation against a weak pound in 1992, which resulted in an effective devaluation, Britain withdrew from the ERM and again allowed the pound to float. Critics argue that this allowed the British economy to recover, since it was not tied to the ERM and could pursue its own economic policies.

In 1993–4, Britain came slowly out of recession, with manufacturing, financial and industrial performance improving and unemployment, inflation and interest rates falling. By 1997, the economy was one of the most successful in the world with strong growth, low inflation and the lowest unemployment since 1980. The Labour government (1997) inherited a strong economy and is continuing similar economic policies to the Conservatives. But

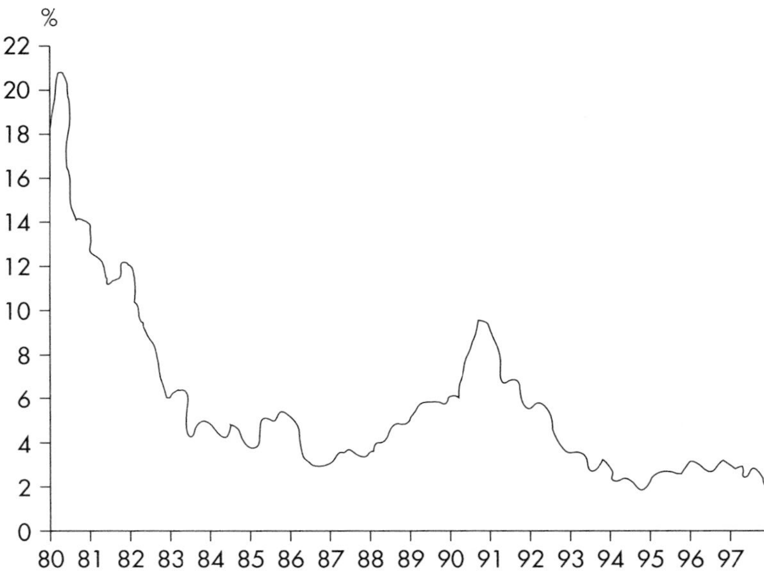

FIGURE 7.1 Inflation rate, 1980–97 *Datastream 1997*

government spending, in spite of cuts in public services, is still high and illustrates the continuing problem of how to combine a 'free-market economy' with a social services sector.

Social class, the workforce and employment

Social class

Class in Britain has been variously defined by material wealth; ownership of the means of production as against the sellers of labour; education and professional status; accent and dialect; birth and breeding; and sometimes by lifestyle.

Historically, the British class system was divided into upper, middle and working classes. Earlier, hierarchies based on wealth, the ownership of property, aristocratic privilege and political power were adhered to rigidly, but a small middle class of traders, merchants and skilled craftsmen began to make inroads into this system. Industrialization in the nineteenth century further fragmented class divisions. The working class divided into skilled and unskilled workers, and the middle class split into lower, middle and upper sections, depending on job classification or wealth. However, the upper class was still defined by birth, property and inherited money rather than by association with any particular profession.

The spread of education and expansion of wealth to greater numbers of people in the twentieth century allowed greater social mobility (moving upwards out of the class into which one was born). The working class was more upwardly mobile, the upper class (due to a loss of aristocratic privilege) merged more with the middle class, and it was felt that the old rigid class system was breaking down. But class structures still exist, although the proportions of people belonging to the various levels have changed substantially.

Some researchers now employ a six-class model based on occupation, income and property ownership, such as:

1 Higher-grade professional, managerial and administrative workers (e.g. doctors and lawyers)
2 Intermediate professional, managerial and administrative workers (e.g. school teachers and sales managers)
3 Non-manual skilled workers (e.g. clerks and shop assistants)
4 Manual skilled workers (e.g. coal miners)
5 Semi-skilled workers (e.g. postmen)
6 Unskilled workers (e.g. dustmen, cleaners and labourers)

In addition, a further group (the underclass) has been used in recent years. This consists of people who fall outside the usual classes and includes the unemployed, single-parent families, the very poor and those with alternative lifestyles.

This model indicates two broad social/occupational groupings for contemporary Britain: a 'middle class' made up of classes 1, 2 and 3 and a 'working class' consisting of classes 4, 5 and 6. Research indicates that the British population today consists of a middle class (60 per cent) and a working class (40 per cent).

The working class has shrunk in size and there has been more upward mobility in recent years, with more people advancing socially because of economic progress and changes in occupational structures.

Polls suggest that the British themselves feel that they are becoming more middle class, and commentators argue that many people have the sort of lifestyle, jobs and income that classify them as middle class. It also seems that class is now as much a matter of different social habits and attitudes as it is of occupation and money. The old gaps between the classes have lessened, and class today is a more finely graded hierarchy dependent upon a range of characteristics. But inequalities of wealth, the majority ownership of the means of production and services, difficulties of social mobility for some people, poverty and questions of prestige remain.

The workforce and employment

The total workforce in 1996 was 28 million. Of these, 22.1 million were classed as employees, 3.3 million were self-employed, and the rest comprised the unemployed, the armed forces and people on work-related training programmes.

Despite twentieth-century occupational changes, the majority of British people, whether part-time or full-time workers, are employed by an organization. It may be a small private firm, a large company, a public sector industry or service, or a multinational corporation. Most people are therefore workers who sell their labour in a market dominated by concerns that own and control the means of production and services. The class-defining boundaries of employees and employers have remained constant, and the top 1 per cent of British society still own more than 18 per cent of marketable wealth, and the top 10 per cent have 49 per cent.

The deregulated economy has created a complexity of work patterns. Manufacturing has declined; service trades have increased; unemployment has grown; self-employment has risen; managerial and professional fields have expanded; and there are

PLATE 7.3 An open-plan office *(Rex Features, London)*

more part-time (24 per cent of the workforce in 1996) and temporary jobs. Manual jobs have decreased; non-manual occupations have increased; and the old working class has been eroded by a growth of salaried jobs. The British workforce has also become increasingly 'white-collar' and better educated.

Two-thirds of British women are now in the labour force and are 46 per cent of the total. They are the principal (and often the only) breadwinner in 30 per cent of households. But a majority of female workers are badly paid, part-time and often unprotected by trade unions or the law. Although women form a 52 per cent majority of the population and are increasing their numbers in higher education (where they form a majority of students), the professions and white-collar jobs, they have problems in progressing to the senior ranks. Yet in 1996, three out of every 10 new businesses were started by women, and in the service sector it was almost five out of 10.

Since the 1960s, women have campaigned for greater equality with men in job opportunities and rates of pay. Legislation has attempted to redress the balance, with varying degrees of success. Equal Pay Acts stipulate that men and women who do the same or similar kinds of work should receive the same wages. The Sex Discrimination Act makes it unlawful for the employer to discriminate between men and women when choosing a candidate for most jobs. The Equal Opportunities Commission monitors this legislation and brings cases when there have been breaches of the Acts. But the average weekly wage of women is still only 79 per cent of the average paid to men, particularly in industry and the service sector.

There has been a recent need for more women to enter the workforce at all levels, in order to compensate for a reduced birthrate and the shortage of skilled labour. This situation requires improved financial, social and child-care benefits for women to enable them to work, as well as more flexible employment arrangements. Some employers and the government are responding positively in these areas, and Britain now seems to be much more egalitarian on women's work than it has been.

Unemployment, although continuing to be a major source of public concern, has dropped steadily from 1992 with the upturn in the economy, and was about 1.5 million (5 per cent of the workforce) in 1997. But it remains proportionally high in Northern Ireland, the industrial English Midlands, Merseyside, north-east England, Scotland and South Wales. Since the late 1980s, it has also affected the normally affluent south of England and includes professional and higher-grade workers.

The creation of jobs is important for all political parties. The Labour government introduced (1997) a Welfare to Work programme in which government money is processed to companies willing to create jobs for the unemployed. But firms seem to be lukewarm about participating in the scheme, and many of the unemployed are not enthusiastic. The need is for genuine job-creation rather than temporary fixes.

Although the British workforce is now more mobile, deregulated and flexible, many vacant jobs are low-paid and part-time.

FIGURE 7.2 Unemployment rate, 1980–97 *Datastream 1997*

Others are in technical and skilled areas, for which the educational and industrial systems have not adequately provided. Traditional apprenticeships have been greatly reduced, and technical education suffers from a lack of investment and facilities. Although Conservative governments have established technological colleges in the major cities (financed jointly by government and private companies), over three-quarters of firms in 1997 were experiencing skills shortages, and over 40 per cent had unfilled vacancies.

In order to provide the unemployed with job experience and training, governments have introduced employment-related programmes under the control of Training and Enterprise Councils. These attempt to train the unemployed workforce, in the hope that permanent jobs may be found for them. Young people between the ages of 16 and 18, who become unemployed on leaving school, do not receive social security benefits but must undertake a training scheme or further education. But the training programmes have been criticized and there is no guarantee that trainees will obtain a job afterwards. Despite the relative success of some programmes, Britain still lacks adequate training schemes for the unemployed and young people, particularly in those technical areas that are essential for a modern industrial state. According to the World Economic Forum's 1997 global competitiveness report, Britain ranks 23rd out of 53 countries for the quality of its employee training.

Traditional manufacturing industry has been progressively reduced in Britain, but an industrial infrastructure will continue to be important, though it will not be as labour-intensive as in the past, because of technical advances. As the economy improves, high-technology industry and the service trades are set to expand. It is also likely that job opportunities for professional and skilled workers, particularly in managerial, supervisory, personal and financial services, will increase. However, unemployment and an adequately trained workforce will still be problems in this post-industrial society, and will entail revisions of the work ethic and concepts of leisure, as well as more flexible employment arrangements.

Financial institutions

Financial institutions are central actors in the economy. In the 1980s, they responded to a more deregulated economy, which allowed them more freedom of operation. Banks, building societies, insurance firms, money markets and the London Stock Exchange expanded and diversified. They entered new fields and reorganized their traditional areas of expertise, as competition between institutions increased. But they also had problems when the economic situation fluctuated in the late 1980s and early 1990s: unemployment in financial concerns was high, and the future of London as a financial centre looked insecure. This uncertainty has now been largely reversed with the upturn in the economy since 1993.

Many of the major financial institutions have their headquarters in London, but also have branches throughout Britain. The square mile of the *City of London*, with its banks, insurance businesses, legal firms and financial dealers' offices, has always been a centre of British and world finance. Its monetary resources have financed royal wars, military and colonial exploration and trading companies. Today it provides financial and investment services for commercial interests in Britain and overseas. Many City institutions were founded in the seventeenth and eighteenth centuries, as Britain's prosperity and overseas trade grew, such as the insurance market of Lloyd's (1680s), the London Stock Exchange (1773) and the Bank of England (1694).

The *Bank of England* (popularly known as 'the old lady of Threadneedle Street') is the country's central bank. Although previously nationalized, it is now largely independent (1997) of the government and able to set interest rates in order to control inflation and monetary policy. Other domestic institutions adjust their interest rates accordingly. It is organized by a governor and directors who are appointed by the government. It is the government's banker and the agent for British commercial and foreign central banks. It prints money notes for use in England and Wales; manages the national debt; supervises the country's gold reserves; and supports the pound by buying pounds on foreign currency exchanges.

The other main banks that provide banking services throughout Britain are the *central clearing banks*, of which the most important are the Midland, National Westminster, Barclays, Lloyds and the Bank of Scotland. They provide their customers with current and deposit (savings) accounts, loans and financial advice. But they have been criticized for their banking charges to clients and their unwillingness to provide funds for small businesses. They are involved in international finance, have foreign interests, investments and branches, and in recent years have expanded their traditional activities.

In addition to these high street banks, there are the long-established *merchant banks*, which are mainly located in London. They give advice and finance to commercial and industrial businesses, both in Britain and overseas; advise companies on takeovers and mergers; provide financial assistance for foreign transactions; and organize a range of financial services for individuals and corporations.

The *International Stock Exchange* is a market for the buying and selling of quoted (or listed) stocks and shares in British public companies and a few overseas companies. Dealings on the Stock Exchange reflect the current market trends and prices for a range of securities, which may go up as well as down.

The Stock Exchange was revolutionized in 1986 by new developments, known popularly as 'Big Bang'. The changes deregulated the financial market, resulting in greater freedom of operation. Rules on membership were changed, financial dealers were given greater powers of dealing for themselves and their clients, and competition increased. However, some companies were too ambitious, over-expanded, and consequently suffered from the effects of the world stock market crash of 1987. The London market returned to earlier profitability levels only after many redundancies among dealers and closure of some companies. From 1997, financial transactions have been organized directly from computer screens in corporate offices by an order-driven system that automates the trading process.

The *Foreign Exchange Market* is also based in London. Brokers in corporate or bank offices deal in the buying and selling of foreign currencies. The London market is the largest in the world in terms of average daily turnover of completed transactions. Other money markets arrange deals on the Euromarkets in foreign currencies; trade on financial futures (speculation on future prices of commodities); arrange gold dealings on the London Gold Market; and transact global deals in the commodity, shipping and freight markets.

Lloyd's of London is a famous name in the insurance market, and has long been active in its traditional fields of shipping and maritime insurance, though it has now diversified into many other areas, and insures against a multitude of events. Lloyd's operates as a market, where employed underwriters (or insurers), together with external Names who invest capital in

Lloyd's, carry on their business. However, many underwriters and Names have suffered in recent years due to heavy insurance losses and their unlimited liability. In 1997, Lloyd's embraced corporate membership, and hence limited liability for its membership.

In addition to the Lloyd's market, there are many individual insurance companies with headquarters in London and branches throughout the country. They have international connections and huge assets. They play an important role in British financial life because they are the largest investors of capital. Their main activity has traditionally been in life insurance, but many have now diversified into other associated fields, such as pensions and property loans.

British financial institutions have traditionally been respected for their honesty and integrity. But, as money markets have expanded and become freer, there have been a number of fraud cases, collapse of financial organizations and financial scandals. Such features, which give the City a bad image, have forced governments and the City ruling bodies to institute legislative and self-regulatory provisions, such as a Securities and Investments Board (SIB), a Financial Services Act and a Serious Fraud Office, in order to tighten the controls on financial dealings.

Some critics, however, argue for stronger independent controls of the City's dealings. The Labour government, although now much more friendly towards the business world than in the past, intends to create a single watchdog (a new SIB) to oversee all financial dealings. Other commentators maintain that the City should be more nationally and socially conscious and forced to invest in British industry rather than overseas. The City insists that it should be allowed to invest how and where it likes in order to make a profit. However, it seems that City organizations are conscious of the negative criticisms and are prepared to put their houses in order.

The composition of those who create and control wealth in Britain has changed since the Second World War. Bankers, aristocrats, land owners and industrialists were the richest people in

PLATE 7.4 Lloyd's of London *(Clive Dixon/Rex Features, London)*

the nineteenth and early twentieth century. Today the most affluent are retailers and those who service the consumer society, although holders of inherited wealth are still numerous. The number of millionaires is now estimated at 120,000, of which a large percentage are self-made, from lower-middle- and working-class backgrounds.

The Labour Party in opposition stated that anyone earning more than £27,000 a year should be classified as rich (and taxed accordingly), while opinion polls suggest that the general public considers earnings above £30,000 a year to be real wealth. Talking about what one earns and about money generally has traditionally been regarded as unseemly in Britain, and too much involved with the cruder elements of existence and survival. But this mentality has slowly changed, particularly since the arrival in the 1980s of 'yuppies' (young upwardly mobile professional people) in business and the money markets. Although the yuppies were affected by the 1987 Stock Market crash and the economic downturn from mid-1988, they are now returning to the financial markets.

Industrial and commercial institutions

The trade unions

Trade unions obtained legal recognition in 1871 after long and bitter struggles. The fight for the right of workers to organize themselves originated in the trade guilds of the fourteenth century and later in social clubs that were formed to give their members protection against sickness and unemployment.

The modern trade unions are associated with the Labour Party, and campaign for better working, health and pay conditions for their members. The trade-union movement is highly organized and has a membership of 8.3 million people, though this marks a fall from over 12 million in 1978. The reduction has been due to rises in unemployment; changing attitudes to trade unions among workers; industrial decline; and regulatory legislation by Conservative governments.

Today there are some 350 trade unions and professional associations of workers, which vary considerably in size and influence. They represent not only skilled and unskilled workers in industry, but also white-collar workers in a range of businesses, companies and local and central government. Other professional associations like the Law Society, the Police Federation and the British Medical Association carry out similar representational roles for their members.

Members of trade unions pay annual subscriptions to their unions and frequently to the Labour Party, unless they elect not to pay this latter amount. This funding provides for union activities and services, such as legal, monetary and professional help. The richer unions are able to give strike pay to members who are taking part in 'official strikes', which are those legally sanctioned by members. Trade unions vary in their wealth and in their political orientation, ranging from the far left to the right wing of the political spectrum.

Some unions admit as members only those people who work in a specific trade or profession, such as miners or teachers. Other unions comprise workers who are employed in different or more general areas of industry or commerce, like the Transport and General Workers' Union. Smaller unions have frequently joined with others in similar fields to form new unions, such as Unison, which comprises public service workers and which is now the largest in Britain with 1.4 million members. Workers may choose, without victimization, whether they want belong to a particular union or none at all.

Many trade unions are affiliated to the Trades Union Congress (TUC), which was founded in 1868 and serves as an umbrella organization to coordinate trade union interests. It holds an annual conference and can be successful in promoting cooperation among workers. In the past, it exerted some political pressure on government, usually when Labour has been in power. It is currently seeking to extend its contacts in industry and commerce and with employers as well as workers.

The influence of the TUC and trade unions has, however, declined, due to the effects of unemployment, the restructuring of industry after recession, and Conservative legislation. Laws were passed to enforce secret voting by union members before strikes can be legally called and for the election of union officials. The number of pickets (union strikers) outside business premises has been reduced, secondary (or sympathy) action by other unionists is banned, and unions may be fined by the courts if they transgress legislation. Such laws (which the Labour government accept) and the economic climate forced trade unions to be more realistic in their wage demands in the 1980s. But pay claims are now escalating again, and there is also pressure for the legal recognition of unions in those workplaces where a majority of workers want them.

Legislation has controlled extreme and dubious union practices and introduced democratic procedures into union activities. The grassroots membership has become more independent of union bosses and activists, is more determined to represent its own wishes, and is concerned to cure abuses in the labour movement. The initiative in industry has shifted to employers and moderate unions, who have been moving away from the traditional 'class-war' image of unionism, and are accepting new technology and working patterns in an attempt to improve competitiveness and productivity.

A MORI public opinion poll in 1990 found that while 80 per cent of those interviewed believed that unions are essential to protect workers' interests, 38 per cent felt that unions still have too much power in Britain and 50 per cent believed that the unions are dominated by extremists. Forty three per cent of trade unionists themselves agreed with this latter point of view and 44 per cent disagreed.

Strike action by unions can be damaging to the economy and has been used as an economic and political weapon in the past. In some cases, strikes are seen as legitimate and find public support, but others that are clearly political or unpopular are rejected. Britain historically seemed to be prone to industrial disputes. However, statistics show that fewer working days are lost through strikes in Britain each year than in other industrial nations, although the number has increased recently. On average, most manufacturing plants and businesses are free of strikes, and media coverage is often responsible for giving a distorted picture of industrial relations.

Industrial problems should be placed in the context of financial rewards. Britain has a low-wage economy, compared with other major European countries, with an average gross wage in 1997 of £367 per week. The unions are pressing the Labour government to set a minimum wage of £4.61 an hour, which is at least a pound higher than most companies say they can afford. Many workers (especially women) receive less than the average wage, and all are taxed at the lower rate of 20 per cent and the basic rate of 25 per cent. The British tend to believe that they are over-taxed, but their basic rates of taxation, and a top rate of 40 per cent, are in fact lower than in many other western countries, and the Labour government is aiming for a lower tax rate of 10 per cent.

Employers' organizations

There are some 140 employers' and managers' associations in Britain, which are associated with companies in the private sector. They promote industrial relations between businesses and their workforces, try to settle disputes, and offer legal and professional advice.

Most are members of the Confederation of British Industry (CBI). This is an umbrella body that represents its members nationally; negotiates on their behalf with the government and the TUC; supports industrial growth and planning; campaigns for greater investment and innovation in industry and new technology; and is often more sympathetic to Conservative governments than Labour ones. However, it can be very critical of Conservative policies. It also acts as a public relations organization, relays the employers' points of view to the public, and has considerable economic influence and authority.

Industrial relations

Complaints are often raised about the quality of industrial relations in Britain. This has tended to be confrontational rather than cooperative and based on notions of 'class-warfare' and 'us-and-them'. Trade union leaders can be extremist and stubborn in pursuing their members' interests, but the performance of management and employers is also criticized, and insensitive managers can frequently be responsible for strikes arising in the first place. Relations between management and workers still leave much to be desired, and industrial unrest, which was largely dormant in the 1980s, has broken out again in recent years. A MORI poll in 1990 found that 58 per cent of those people interviewed believed that bad management is more to blame than the unions for poor industrial relations and Britain's economic problems.

The Advisory, Conciliation and Arbitration Service (ACAS)

ACAS is an independent, government-financed organization that was created in 1974 to improve industrial relations. It may provide, if requested, advice, conciliation and arbitration services for the parties involved in a dispute. But ACAS does not have binding power, and the parties may disregard its advice and solutions. There is also no legal requirement to bring ACAS into a dispute, for industrial relations in Britain consist of free collective bargaining between employers and workers. It has been argued that arbitration should be made compulsory and that findings should be binding on the parties. However, strike action is not illegal for most workers if legally called, and the government has no power to intervene. Nevertheless, ACAS has performed much valuable work, even within the present framework, and has been responsible for settling a wide range of disputes.

ACAS also oversees the operation of employment law and examines abuses of workers' rights under legislation. These may involve complaints of unfair and unlawful dismissal; claims under the Equal Pay Acts of 1970 and 1984; grievances under the Sex Discrimination Acts of 1975 and 1986; and unlawful discrimination under the Race Relations Act of 1976. There is now a large body of employment and regulatory law, which makes conditions of work more secure and less arbitrary than they have been in the past, particularly in the cases of women, ethnic minorities and the low-paid. But there is still concern about the real effectiveness of such legislation.

Consumer protection

In a competitive market, consumers should have a choice of goods and services, information to make choices, and laws to safeguard their purchases. Statutory protection for consumers has grown steadily in Britain and is harmonized with European Union law. The public can complain to tribunals and the courts about unfair trading practices, dangerous and unsafe goods, misrepresentation, bad service, misleading advertising, and personal injuries resulting from defective products.

The Office of Fair Trading is a government department that oversees the behaviour of trade and industry in the consumer field. It promotes fair trading, protects consumers, and has helped to improve consumer protection and awareness. It has drawn up codes of practice with industrial and commercial organizations, keeps a close watch for any breaches of the codes, and publishes its findings, often to the embarrassment of the manufacturers concerned. It can suggest legislation to the government where needed.

Organizations that provide help on consumer affairs at the local level are Citizens Advice Bureaux, Consumer Advice Centres and consumer protection departments of local councils. Private consumer protection groups, which investigate complaints and grievances, may also exist in some localities.

At national level, the independent National Consumer Council monitors consumers' attitudes, although there is doubt about its effectiveness. A more active body is the Consumers' Association, funded by the subscriptions of its 1 million members. Its magazine *Which?* is a champion of the consumer, and applies rigorous tests to anything from television sets to insurance and estate agents. *Which?* is the 'buyers' bible', and its reports have raised the standards of commercial products and services in Britain.

Critics argue that much remains to be done in the consumer field to achieve minimum standards and adequate protection. The Conservative government introduced (1991) a Citizens' Charter programme which, by promoting greater openness and providing more information, attempts to improve standards of service for the consumer. Members of the public can complain about the quality of state businesses, such as education, health, the Post Office, transport and employment.

ATTITUDES

Attitudes to the economy and economic structure

Opinion polls have echoed the changing and volatile economic climate since 1979. There has been a recent lack of faith in Conservative government ability to manage the economy, even though the economy was booming. Instead, the 1997 general election showed that the electorate was willing to trust the Labour Party in economic matters because it had adopted more centrist, pragmatic and low taxation market policies.

The economy concerns many British people in areas like unemployment, industrial decline, inflation, prices and taxation, and it is felt that governments could do more about unemployment and invest more in industry. In an insecure deregulated market, job security is the first priority of job seekers, and is ranked ahead of work satisfaction, promotion and working conditions. In terms of job satisfaction, however, a 1990 MORI opinion poll found that, of those people interviewed, 82 per cent were very or fairly satisfied with their jobs, and only 10 per cent were either fairly or very dissatisfied.

However, a majority of respondents to polls believe that business and economic arrangements in Britain are unfair, and that the values of managers and workers are opposed. They feel that the country's wealth is unfairly

ATTITUDES

distributed, and that this favours the owners and the rich at the expense of employees and the poor. A Leeds University survey in 1997 found that people believed that the gap between rich and poor is growing, the notion of a 'job for life' is dismissed, and that businesses did not care about the community, the environment or individual customers. Most people now support the idea that workers should be given more control over and say in the organization of their places of work. The Labour government's acceptance of the EU Social Chapter, with its provision for workers' councils, may improve this situation.

Critics argue that Britain's economic ills are due to cultural factors; that there has been a traditional reluctance for educated people to enter trade and industry; that the workforce has a lower productivity rate than other comparable competitors; that there has been insufficient investment in industry; that management is weak and unprofessional; and that there has been too little investment in and encouragement of the technical, scientific and research fields.

EXERCISES

■ Explain and examine the following terms:

diversify	privatization	monopoly	invisible exports
merger	Lloyd's	shares	balance of payments
private sector	deficit	TUC	service industries
laissez-faire	Barclays	ACAS	deindustrialization
the City	inflation	*Which?*	mixed economy
devaluation	consumer boom	CBI	Stock Exchange deregulation
Keynesian	Clause 4	GDP	

■ Write short essays on the following topics:

1 Examine British economic policy and performance from 1979 to the present.

2 Discuss the role of the trade unions in British life.

3 Consider the financial institutions in Britain. Should they be more closely regulated by government? If so, why?

Chapter 8

Social services

STATE (OR PUBLIC) PROVISIONS for social security, health care, personal social services and housing are very much taken for granted by British people today. But it was not until the 1940s that the state accepted substantial responsibility for providing basic help for its citizens. Previously, there had been few public facilities and it was felt that the state was not obliged to supply social services. British social amenities have developed considerably since the mid-twentieth century as society and government policies have changed. They are now divided between state (public) and private sectors.

The state gives services and benefits for sick, retired, disabled, elderly, needy and unemployed people and their children. They are provided by local agencies and authorities under the central direction of the Departments of Health and Social Security. The cost of this welfare state is financed mainly by taxation revenues and by a National Insurance Fund to which employers and employees contribute.

In the private sector, there are many voluntary organizations that continue the tradition of charitable help for the needy, and which depend for their funding upon donations from the general public. Other private social and health services are financed by personal insurance schemes and by those people able to pay for such facilities out of income or capital.

Conservative governments (1979–97) introduced reforms in the state sector in order to reduce expenditure, improve efficiency, encourage more self-provision by individuals, and target benefits to those most in need. Critics argued that this was based on a market orientation and a return to the old mentality on social services. Such policies were widely attacked and some reforms were unpopular with the public.

State social services are controversial. They show the difficulty of reconciling such services with a 'free-market' economy and of deciding how much dependence there should be upon the state. The Labour government (1997) intends to reform the hugely expensive welfare system and to reduce dependency on the state. It seems that in future people will be encouraged to insure themselves against unemployment and sickness and to take out pensions and care insurance for their old age. These ideas suggest that people will build their own do-it-yourself welfare plans, and government's role would be to organize rather than fund such provision. The Welfare-to-Work programme is also intended to take people off state benefits.

Social services history

Historically, state social services were non-existent for most of the British population. The churches, charities, the rural feudal system and town guilds (organizations of skilled craftsmen) did give some protection against poverty, illness and unemployment, but this help was limited in its application and effect. Most people were therefore thrown upon their own resources, which were often minimal, in order to survive.

In Elizabeth I's reign (1558–1603), a Poor Law was established in England, by which the state took over the organization of charity provisions from the church. Parishes became responsible for their own poor, sick and unemployed, and were supposed to provide housing, help and work opportunities. The Poor Law marked the start of state social legislation in Britain, but it was grudging and limited, and discouraged people from relying on the parish relief system. Poverty and need were thought to be the result of an unwillingness to work and provide for oneself. The state was not considered to have extensive responsibility for social services.

These attitudes persisted in later centuries, but urban and rural poverty continued. Conditions worsened in the eighteenth and nineteenth centuries under the industrial revolutions, as the population increased rapidly. The urban workforce was obliged to work long hours in bad conditions in low-quality factories for low wages. Families frequently inhabited slums of overcrowded, back-to-back dwellings that lacked adequate sewage, heating or ventilation. The situation of many rural agricultural workers was just as bad.

Public health became an inevitable problem, and the poor conditions resulted in infectious epidemics in the nineteenth century, such as diphtheria, typhoid, tuberculosis and smallpox. Some diseases remained endemic in the British population into the twentieth century because of bad housing and the lack of adequate health and social facilities.

The Elizabethan Poor Law was eventually replaced by the Poor Law Amendment Act of 1834. This was designed to prevent the alleged abuse of the social relief provided by parishes. It created a system of workhouses in which the destitute and needy could live. But the workhouses were unpleasant places and people were discouraged from relying upon them. They were dreaded by the poor and accepted as a last alternative only when all else failed. Since nineteenth-century Britain was subject to economic slumps and unemployment, the workhouse system resulted in misery and the separation of families.

Successive governments until the end of the nineteenth century also refused to allow workers to organize themselves into trade unions, through which they might agitate against their working and living conditions. This forced workers into establishing their own social and self-help clubs in order to provide basic protection for themselves. Some employers were more benevolent than others, and provided good housing and health facilities for their workforces, but these examples were few and life continued to be harsh for many people.

The social misery of the nineteenth century persuaded some towns to establish local boards to control public health and initiate health schemes, but an effective apparatus was not created until the Public Health Act of 1848, and a national system of public health was not created until a second Public Health Act in 1875. Other legislation was passed to clear slum areas, but large-scale slum clearance was not achieved until the middle of the twentieth century. Reforms relating to housing, health, factory and mine conditions, sanitation and sewage, town planning and trade unionism were implemented in the nineteenth century. But they were limited in their effects, and have been described as paternalistic in their intention.

The social welfare problems of the nineteenth century were substantial. The failure of the state to provide for a reasonable security against illness, unemployment and poverty made the situation worse. The prevailing mentality was that suffering was the fault of the destitute themselves and that the remedy for their ills was in self-help. Social reformers, who were responsible for legislation that gave some relief from the effects of nineteenth-century industrialization, had to struggle against the apathy and hostility of the vested interests in Parliament and the country.

However, some small victories had been won, and it was gradually admitted in the early twentieth century that the state did have social responsibility for society as a whole, though this admission was not universally accepted. It was largely left to the Liberal government between 1906 and 1914 to introduce some reform programmes, but such measures affected only a minority of people, and the state was unwilling or unable to introduce further provisions in the early twentieth century. The financial and physical exhaustion resulting from the 1914–18 World War and the economic crises of the 1920s and 1930s halted social services expansion.

The underlying need for more state help continued, and the model for a welfare state appeared in the Beveridge Report of 1942. It recommended that a comprehensive system of social security and free health care for all should be established to overcome the suffering and need experienced by many people. It was intended that the system would be largely financed by a national insurance scheme, to which workers would contribute, and out of which they and their families would receive benefits when required. Although Conservative governments passed some of the necessary legislation to implement these proposals, it was the Labour government from 1945 to 1951 that radically altered the social and health systems and created the present welfare state.

Changing family and demographic structures

The provision of contemporary social services, in both public and private sectors, is conditioned by changes in family structures and demographic factors, governmental responses to social needs, and the availability and cost of services.

It is often argued that the traditional British family unit is falling apart; failing to provide for its elderly and disabled; suffering from social and moral problems; and looking automatically to the state for support. Family life has changed recently as the nuclear family (two parents and children living together) has decreased. But some traditional features continue even as new family structures have emerged.

Marriage is still popular in Britain. In 1993 there were 332,600 marriages, and 38 per cent of these were remarriages of one or both parties. Of the population aged 16 and over in 1994, 57.5 per cent were married, 21 per cent were single, 8.5 per cent were widowed, 6.5 per cent were cohabiting (living together outside marriage), 5 per cent were divorced and 1.5 per cent were separated.

More people are delaying marriage until their late twenties, with an average age of 28 for men and 26 for women. This suggests that the British are postponing marriage for a number of reasons, such as career considerations, rather than rejecting it as a social institution. Some 70 per cent of those marrying for the first time have a religious ceremony.

However, four out of every ten marriages end in divorce, and Britain has the highest divorce rate in the European Union. Remarriages are at greater risk than first marriages, and people who marry under 21 are the most susceptible to divorce. The average length of marriages ending in divorce is 10 years, and the average divorce age is 37 for women and 39 for men.

Divorce is based on the irretrievable breakdown of a marriage. In an attempt to save some marriages, couples now seeking divorce must go through a period of at least one year for reflection and possible conciliation. Divorce is painful for most people and affects a considerable number of children under 16.

The trauma is increased by the confrontational nature of the divorce system, with conflicts over property, financial support and custody of children.

Despite the popularity of marriage, there has been a big increase in cohabitation. This occurs mostly in the cases of separated or divorced women, although an increasing number of single women now cohabit. Many of these relationships are stable and long-term, and half of the resulting births are registered by both parents, rather than one as previously.

Non-matrial (or illegitimate) births arising from cohabitation and single mothers are now 31 per cent of live births. This has caused controversy on moral grounds, since illegitimacy still retains some of its traditional stigma, but legislation has improved the legal standing of such children by removing restrictions in areas like inheritance.

There were 732,000 live births in Britain in 1995, and births outnumbered deaths at 626,000. The average family size has declined, however, and is below 2.1 children per family, or the level necessary to replace the population in the long term. This means that the proportion of young people under 15 fell from 24 per cent of the population in 1971 to 9.4 per cent in 1995. However, the birth rate is now estimated to have risen slightly.

The low birth rate is due to several factors. Child bearing is being delayed, with an average age of 28 at which women have their first child. Some career women are delaying even longer, and there has been an increase in the number of single women and married couples who choose to remain childless, or to limit their families. Contraception has become more widespread, voluntary sterilization of both sexes is more common, and legal abortions have increased.

Increased divorce, separation and individual lifestyles have led to a growth in the number of one-parent families. It is estimated that some 2 million children are being raised in 1.3 million one-parent units, where 90 per cent of the parents are women. Of the women bringing up one-parent families, 16 per cent are single, 34 per cent are divorced, 22 per cent are separated and 17 per cent are widowed. Many of these families, the highest proportion of which live in inner London, are struggling with reduced living standards and are dependent upon social security benefits.

The proportion of married women in employment is now some 49 per cent. More women are returning to work more quickly after the birth of a child, and women make up 46 per cent of the workforce. But although Britain has a high percentage of working mothers and wives, provisions for maternity leave and child care are the lowest in Europe.

The various nuclear, one-parent, cohabiting and extended families have to cope with increased demands upon them, which may entail considerable personal sacrifice. Families carry out the greater share of caring roles in British society, rather than state professionals. Only 5 per cent of people over 65 live in state or private institutions, and only 7 per cent of disabled adults live in communal establishments. Most handicapped children and adults are cared for by their families, and most of the elderly are cared for by families or live alone. This is a big saving to the state, without which the cost of state health and welfare care would rise steeply.

However, the burden upon families and the state will grow as the population becomes more elderly, the disabled (currently 6 million adults) and the disadvantaged increase, and unemployment remains relatively high. Some 18 per cent of the population are over the state retirement ages of 60 for women and 65 for men. Life expectancy of men is 73 years and women 79 years, so there are more women among the elderly. It is estimated that Britain will have 4.5 million people over 75 and 0.5 million over 90 by the year 2001. Critics argue that more government aid should be given to families and local authorities to lighten their burden.

The picture that emerges from these statistics is one of smaller families; more people (both young and elderly) living alone; an increase in one-parent families and non-matrial births; rising divorce rates; more people living longer and contributing to an ageing population; more working mothers and wives; more couples cohabiting before and outside marriage; but with the institution of marriage itself remaining popular.

However, the traditional nuclear family is surviving, despite changes in family structure. Most adults marry and have children inside marriage, most children are raised by their natural parents, and most marriages continue until ended by the death of one of the partners. These features form a background to the contemporary state and private provisions for social security, health, social services and housing.

Social security

The social security system gives a basic standard of living for people in financial need and retirement through benefits and pensions. It is the government's most expensive programme at 32 per cent of total public spending (£100 billion), and 27 per cent of the population are on income-related benefits. It is financed from taxation revenue and from compulsory payments by employers and most workers over 16 to the National Insurance Fund. It is operated by the Department of Social Security (DSS) through local agencies nationwide.

Social security provides benefits for workers who pay into the National Insurance Fund (contributory); income-related benefits to those people whose income from all sources falls below certain levels; and other benefits that are conditional on disability or family needs.

The contributory system gives, for example, state retirement pensions for women at 60 and men at 65 (to be equalized at 65 for both sexes from 2010); maternity pay for pregnant working women; sick pay or incapacity benefit for people who are absent from work because of sickness; disability allowances for people who become incapable of work; and allowances to widowed mothers. The former unemployment benefit has become a Jobseeker's Allowance, which is dependent upon people actively seeking work.

Income-related benefits are also provided by the state. Income Support depends upon savings and capital and is given to some 5.6 million people in great financial need, such as one-parent families, the elderly and long-term sick or disabled. This benefit covers basic living requirements, although the sums involved are relatively low. It also includes free prescription drugs, dental treatment, opticians' services and children's school meals. Family Credit is a benefit whereby families with children and at least one parent in work receive an additional sum to their low wages, which includes the same extra benefits as Income Support. It is dependent upon income, savings and capital, and may be replaced by an earned income tax credit that effectively gives low-earners extra cash. Housing Benefit is paid to people on Income Support and other low-income claimants (4.8 million in 1996) and covers the cost of rented accommodation. A tax-free Child Benefit (£10 per week for the eldest child and £8 for each other child) is paid to all mothers for each of her children up to the age of 18, irrespective of family income.

In the past, people in great need were also able to claim a wide range of non-contributory single payments, such as the cost of clothes, cookers, children's shoes and funeral expenses, in the form of grants or loans, but these have now been sharply cut and replaced by a limited Social Fund, to which people have to apply. The Fund is being applied restrictively and has been widely attacked as an example of government's alleged reduction of social security aid.

The social security system does provide a degree of security. It is supposed to be a safety-net against the most urgent needs, but this does not prevent hardship. It is estimated that some 13.7 million people in Britain exist on the poverty line, which is sometimes measured on European Union scales as half the average national income. Accurate figures of poverty are difficult to obtain, however, because of the variable presentation of official statistics and because there are different definitions of what constitutes poverty.

Social security is very expensive and will become more so as the old age population grows and as the numbers of the long-term sick, disadvantaged, poor and unemployed persist. It is also very complicated with its large array of benefits, and is subject to considerable fraud, particularly in the cases of Income Support and Housing Benefit. From 1988, the Conservative government reshaped the system, attacked fraud and reduced benefits.

It argued that the reforms would save public money, preserve the safety-net commitment and target those people with the greatest needs. Critics argued that the changes meant a reduction in social security, particularly the Social Fund, Housing Benefit and Income Support. The young unemployed between 16 and 18 were also affected and are now ineligible for benefits until they are 18. But the government maintained that it was increasing its expenditure in real terms.

It was also concerned that people should look after themselves more, without automatic recourse to the state for help, and that they should seek employment more actively. Employees were encouraged to take out personal pension insurance to add to their state pensions, and to insure privately against health and other costs. But the record of the insurance companies in these areas has been criticized, as many people were wrongly advised to leave their company pension in favour of a personal pension plan that will, in fact, produce a smaller future income.

Conservative reforms of social security, driven by cost considerations and a market ideology, were controversial. But it is difficult to create a satisfactorily simple and fair system that will protect the genuinely needy and still encourage people to become more self-reliant and economically independent. The Labour government also accepts that the cost of social security is unsustainable. It will cut expense and some state benefits, such as Disability and Single Parents' additional benefits, use insurance to replace some state benefits, and encourage greater self-provision through work rather than dependency. Its Welfare-to-Work policy aims to provide work, education and training programmes for the unemployed, and automatic reliance on state benefits is not an option.

The National Health Service (NHS)

The Labour government (1945–51) created the NHS by the National Health Service Act of 1947. The NHS was based on the Beveridge Report recommendations, and replaced a private system of payment for health care by one of free treatment for all. The medical profession, which wished to retain private medicine, opposed the establishment of the NHS, but this was countered by the Labour government.

It was originally intended that the NHS would be completely free of charge in its provision of consultations, treatment and medicines. But prescriptions, which are written notes from a doctor enabling patients to obtain drugs from a chemist, now have to be paid for, as do some dental work, dental checks and eye tests. Such payments are, however, dependent upon employment status, age and income, so that children under 16, recipients of social security benefits and most old age pensioners usually receive free health services. In practice, some 80 per cent of medical prescription items are supplied free. Similarly, hospital care and treatment under the NHS is free for British and European Union citizens.

The NHS now provides a comprehensive range of medical and dental services for the whole country. It includes hospitals, doctors, dentists, nurses, midwives, blood transfusion and ambulance services and other health facilities.

The NHS is mainly financed from taxation. Its cost is £41,793 million per year (some 14 per cent of total government spending), and the NHS is also the biggest single employer of labour in Western Europe. Yet health expenditure in Britain is only 6 per cent of the gross domestic product (GDP) and lower than other major western countries, though its actual health coverage is better and more comprehensive than most.

Central government is responsible for the NHS, and the Secretary of State for Health initiates and implements health policy. But the system is devolved and is administered by local health authorities in England and Wales and health boards in Scotland and Northern Ireland. They are funded by central government to purchase health care for their local residents by arranging contracts with hospitals, doctors and health care units in both the public and the private sector. These management structures result from reforms by the previous Conservative government, which created an 'internal market' for health care where 'money followed the patient'.

Doctors

Most people who require health care will first consult their local NHS or state-employed doctor, who is a GP or non-specialist general practitioner, and of whom there are about 35,000 in Britain. Doctors have an average of about 1,900 registered patients on their panel (or list of names), although they will see only a small percentage of these on a regular basis. The majority of GPs are now members of group practices, where they share larger premises, services and equipment. However, a patient will usually be on the panel of one particular doctor, who will often be a personal choice.

Following reforms by the previous Conservative government, doctors (GPs) belonging to large practices may apply to become 'fundholders'. This means that they receive an annual budget from the local health authority; are free to determine the need for patient services; and are able to buy these from hospitals (private and state) inside and outside their local area. There are now two types of GPs – fundholders and state-paid non-fundholders. In 1996, some 14,000 GPs in 3,000 practices had become fundholders, covering 47 per cent of the population. Critics maintain that the two types of doctors effectively compete against each other and that patients receive better services from fundholders, but the Labour government intends to abolish fundholder status by 1999 and to give budgets and control over patients to large groups of local GPs, who will provide primary care.

Hospitals

If patients require further treatment or examination, the GP will refer them to specialists and consultants, normally at the local NHS hospital. These hospitals have about 370,000 beds and provide medical, dental, nursing and midwifery staff. Britain has some of the world's most modern hospitals, expertise and facilities, and more hospitals are being constructed. But it also has many buildings that were erected in the nineteenth century and that are in urgent need of modernization and repair. There is a shortage of beds in some hospitals, wards and hospitals are being closed, and waiting times for admission to hospital increased in 1997. The blame for this situation is placed on government spending cuts and an alleged unwillingness to spend more public money on health.

The funding of hospitals is now based on contracts with local health authorities/boards and is tied to the number of patients they treat. Some big hospitals have opted out of local health authority control and become 'self-governing Trusts'. They are then responsible for managing their own affairs with their own budgets, although they are still state hospitals within the NHS. However, the Labour government intends to create an integrated relationship between hospitals and the local GP groups, with the latter buying hospital care for their patients.

The state of the NHS

The NHS has an ambivalent position in the public mind. On the one hand, it is praised for its work as a free service and its achievements. It is considered a success in terms of consumer demand. Today, people are in general receiving help when they need it, and many who would previously have died or suffered are surviving and being cared for. Standards of living and medicine have risen, better diets have been devised, and there is a greater health awareness in the population at large.

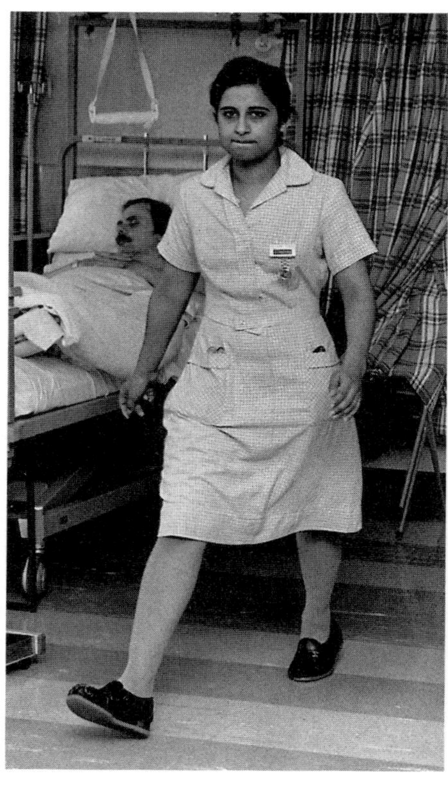

PLATE 8.1 A hospital nurse
(Judy Harrison/Format)

On the other hand, the NHS is criticized for its alleged inefficiency, inadequate standards and vast bureaucracy, and its objectives are considered too ambitious for the money spent on it. The media constantly draw attention to shortcomings and forecast breakdown. Workers in the NHS, like doctors, nurses and non-medical staff, complain about low pay, long hours, bureaucracy, levels of staffing and cuts in services. Such critics seem to feel that many of the problems could be solved simply by injecting more finance into the NHS.

The previous Conservative government maintained that it had increased spending and that the NHS was safe in its hands. But the facts of inflation, rising costs and increased demand arguably contribute to alleged underfunding. The NHS is in many ways a victim of its own success and of the demands that the British place upon it as of right. It is inevitable that a free, consumer-led service will require increasing levels of expenditure, better management of existing resources or alternative funding. Yet, despite problems, the NHS works well and gives great value for the money spent on it. Outsiders may often feel that the British do not always appreciate what a good health system they have compared to many other countries

The public is concerned about reforms of the NHS. The Conservative government privatized parts of the NHS such as hospital laundry, cleaning and catering services in order to save money and introduce competition. Later reforms altered the way in which the NHS is managed and funded. They were intended to create a competitive and demand-led 'internal market' in order to provide better health facilities and greater choice. Local health authorities/boards are now purchasers of health care for their local residents rather than providers of hospitals and services.

The reforms have been controversial, but have also won some acceptance as ways of simplifying the bureaucratic procedures of the NHS. It was hoped that they would result in competitive, patient-led services, where finance is diverted to real needs and skills. But critics argue that patient care has suffered, as Trust hospitals and fundholding doctors spend more time on financial and management matters than health.

Many people are confused and concerned about the NHS reforms under both Conservative and Labour governments. The debate is one of how to manage limited resources more efficiently, and whether this should be done through traditional local planning or competitive units. The Labour government will abolish the 'internal market' and fundholding GPs; cut down on management costs; transfer money to medical care and staff; reorganize the administrative base; possibly introduce some charges and insurance schemes for medical care; and involve private groups and finance in the running of the NHS.

The private medical sector

The previous Conservative government encouraged the growth of private health institutions and private medical insurance. It saw the private sector as complementary to the NHS. It would release pressure on state funds; give choice to patients; provide medical resources and flexibility of services; result in cost-effective cooperation with the NHS; share expensive facilities and equipment; and allow treatment of NHS patients at public expense in the private sector.

However, the scale of private practice in relation to the NHS is very small. Most private treatment is confined to relatively minor medical cases, and the very expensive, long-term care is still carried out by the NHS. Yet critics have long argued that health care should not be a matter of who can pay for it, but a responsibility of the state.

A quarter of patients pay for private health care out of their income or capital. Some 5.5 million other people, or 10 per cent of the population, are covered by private medical insurance taken out with businesses such as the British United Provident Association (BUPA). Concern about waiting lists and standards of health care in the NHS has persuaded many to take out private health insurance.

The insurance policy pays for private health care either in private hospitals and clinics, or in NHS hospitals that provide 'pay-beds'. These are beds for the use of paying patients, which still exist in NHS hospitals, despite opposition and the political threat (mainly from the Labour Party) to stop the practice. Pay-beds were a concession in 1946 to those doctors who agreed to join the NHS but who still wished to keep a number of private patients.

The personal social services

The social services provide facilities for assisting people, for example the elderly, the disabled, the mentally ill, families and children in the community. Trained staff, such as district visitors, home nurses and social workers, cater for these personal needs. The services are organized by local health and government authorities with central government funding, which currently amounts to some £431 million a year.

An increasing pressure is being put upon the social services and families as the elderly population grows and the number of the disadvantaged rises. More public residential homes are being provided, and greater financial resources are being devoted to family carers and the social services.

The previous Conservative government introduced a 'Care in the Community' programme, under which financial and material support is given to families caring for elderly or disabled relatives in the latters' own homes, or for handicapped children and adults in the family home. It allows hospital patients who do not need long-term care to be transferred to the community under the social services supervision, and for some elderly and disabled people to be cared for in their own homes by the social services. The aim is to prevent the institutionalization of people and to give them independence.

The scheme is financed by central government and operated by local government authorities. But it has caused controversy and difficulties, with mentally ill and handicapped patients becoming homeless or housed in inadequate temporary accommodation. There needs to be more support for local authorities and a greater awareness of implementation problems if the policy is to be more successful than at present.

The private social services (voluntary) sector

While there have been substantial improvements in social services in the twentieth century, there is still a shortage of finance to support the needy in a comprehensive fashion. It is therefore important that private residential care for the elderly is growing and that voluntary charities and agencies have continued. They form a complementary welfare service to the state facilities, and provide an essential element in the total aid pattern. The state system would be unable to cover all needs without them.

Most of the voluntary agencies have charitable status, which means that they receive tax concessions on their income, but receive no (or very little) financial support from the state. However, some groups, such as those dealing with drug and alcohol addiction, do receive financial grants from central and local government. There are many thousands of voluntary organizations in Britain, operating at national and local levels and varying considerably in size. Some are small and collect small amounts of money from the public. Others are very large and have professional staffs who receive millions of pounds from many different sources. Some groups, such as Oxfam (for the relief of famine) and the Save the Children Fund, have now become international organizations.

The following are examples of the voluntary agencies. Barnado's provides care and help for needy children; The Church of England Children's Society cares for children in need and is Britain's largest adoption agency; the Cancer Research Fund gathers finance in order to carry out research into potential cures for cancer; the People's Dispensary for Sick Animals (PDSA) provides medical and veterinary aid for people's pets; the Samaritans give telephone help to the suicidal; women's groups have founded refuges for abused women; and Help the Aged campaigns for the elderly.

Housing

Housing in Britain is divided into public and private sectors. Of the 22 million domestic dwellings, the great majority are in the private sector, with 67 per cent being owner-occupied and 7 per cent rented out by private landlords. The remaining 26 per cent are in the public or subsidized sector and are rented by low-income tenants from local government authorities or housing associations. Housing associations are non-profit making organizations that are becoming the main providers of new or refurbished housing in the subsidized rented sector.

In both public and private sectors, it is estimated that over 80 per cent of the British population live in houses or bungalows (one-storey houses) and the remainder in flats and maisonettes. Houses have traditionally been divided into detached, semi-detached and terraced housing, with the greater prices and prestige being given to detached property.

Public sector or social housing in England is controlled centrally by the Department of the Environment and by Secretaries of State in Wales and Scotland. A declining amount of the actual

PLATE 8.2 A Tudor house, Dedham, Suffolk *(The Hutchison Library)*

organization and provision of public housing is done by local government authorities. However, should public sector tenants be dissatisfied with the services provided by their local authorities, they can by ballot substitute the local authority for another landlord, which may be a cooperative, a trust, a private company approved by the Housing Corporation, or their own Tenant Management Organization.

The previous Conservative government encouraged the growth of home ownership in the housing market, as part of its programme to create a property and share owning democracy in Britain. In the public sector, it introduced (1980) a 'right to buy' policy, by which local government sells off council housing to sitting tenants at below-market prices. This policy has increased the number of home owners by over 1 million and relieved local authorities of the expense of decoration, upkeep and repair. The Labour Party, after initially opposing the policy, accepted it, mainly because it has proved attractive to tenants. The current Labour government has ploughed back the revenue from council sales into local government (which previously had not been able to spend it) so that they can provide more low-cost accommodation.

The Conservatives were critical of local government housing programmes. They intended that local authorities should divest themselves of council housing management. Instead, they would work with housing associations and the private sector to increase the supply of low-cost housing for rent, without necessarily providing it themselves. They would then concentrate their resources on improving the management of their existing housing stock. The Labour government apparently intends to return housing policies and control back to local government.

The construction of new publicly funded houses has, however, been radically reduced, and the private sector is not building enough low-cost properties. Critics argue that previous Conservative government housing policies contributed to a serious shortage of cheap rented accommodation in towns and rural areas for low-income groups, single people and the unemployed, at a time when demand is increasing.

Home ownership in the private sector has increased by 10 per cent since 1979. The normal procedure when buying a house or flat is to take out a loan on the security of the property (a mortgage) from a building society, bank or other financial institution. The amount of money advanced on a loan depends mainly on the borrower's salary, and it is usual to borrow twice one's gross annual salary. This long-term loan is usually paid off over a 25-year period, and includes interest. Tax relief is partially given on the interest on loans of up to £30,000 for each property, so that a government subsidy helps the purchasers of private property. But mortgage relief is being reduced and may soon be totally abolished.

House prices can vary considerably throughout the country, with London and south-east England having the highest prices, and northern England, Scotland and Wales having the lowest. Prices increased dramatically at the beginning of the 1970s, and much property speculation occurred. Price increases then stabilized for some years at 7–10 per cent each year.

A price boom from 1986 to 1988, however, was followed by high interest rates and an increase in mortgage foreclosures. This means that, when people cannot afford to continue their repayments on the loan, the lending institution takes over the property, and the occupier becomes homeless. The number of foreclosures has now been reduced. There was also a fall in house prices, a property slump and a growth in negative equity that was only slowly reversed from 1994, as interest rates were reduced and the property market slowly recovered.

British homes still have variable construction standards. Many are old and cold, are frequently badly built, and lack central heating and adequate insulation. But there has been some improvement in housing standards in recent years, and most new houses have a high percentage of the basic amenities. Greater attention has been paid to insulation, energy saving and quality. However, as building costs rise and available land becomes scarcer, the trend in new property construction has been towards flats and smaller rooms in houses.

Nevertheless, there are still districts, particularly in the centres of the big cities, where living conditions are bad and

PLATE 8.3 A house in Maidenhead *(The Hutchison Library)*

the equivalent of contemporary slums. Nearly half of the property in the inner-city areas was built before 1919 and, in spite of large-scale slum clearance in the 1950s and 1960s, much existing housing here is in barely habitable shape. Some recently completed high-rise blocks of council flats and estates in the public sector have had to be demolished because of defective and dangerous structures. According to the National Housing Forum, one in 13 British homes (or 1.8 million) are unfit for human habitation

Twentieth-century town renovation and slum clearance policies from the 1930s were largely devoted to the removal of the populations of large city centres to new towns, usually located in the countryside, or to new council estates in the suburbs. Some of the new towns, such as Crawley and Stevenage, have been seen as successes, although they initially had their share of social and planning problems. The same cannot be said of many council estates, which have tended to degenerate very quickly. The bad design of some housing estates, their social deprivation and lack

PLATE 8.4 An inner-city council estate, London *(The Hutchison Library)*

of upkeep are often blamed for the crime and vandalism that affect some of them. However, some local councils are now modernizing decaying housing stock, rather than spending on new development, in an attempt to preserve local communities. Similar work is also being done by housing associations (with government grants) and by private builders.

The provision of sufficient adequate and varied housing in Britain, such as one-bedroom properties for young and single persons, has been a problem for many years. Young people on low wages, whether married or single, are often unable to afford the cost of a mortgage, even for suitable private property. It is frequently difficult for them to obtain council housing because of long waiting lists, which contain people with priority over them. Additionally, the 'right to buy' policy has reduced the number of available council houses and flats for low-income groups and the unemployed. An alternative for many was either to board with parents or to rent property in the private sector.

However, Rent Acts and other legislation have strictly controlled rents and security of tenure, and these measures have resulted in the private rented sector being greatly reduced, because landlords could no longer charge true market prices and were unwilling to suffer the restrictions. The previous Conservative government lessened the effects of the Rent Acts by introducing new lease structures and encouraging landlords and other agencies to provide more privately rented accommodation. But the relaxations have led to accusations of exploitation of tenants by landlords.

The inadequate overall housing market has partly contributed to the considerable number of homeless people, particularly in London and other large cities, which in turn has led to increased social problems. It is admitted officially that there are some 150,000 homeless people who must be housed in temporary accommodation, which is usually inadequate. But unofficial figures put the real homeless total for all age groups at about 300,000, and some of them are clearly visible on the streets of Britain's large cities, particularly London. The causes of homelessness are complex and affect all age groups and types of people, but critics suggest that the problem could be better handled than at present. Independent research suggests that there are some 870,000 homes in Britain in both the private and the public sectors that remain empty and unoccupied for a variety of reasons. They could eradicate the

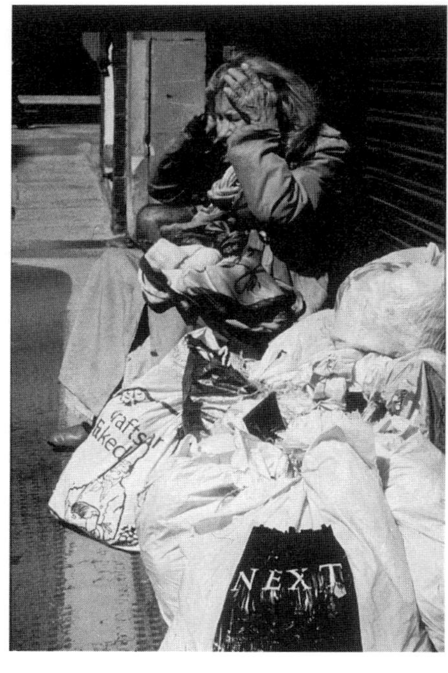

PLATE 8.5 Homeless
(Rex Features, London)

problem of homelessness and the housing shortage if they were refurbished and if private renting were made more attractive to landlords.

Charities such as Shelter and religious organizations like the Salvation Army provide accommodation for the homeless for limited periods, and campaign on their behalf. Local organizations, such as Housing Advice Centres and Housing Aid Centres, also provide help. But the problem of housing in Britain is still a major one and a focus of public concern. The high prices of many private houses, mortgage interest rates and persisting unemployment suggest that the problem will remain. The number of new starts for construction in both the public and private sectors has decreased, although the slump in building was reversed slightly from 1994.

ATTITUDES

Attitudes to social security, health and housing

Opinion polls consistently show that a large majority of British people demonstrate a concern for and dissatisfaction with the condition of the National Health Service and hospitals. Respondents place a high priority for increased public spending on health and medical provisions.

There has also been opposition to reforms in the NHS, with fear expressed about the possible privatization of health services. Respondents do not consider that the NHS is as well run as other national institutions, and there has been growing support for a comprehensive, better-funded state health care service. However, doctors and nurses always head the lists of those professionals with whom the public are most satisfied.

Concern is also felt about the provision of public housing, social security benefits, the personal social services and the community care programme. Most people, at least in response to poll questions, indicate that they would be

ATTITUDES

willing to pay higher taxes in order to ensure better public social and health services.

EXERCISES

Explain and examine the following terms:

welfare state	chemist	'fundholder'	social services
Social Fund	benefits	GP	nuclear family
'pay-beds'	rent	Shelter	council housing
workhouses	landlord	Oxfam	Beveridge Report
Poor Law	bungalow	mortgage	Income Support
charities	DSS	cohabitation	building society

Write short essays on the following topics:

1. Describe the structure and condition of the National Health Service.
2. Does the social security system provide a comprehensive service for the needy in Britain?
3. Discuss the different types of housing in Britain, and the mechanics of buying property.

Chapter 9

Education

THE BRITISH EDUCATIONAL SYSTEM has three levels: schools, further education (post-school) and higher education (universities). Schools are divided into state (maintained from public funds) and independent (privately financed) sectors, and there is no common organization for the whole country. England and Wales (with which this chapter is mainly concerned), Northern Ireland and Scotland have different school systems, though further and higher education generally has much the same structure throughout Britain, and is mostly funded by the state.

British education at many levels is of concern to parents, employers, politicians, students and schoolchildren. School inspectors have criticized standards in mathematics, technology, writing and reading skills and English. An Office for National Statistics survey (1997) showed that 8 million adults (or one in five) are poor readers, suggesting that standards of literacy in Britain are lower than previously believed.

The Sunday Times (5 October 1997) reported that

> Britain ranks 32nd out of 53 countries for the quality of its primary and secondary education system . . . according to the World Economic Forum's global competitiveness report. A National Institute of Economic and Social Research study showed British 13- and 14-year-olds are the equivalent of one year behind most other European countries and even further behind Japan, Korea and Singapore. At age 8–9, 91 per cent of European pupils could do a simple sum compared with 15 per cent in Britain. A Manchester University study . . . said reading standards at age 11 have declined since the mid-1980s. [The Labour government's] pledge to put 500,000 more students into further and higher education comes when there is already criticism of degree standards

. . . and some university courses.

However, British education should not be seen in a totally negative light. National school examination results have improved considerably in recent years, although some critics attribute this to lower standards. Many schools in the independent and state sectors do an excellent job, as do their teachers. It is the failing and underperforming state schools (some 50 per cent according to Labour government ministers) that tend to catch the media headlines. Nevertheless, the Labour government has prioritized education and intends to make it a lifelong experience and improve its quality.

English school history

The complicated nature of contemporary English schooling and current controversies have their roots in school history. State involvement in education was relatively late, and the first major attempt to establish compulsory elementary schools funded by the state came only in 1870 for England and Wales (1872 for Scotland and 1923 for Northern Ireland). It was not until 1944 that the state supplied a comprehensive system of free and compulsory primary and secondary school education.

However, church schools had existed for many centuries, and they influenced the later state system. After England, Scotland, Ireland and Wales were converted to Christianity in the fifth and sixth centuries, the church's central position in society enabled it to create the first schools. Its schools were initially intended to prepare boys for the priesthood, and it maintained its educational role in succeeding centuries.

Other schools were also periodically established, either by rich individuals or by monarchs. These were variously known as grammar, high and public schools, and were later associated with both the modern independent and state educational sectors. But these schools were largely confined to the sons of the rich, aristocratic and influential. The majority of the population received no formal schooling, and most people remained illiterate and innumerate.

In later centuries, more children benefited as the church created new elementary schools; some local areas developed secular schools; and school opportunities were provided by wealthy industrialists and philanthropists for working-class boys and girls. But the minority of children attending such institutions received only a basic instruction in reading, writing and arithmetic. Adequate education for the majority of children was non-existent.

By the nineteenth century, England had a haphazard school structure. But changes had occurred. The Church of England lost its domination of education and had to compete with the Roman Catholic Church, Nonconformist churches and other faiths. Although they had their separate schools and guarded their independence from state and secular interference, they provided much of the available schooling. The ancient high, grammar and public schools also continued to train the sons of the middle and upper classes for leadership and professional roles in society. But, at a time when the industrial revolutions were proceeding rapidly and the population was growing strongly, the state did not provide a system that could educate the workforce. Many members of the working class still received no formal or adequate education.

However, local and central government began to show some regard for education in the early nineteenth century, although new developments were limited. Grants were made to local authorities for use in their areas, and in 1833 Parliament supplied finance for the construction of school buildings. But it was only in 1870 that the state became more actively involved at the national level. An Education Act (the Forster Act) created local school boards, which had authority to provide schools in their areas. New state elementary schools supplied non-denominational training, while existing religious voluntary schools served denominational needs. By 1880, a national system provided free and compulsory elementary schooling for all children between the ages of 5 and 10. The Balfour Act in 1902 gave further impetus, by making local government responsible for state education and providing finance for voluntary schools. By 1918, schools were able to provide elementary education for children up to the age of 14.

Secondary school education still remained largely the province of the independent sector, and consequently of those people who could pay for its provisions. After a period when the old public schools had declined in quality, they revived in the nineteenth century. Their weaknesses, such as the narrow curriculum and indiscipline, had been reformed by progressive headmasters such as Thomas Arnold of Rugby, and their reputations increased. The grammar and high schools, which imitated the classics-based education of the public schools, also expanded. These schools drew their pupils from the sons of the middle and upper classes, and were the training grounds for the established elite and the professions.

A number of Acts in the early twentieth century marginally extended secondary education to those children whose parents could not afford school fees. The 1902 Act provided scholarships (financial grants) so that clever elementary schoolchildren could enter fee paying secondary schools. An Education Act of 1918 (the Fisher Act) established a few state secondary schools, but this increased state help did not appreciably expand the provisions for secondary education, and only a small number of children were able to enter the secondary school system on a non-fee paying basis. The English school system in the early twentieth century was consequently still inadequate for the demands of society, and governments avoided any further large-scale involvement.

The 1944 Education Act

In 1944, an Education Act (the Butler Act) reorganized the state primary and secondary school system in England and Wales and greatly influenced future generations of schoolchildren. State schooling became free and compulsory up to the age of 15 and was divided into three stages: primary schools (5–12 years old), secondary schools (12–15) and further, post-school training. The Act created a Ministry of Education, headed by a Minister of Education. A decentralized system resulted, in which the Ministry drew up policy guidelines, and local education authorities (LEAs) decided which forms of schooling would be used in their areas.

Two main types of state schools resulted from the Act: county and voluntary. Primary and secondary county schools were provided by the local authorities of each county. Voluntary schools were mainly those elementary schools that had been founded by religious and other groups and which were now partially financed and maintained by local authorities, although they still retained their religious affiliation. This resulted in non-denominational state schools coexisting with maintained voluntary schools, and this situation continues today.

Most state county schools at the secondary level were divided into grammar schools and secondary modern schools, with some areas having a third type, the secondary technical school or college. Some of the grammar schools were new, while others were old foundations that now received direct state funding. Some other ancient grammar schools decided to become independent and so stayed outside the state system.

The secondary division was dependent upon an examination result. The 11-plus examination, which was adopted by most LEAs, consisted of tests that covered linguistic, mathematical and general knowledge, and it was taken in the last year of primary school at around the age of 11. The object was to select between academic and non-academic children, which introduced the notion of 'selection' based on ability. Those who passed the 11-plus went to grammar school, while those who failed went to the less

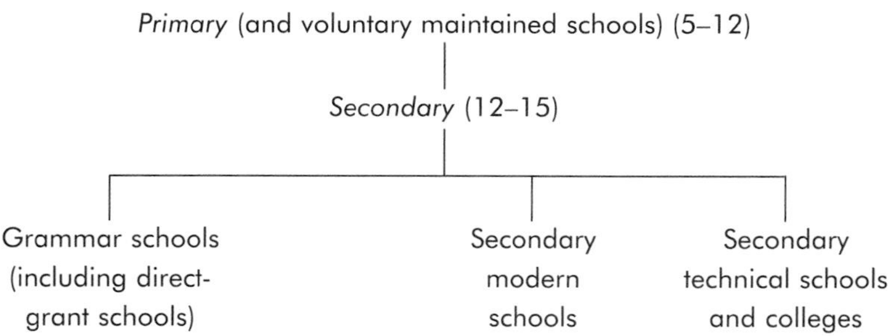

FIGURE 9.1 The 1944 organization of state schools

academic secondary modern school or technical college. Although schools were supposed to be equal in terms of their educational targets, success at the 11-plus led parents, pupils and teachers to equate the grammar schools with a better (more academic) education and a socially more respectable role.

The grammar schools prepared children for national examinations like the Matriculation Certificate, which later became the General Certificate of Education (GCE) at ordinary and advanced levels. These examinations qualified children for the better jobs and entry into higher education and the professions. Education in secondary modern schools was based on practical schooling without examinations, although GCE and other examinations were later introduced.

The intention of the 1944 Act was to provide universal and free state primary and secondary education. In addition, day-release training at local colleges was introduced for employed people who wanted further education after 15, and local authority grants were given to students who wished to enter higher education. It was hoped that such equality of opportunity would expand the educational market, lead to a better-educated society, encourage more working-class children to enter university, and achieve greater social mobility.

Objections to the 1944 Act provisions

However, it was widely felt in the 1950s that these aims were not being achieved under the selective system of secondary education. Education became a party-political battlefield on which ideological battles are still fought. The Labour Party and other critics argued that the 11-plus examination was wrong in principle, socially divisive, and had educational and testing weaknesses. It was maintained that the 11-plus led middle-class children to predominate in the grammar schools and in higher education, thus perpetuating the class system.

The Labour government in 1964 was committed to abolishing the 11-plus, selection and the secondary school divisions. They would be replaced by non-selective 'comprehensive schools', to which children would automatically transfer after primary school. These would provide schooling for all children of all ability levels and from all social backgrounds.

The battle for the comprehensive and selective systems was waged between 1964 and 1979, accompanied by fierce debate. Labour governments tried to introduce comprehensive schools (both by persuasion and legislation), while some LEAs fought to retain grammar schools and the selective system. Although more schools became comprehensive under the Conservative government from 1970, it decided against legislative compulsion. Instead, LEAs were allowed to choose the type of secondary education that was best suited to local needs. Some decided for comprehensives, while others retained selection.

The next Labour government introduced an Education Act in 1976 that was intended to establish comprehensive schools nationwide and to phase out direct-grant grammar schools, many of which, when faced with the threat, chose to become independent of the state. However, before a totally comprehensive system could be implemented, a Conservative government came to power in 1979. The state secondary school sector consequently remains divided, although with greatly reduced effect, between the selective and non-selective options, since a minority of LEAs do not have comprehensives and there are 163 grammar schools left.

The comprehensive/selection debate continues, and education is still subject to party-political and ideological conflict. A MORI public opinion poll in 1987 found that only one parent in three supported comprehensive education, and that 62 per cent of parents with children in state secondary schools wanted a return to a selective system of grammar schools and secondary moderns. However, only 17 per cent favoured the 11-plus, and 45 per cent wanted entry to grammar schools to be determined by continuous assessment rather than by examination. It is often maintained that the continuous arguments about the relative merits of different types of schooling have not benefited schoolchildren or the educational system as a whole, but reforms to the state school system are still made by both Conservative and Labour governments.

The present state school system

State education is free (except for some specialist tuition in areas such as music) and compulsory for children between the ages of 5 and 16. Some 93 per cent of all children in England and Wales are educated in the state primary and secondary sectors, but the present state school system is complicated by remnants of the 1944 Act, Conservative reforms from 1979–97, and proposals for change tabled by the Labour government.

The Department for Education and Employment (DfEE), under a Secretary of State, initiates policy, and the LEAs retain a degree of decentralized administrative choice in many educational matters. They are controlled by the education committees of local councils, and organize school planning and the hiring of teachers in their areas. Although most of the finance for local education is provided by central government, governments in the past have interfered very little in the activities of the LEAs and the schools.

The LEAs have also traditionally left the academic organization of schools to headteachers. These have allowed freedom to the staffs of their schools to organize their own programmes, books and methods of teaching. Many state schools also have boards of unpaid governors, who are usually local citizens prepared to give help and guidance and who may also be involved in the hiring of headteachers and teachers.

This overall situation has been affected by Conservative government policies from 1979–97. Under the local Management of Schools policy, headteachers were given financial control over their school budgets and took on management roles; greater powers of decision making were transferred to school governors; and parents now have a greater voice in the actual running of schools, as well as a right to choose a particular school for their children. Some schools were also allowed to 'opt out' of (transfer from) local authority control if a majority of parents voted for such a move. These grant-maintained (GM) schools are still state schools, but are self-governing; receive their funding directly from the DfEE; and the headteachers and governors are responsible for their own school budgets and management. Some 18 per cent of secondary schools in England and 5 per cent in Wales are GM schools. Such schools are also allowed to select up to 50 per cent of their pupils.

As a result of these reforms, LEAs have lost some authority in the state school sector. Greater responsibility is now held by headteachers, governors, teachers and parents in the organization of state schools. This has meant a shift from purely educational to management roles, and involves increased burdens of time and administration.

However, the Labour government intends to find a new role for LEAs that would oversee admissions policies for all types of state schools and provide central services. It will abolish GM schools, and has outlined a new structure for state schools with three different categories: LEA schools would become community schools; those associated with church or charitable bodies would be known as aided schools; and previous GM schools are offered the halfway house of 'foundation' status, sharing responsibility for admissions with the LEAs.

State schooling before the age of 5 is not compulsory in Britain, and there is no statutory requirement on the LEAs to provide such education. But more parents (particularly those at work) are seeking school provisions for young children, and there is concern about the lack of opportunities. At present, 57 per cent of 3 and 4 year olds benefit from a state nursery education, whilst others attend private playgroups. The Labour government wants to expand state nursery education, reduce class size and devote more funding to the sector.

Pupils attend primary school in the state sector from the age of 5 and then move to secondary schools normally at the age of 11. Some 90 per cent of secondary school children go to comprehensives from the ages of 11–16/18, and there are only a small number (some 3 per cent) of grammar and secondary modern schools left in the state system. The continued existence of these schools depends partly upon local government decisions, partly upon parent power, and partly upon Labour government policy.

PLATE 9.1 A multiracial class in a primary school
(Liba Taylor/The Hutchison Library)

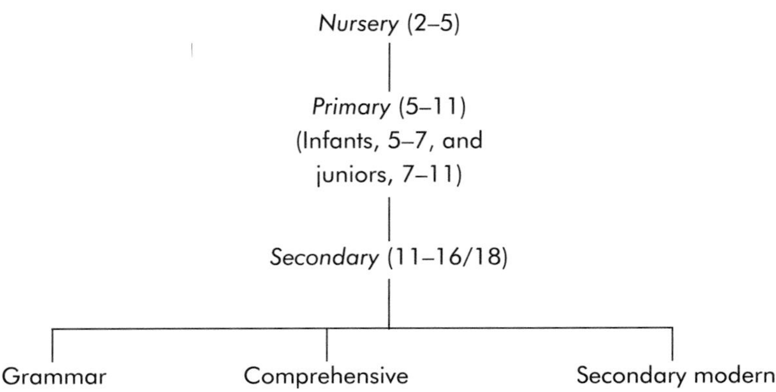

FIGURE 9.2 The current state school system

Comprehensive school pupils are of mixed abilities and come from a variety of social backgrounds in the local area. There is still much argument about the quality and performance of the system. Some critics maintain that bright, academic children suffer, although 'streaming' into different ability classes occurs, and examination results can be excellent. The Labour government will introduce 'setting', which essentially divides children into ability and interest classes. Arguably, therefore, 'selection' continues even in the comprehensives. There are some very good comprehensive schools, which are not necessarily confined to privileged areas. But there are also some very weak ones, which suffer from a variety of social, economic and educational problems.

Scotland has an ancient educational system, with colleges and universities that are among the oldest in Europe. Its state school system, under a Scottish Education Board that decides policy, has long been comprehensive, and it has different school examinations from those in the rest of Britain. The Scottish 'public schools' are state and not private institutions (although independent schools exist), and children transfer from primary to secondary education at 12.

In Northern Ireland, the state schools are mostly divided on religious grounds into Catholic and Protestant, and are often single-sex. However, there are some tentative movements towards integrated coeducational schools. The comprehensive principle has not been widely adopted, and a selective system with an examination at 11 gives entrance to grammar schools. Performances at these schools have been generally superior to their counterparts in England and Wales, although examination results in the other secondary schools are comparatively poor.

The independent (or private fee-paying) school sector

The independent school sector is separate from the state school system and caters for some 7.6 per cent of all British children, from the ages of 4–18 at various levels of education in some 2,400 schools.

Its financing depends upon investments and from the fees paid by the pupils' parents for their education, which vary between schools and can amount to several thousand pounds a term. The independent sector is dependent upon its charitable and tax-exempt status to survive. This means that the schools are not taxed on their income if it is used only for educational purposes. There are a minority of scholarship holders, whose expenses are covered by their schools. But the Labour government is now phasing out the 'assisted places scheme', whereby gifted children from poorer families benefit from independent education at state

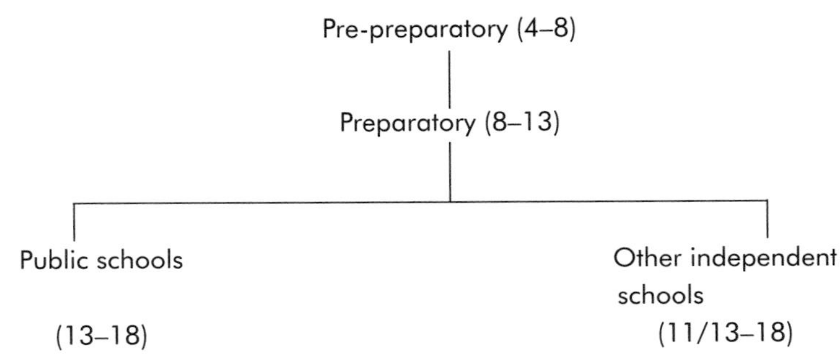

FIGURE 9.3 The independent school sector

expense. The saving is to be invested in reducing state primary school class size.

Some 250 public schools, such as Eton, Harrow and Winchester, are the most famous of the independent schools, and are usually defined by their membership of the Headmasters' Conference. They were originally created (often by monarchs) to provide education for the sons of the rich and aristocratic. Such schools are mainly boarding establishments, where the pupils live and are educated during term time, although boarding has declined in recent years and many of them now take day-pupils who do not board in.

Public schools play a significant role in British education, and many leading figures have been educated at them. Entry today is competitive, normally by an entrance examination, and is not confined to social class, connections or wealth, although the ability to pay the fees is obviously important. Independent preparatory schools (primary level) prepare their pupils for public school entrance, and parents who decide to send their children to a public school will often give them a 'prep school' education first.

There are many other independent schools in addition to the public schools, which can vary considerably in quality and reputation. Insurance schemes for the payment of fees mean that there are opportunities for independent education for the less affluent, but some parents make great financial sacrifices so that their children can be independently educated. In a 1987 MORI poll, 48 per cent of parents said that they would send their children to an independent school if they could afford it. Bristol University research (1997) found that bright pupils who go to independent schools are more likely to win places at top universities and secure well-paid jobs than children of similar ability educated at state schools. These findings query the assumption that bright children will fulfil their potential in any environment. They suggest that parents give an advantage to their children by investing in school fees.

The independent sector is criticized for being elitist, socially divisive and based on the ability to pay for education. In this view it perpetuates the class system. The Labour Party in opposition

PLATE 9.2 Harrow school boys on Speech Day *(Philip Wolmuth/ The Hutchison Library)*

argued for the abolition of independent schools and the removal of their tax and charitable status. But, while the Labour government is phasing out the assisted places scheme, it has no stated plans to abolish the independent sector. Independent schools are now firmly established and for many provide an element of choice in what would otherwise be a state monopoly on education.

School organization and examinations

The school day in most state and independent schools, except for infant and junior schools, usually runs from 9.00 am until 4 pm, and the school year is divided into three terms (autumn, spring and summer). Classes in British schools used to be called 'forms', and in secondary schools were numbered from one to six. But most schools have adopted year numbers from seven to 11 in secondary schools, with a two-year sixth form for advanced work. Corporal punishment was abolished in state schools in 1986, but is permissible in the independent sector.

The reduced birth rate in recent years has led to a decrease in the number of schoolchildren at all levels. The birth rate continued to decline in the mid-1990s, but has now started to increase again. The reduced pupil numbers have resulted in the closure of schools in rural and urban areas, and the average pupil–teacher ratio for all state schools is now about 17 to one, although many schools have larger classes.

Most teachers are still trained at the universities and other colleges, although attempts have been made to broaden their training by increased practice in the actual school system. There is a shortage of teachers in some parts of the country and in specialized subjects like mathematics, technology and physics. Potential teachers increasingly see the profession as unattractive, and many practising teachers leave for better-paid jobs or retire early. Teachers at present are suffering from low morale after battles with the government over pay, conditions and educational reforms, and from what they perceive as the low status afforded them by government and the general public. The teaching

PLATE 9.3 A science class in a state comprehensive school
(Michael Ann Mullett/Format)

profession has become very stressful and subject to greater pressures, such as assaults upon teachers by pupils, than in the past. The standards of teaching, particularly in state schools, have attracted a good deal of criticism from all quarters in recent years. The Labour government intends to remove incompetent and underperforming teachers and to close 'failing schools'.

However, the effect of public spending cuts in education has been considerable and has attracted much criticism. They have prevented the building and modernization of schools, especially in inner-city areas. The cuts have also resulted in a shortage of books and equipment for pupils, teachers and libraries, in addition to other reduced services. But the previous Conservative government established (jointly with local industry) technological colleges in some cities and tried to attract more specialist teachers.

Conservative governments also introduced school reforms. Attainment tests were set to establish what children should

PLATE 9.4 Children in an inner-city comprehensive school
(Maggie Murray/Format)

reasonably be expected to know at the ages of 7, 11 and 14. The progress of each schoolchild can then be measured against national standards, assessed and reported. But many teachers were opposed to the extra work involved, doubted the validity of the tests and have boycotted them in recent years.

Another radical reform was the establishment of a National Curriculum. The aim was to create an educational curriculum that was standardized, centrally devised and appropriate to the needs and demands of the contemporary world. It was to cover all age groups and include the 'core subjects' of English, mathematics and science, as well as the 'foundation subjects' of history, geography, technology, music, art, physical education and (at the secondary level) a modern foreign language. But this reform generated much controversy, opposition, difficulties of implementation, and problems concerning the content and scope of course material. It has now been reduced to a more manageable level and the emphasis placed on literacy and numeracy skills.

The National Curriculum (which is not applicable to independent schools, although they follow the subject structure) is tied to a system of national examinations at the secondary level. They may be taken in all types of schools in England, Wales and Northern Ireland. The two main examinations are the General Certificate of Secondary Education (GCSE), which is taken usually by 16 year olds, and the General Certificate of Education at Advanced Level (GCE A level), which is normally taken at the end of the second year in the sixth form by 18 year olds. Results in all exams tend to be better in single-sex schools.

The GCSE is taken in a range of subjects, the questions and marking of which are undertaken by independent examination boards whose standards have attracted criticism in recent years. In addition to written examinations, project work and continuous assessment of pupils are also taken into account in arriving at a final grade. The exam can be taken in any available subject(s) according to individual choice, but most candidates will attempt six or seven subjects, and the basic subjects required for jobs and further education are English, mathematics (or a science) and a foreign language. The GCSE was intended as a better evaluation of pupils' abilities than pure examinations, and one that would give prospective employers some idea of the candidate's ability. But, although standards continue to improve, 8 per cent of pupils taking GCSE in 1997 did not pass a single subject.

The GCE A level is normally associated with more academic children, who are aiming for entry to higher education or the professions. Good passes are now essential because the competition for places in the universities and other colleges has become much stiffer. The number of subjects taken at A level varies between one and four, although three are usually required for entry into higher education, and pupils may mix arts and science subjects. The concentration upon a few subjects reflects the high degree of early specialization in the British system. Supplementary examinations to the A levels (AS levels) may also be taken at the end of the first year in the sixth form, and serve as a lower-level alternative. The standards achieved in A levels continue to rise, although some critics argue that this is due to easier examinations. There is continuing discussion about the format and content of A levels, and the Labour government may broaden their base by introducing other subjects, whilst still keeping the emphasis upon specialized academic knowledge in the main subjects.

GCSE and A level results by pupils and schools are the basis of 'league tables', a reform instituted by the previous Conservative government. Examination results and marks at individual schools are published so that parents and pupils can judge a school's performance. The exercise has been criticized for its methodology and for creating a 'results mentality', but it is now firmly established and influential.

Higher education

Should a pupil obtain the required examination results at A level, he or she may go on to an institution of higher education, such as a university or other college. The student, after a prescribed period of study and after passing examinations, will receive a degree and become a graduate of that institution. In the past, only a small proportion of the age group in Britain proceeded to higher education, in contrast to the higher rates in many major industrial nations, but the ratio is now one in three, following a recent rapid increase in student numbers.

The universities

There were 23 British universities in 1960. After a period of expansion in the 1960s and reforms in 1992, when existing institutions such as polytechnics were given university status, there are now some 100, with 1.2 million full-time students in 1995.

The Open University and the independent University of Buckingham are additional university-level institutions.

The universities can be broadly classified into four types. The ancient universities of Oxford and Cambridge (composed of their many colleges) date from the twelfth century, and until the nineteenth century they were virtually the only English universities and offered no places to women. However, other older universities were founded in Scotland, such as St Andrews (1411), Glasgow (1450), Aberdeen (1494) and Edinburgh (1583). A second group comprises the 'redbrick' or civic universities such as Leeds, Liverpool and Manchester, which were created between 1850 and 1930. The third group consists of universities founded after the Second World War and in the 1960s, like Sussex, York

PLATE 9.5 Wadham College, Oxford University *(John Oakland)*

and East Anglia, many of which are in rural areas. The fourth group are the 'new universities' created in 1992, when polytechnics and some other colleges attained university status.

The competition to enter universities is now very strong, and students who do not do well at A level may be unable to find a place. Some 10 per cent of students now drop out of higher education because of work, financial or other problems, but the majority aim for a good degree in order to obtain a good job, or to continue in higher education by doing research (masters' degrees and doctorates). The bachelor's degree (Bachelor of Arts or Bachelor of Science, BA or BSc) is usually taken in final examinations at the end of the third year of study, although some degree courses do vary in length in different parts of Britain. This degree is divided into first-, second- and third-class honours. Some degrees are dependent entirely upon the examination results, while others include continuing assessment over the period of study.

Universities are supposed to have uniform standards, although there are centres of excellence in particular subjects, and there has been recent criticism about levels in some universities and some subjects. Students can choose from an impressive array of subject areas, and teaching is mainly by the lecture system, supported by tutorials (small groups) and seminars. The student–lecturer ratio at British universities is relatively good at about 16 to one. Most students tend to live on campus in university accommodation, while others choose to live in rented property outside the university. Until recently, few British students chose universities near their parents' homes, and many seemed to prefer those in the south of England; but financial costs are now changing these preferences.

Universities are independent institutions created by royal charter, but they are in practice dependent upon government money. This derives mainly from finance given by government to Universities Funding Councils for distribution to the universities through university Vice-Chancellors, who are the chief executive officers of the universities.

The previous Conservative government was concerned to make the universities more accountable in the national interest, tightly controlled their budgets, and encouraged them to seek alternative private sources of finance. The universities have lost staff and research money; have been forced to adopt more effective management and accounting procedures; must market their resources more efficiently in order to attract students; pay greater attention to performance; and must justify their positions financially and educationally. Government consequently intervenes more closely in the running of the universities than in the past. Such policies have provoked considerable opposition from the universities, which argue that the recent large expansion of student numbers has not seen an equivalent rise in funding. But they are being forced to adapt rather than continuing to lose staff, finance and educational programmes.

Other higher education colleges

The 1970s saw the creation of colleges (or institutes) of higher education, often by merging existing colleges with redundant teachers' training colleges, or by establishing new institutions. They now offer a wide range of degree, diploma and certificate courses in both science and the arts, and in some cases have specifically taken over the role of training schoolteachers. They used to be under the control of their local authorities, but the Conservative government granted them independence, and some have achieved university status.

A variety of other institutions also offer higher education. Some, like the Royal College of Art, the Cranfield Institute of Technology, and various Business Schools, have university status, while others, such as agricultural, drama and art colleges like the Royal Academy of Dramatic Arts (RADA) and the Royal College of Music, provide comparable courses. All these institutions usually have a strong vocational aspect to their programmes that fills a specialized role in higher education.

Student finance

In the past, British students who gained a place at an institution of higher education were awarded a grant from their local education authorities. The grant was in two parts: the first covered the tuition fees of a first degree course (paid directly to the institution and resulting in tuition being free for students); the second covered, after means testing of parents' income, maintenance expenses such as the cost of rent, food and books of a course during term time.

The Labour government radically changed this situation from 1998 by abolishing the student grant. Students now have to pay at least £1,000 tuition fees and their maintenance, usually through loans from the Student Loan Company. They start to pay back their loans when they reach certain salary levels. Students are means tested on their parents' income, and those from poor backgrounds may not have to pay tuition fees. But many students will now have to finance their own higher education, and some students are already in financial difficulties. These changes in funding have resulted in a drop in the number of students provisionally applying for university entry.

The Open University

The Labour Party broached the idea of the Open University in the 1960s. It would be an educational service that used television, radio and correspondence courses to teach its students. It was intended to give opportunities (or a 'second chance') to adults who had been unable to take conventional higher education. It was hoped that the courses might appeal to working-class students who had left school at the official school-leaving age and who wished to broaden their horizons.

The Open University opened in 1969; its first courses started in 1971; and by 1996 there were 104,000 registered first degree students and an increasing number of postgraduate and research students. About 7,000 students of all ages and from very different walks of life receive degrees from the Open University each year. First degrees (bachelors) are awarded on a system of credits for each course completed, and now include students from the European Union, Gibraltar, Slovenia and Switzerland.

Dedication, stamina and perseverance are necessary to complete the long, part-time courses of the Open University.

Students, who are often employed, do not attend any one institution, but receive their lessons and lectures at home, partly by correspondence courses and partly by television (BBC 2) and radio broadcasts. Part-time tutors in local areas mark the students' written work and meet them regularly to discuss their progress. There are also special weekend and refresher courses throughout the year, which are held at universities and colleges, to enable students to take part in intensive study. The various television programmes and books associated with the Open University programmes are widely exported throughout the world. The Open University is generally considered to be a cost-effective success, has provided valuable alternative educational opportunities for many people, and has served as a model for other countries.

Further and adult education

An important aspect of British education is the provision of further and adult education, whether by voluntary bodies, trade unions or other institutions. The present organizations originated to some degree in the thirst for knowledge that was felt by working-class people in the nineteenth and early twentieth centuries, particularly after the arrival of elementary state education and mass literacy. Today, a wide range of educational opportunities are provided by self-governing colleges of further education, technical colleges and other institutions. These offer a considerable selection of subjects at basic levels for part- and full-time students.

Adult education is provided by these colleges, the universities, the Workers' Educational Association (WEA), evening institutes, local societies and clubs. Adult courses may be vocational (relating to employment) or recreational (for pleasure), and cover a wide variety of activities and programmes.

Some 4 million students of very varying ages are taking further and adult education courses in one form or another. In the past, a relatively low percentage of the 16–24 age group in Britain were in further and higher education, compared to the very much larger percentages in Japan, the USA and Germany. Although the figures have now improved considerably, it is still a matter of concern that too few people are being educated or trained further after the age of 16. This is particularly true at a time when there will be an increasing shortage of well-qualified people in the future workforce, especially in the scientific and technological fields.

Nevertheless, there has been a recent expansion of continuing-education projects and a range of programmes specifically designed for employment purposes and to provide people with access qualifications for further training. The Labour government intends further and higher education to be part of a lifelong learning process. But further education is suffering at present from a lack of resources and funding.

ATTITUDES

Attitudes to education

There have been continuous and vigorous debates about the quality and goals of British education at all levels since the 1970s. Traditionalist critics feel that state comprehensive schools and 'creative/progressive' methods of child-centred teaching are not producing the kind of people needed for contemporary society. It is argued that pupils lack the basic skills of numeracy and literacy, and are unprepared for the realities of the world outside school. Employers frequently criticize both the schools and higher education for the quality of their products.

The previous Conservative government's reforms from 1986 were based on centralizing and consumer-choice policies. They may be seen as an attempt to rectify the general educational situation, and were aimed at producing accountability, improved standards and skills in both the school and higher education sectors by more formal learning programmes. The government attempted to reform the teaching profession, improve pupils' performances, emphasize science and modern language studies, and increase parental choice.

The Labour government is continuing this process by stressing compulsory homework, contracts with parents, concentration on the '3 Rs' (reading, writing and arithmetic), and grouping children by ability ('setting'). Progressive 'child-centred' practices are dismissed, funds will be provided for school fabric repairs, and computers will be installed in every school within five years.

Critics, however, argue that an educational system should not be solely devoted to elitist standards, market considerations and the 'enterprise culture', but should try to combine the academic/liberal tradition, the technical and the vocational. The future of British education will depend in large part on how government reforms work and how they are perceived by teachers, parents, students and employers.

Concerns about quality and educational policy at all levels, particularly in the schools, rank second only to health care and are consistently voiced by a majority of respondents to public opinion polls. They think that state schools are not well run and that more public money should be spent on education. Education is likely to continue as a major concern in British life.

EXERCISES

■ Explain and examine the following terms:

public schools	grammar schools	WEA
comprehensives	11-plus	tutorial
GCE A level	Open University	scholarships
LEAs	corporal punishment	student finance
Eton	GCSE	'prep school'
the Butler Act	degree	vocational
streaming/setting	'3 Rs'	literacy

■ Write short essays on the following topics:

1 In what ways have government reforms since 1986 changed educational provisions?

2 Describe the structure of British higher education and its roles.

3 Comment upon the desirability, or otherwise, of British education's division into state and independent sectors.

Chapter 10

The media

THE TERM 'MEDIA' may include any communication system through which people are informed, educated or entertained. In Britain today it refers mainly to the press (newspapers), magazines, terrestrial (earth-based) television, cable and satellite television, radio and video. These systems overlap to some extent with each other and with books and film, have become profitable businesses and are closely tied to commerce, industry, advertising and sponsorship.

The media have evolved from simple methods of production, distribution and communication to the present sophisticated technologies. Their growth and variety have greatly improved information dispersal, news availability and entertainment opportunities. They now cover homes, places of business and leisure activities, and their influence is very powerful and an inevitable part of daily life. Surveys indicate, for example, that 69 per cent of Britons obtain their news and views of current affairs from television, 20 per cent from newspapers and 11 per cent from radio. Over 70 per cent of viewers trust television news to be fair and accurate.

However, the media also provoke debates about what is socially and morally permissible in their content and methods. Questions are asked about the role of advertising, the quality of services, concentrated ownership, influence on politics, legal and other restraints upon 'free expression', and the ethical responsibility of the media to individuals and society.

The print media

Print media (newspapers and magazines) began to develop in the eighteenth century. A wide circulation was hindered initially by transportation and distribution problems, illiteracy and government licensing/censorship restrictions. Over the last 200 years, however, an expanded educational system, abolition of government control, new print inventions and Britain's small geographical size have eliminated these difficulties and created allegedly free print media.

The growth of mass literacy after 1870 provided the owners of the print media with a greatly increased market. This led to the popularization of newspapers and magazines, which had previously been limited to the middle and upper classes. The print media were progressively used not only for news and information, but also for increased profits and entertainment. Personal ownership and new varieties of the print media expanded rapidly in the competitive atmosphere of the late nineteenth and early twentieth centuries, and were helped by financially rewarding advertising. Owners also realized that political and social influence could be achieved through control of the means of communication.

National newspapers

National newspapers are those that are available in all parts of Britain on the same day, including Sundays. They are often delivered direct to the home from local newsagents by newsboys and girls. The good internal distribution systems of a rather small country have enabled a national press to develop.

The first British newspapers with a limited national circulation appeared in the early eighteenth century and were followed by others, such as *The Times* (1785), the *Observer* (1791) and the *Sunday Times* (1822). Most were quality papers, catering for a relatively small, educated market.

In the nineteenth century, the growth and composition of the population conditioned the types of newspaper that were produced. The first popular national papers were deliberately printed on Sundays, such as the *News of the World* (1843) and the *People* (1881). They were inexpensive and aimed at the expanding and increasingly literate working class. In 1896, Alfred Harmsworth produced the *Daily Mail*, which was targeted at the lower-middle class as an alternative to the quality dailies. Harmsworth then published the *Daily Mirror* in 1903 for the working-class popular market. Both the *Mail* and the *Mirror* were soon selling more than a million copies a day.

The early twentieth century was the era of mass-circulation papers and of owners like Harmsworth and Arthur Pearson. There was fierce competition between them as they fought for bigger shares of the market. Pearson's *Morning Herald* (later the *Daily Express*) was created in 1900 to compete with the *Daily Mail* for lower-middle class readers.

The *Daily Mirror* was the largest-selling national daily in the early twentieth century. It supported the Labour Party and was designed for quick and easy reading by the industrial and increasingly politicized working class. The *Daily Herald* (1911) also supported the Labour Party, until it was sold in 1964, renamed the *Sun*, and developed different political and news emphases. The competition between the *Sun* and *Mirror* continues today, with each aiming for a bigger share of the mass daily market. Fierce battles are still fought between owners, since newspaper ownership is concentrated in a few large publishing groups, such as Rupert Murdoch's News International and the Mirror consortium (see table 10.1).

The success of the early popular press was due to growing literacy; a desire for knowledge and information by the working class; and political awareness among workers caused by the rise of the Labour Party. Newspaper owners profited by the huge market, but they also satisfied demand. The price and content of mass papers reflected lower-middle- and working-class readerships. This emphasis attracted large consumer advertising, and owners were able to produce cheaply by using modern printing methods and a nationwide distribution network.

The circulation of national papers rose rapidly in the early twentieth century, and it is estimated that there were 5.5 million daily sales by 1920. By 1973 these had increased to 17 million. But newspapers had to cope first with the competition of radio and films, and later with television. Although they have survived in considerable numbers, there has, since the 1970s,

PLATE 10.1 The *Daily Mirror* newspaper building, Central London
(Bill Coward/Barnaby)

been a reduction in sales and in the number of national and other newspapers.

Surveys in 1997 suggested that Britons buy more papers than any other Europeans, although they are least trustful of what they read in them. It is estimated that two out of three people over the age of 15 read a national daily paper, and three out of four read a Sunday newspaper. National newspapers now have sales of nearly 14 million on weekdays and 17 million on Sundays, although the total readership (e.g. family members) is obviously greater than these figures suggest.

The national press in Britain consists of 10 daily morning papers and nine Sunday papers. It is, in effect, a London press, because most national newspapers have their bases and printing facilities in the capital, although editions of some national papers are now published in the north of England, Scotland, Europe and the USA. The majority of them used to be located in Fleet Street in central London, but all have now left the street and moved to other parts of London. The reasons for these moves were high property rents, fierce competition and opposition from trade unions to the introduction of new printing technology. Newspapers and magazines in the 1970s and 1980s also had to face the expense of newsprint and rising production and labour costs.

Heavy labour costs in the print industries were often attributed to the overmanning and restrictive practices of the trade unions, particularly in London. This situation forced owners to consider new ways of increasing productivity while cutting costs. The use of new print technology meant that journalists' 'copy' could be printed directly through computerization, without having to use the intermediate and traditional 'hot metal' typesetting by printers. This change gave owners flexibility in their printing and distribution methods and cheaper production costs. It allowed them to escape from trade union dominance and the concentration of the industry in London, but it also resulted in job reductions, trade union opposition and industrial action.

Regional owners outside London had, in fact, pioneered the movement of newspapers and magazines into new print technology, and London newspapers followed. *The Times* tried to introduce new equipment, but was prevented by union opposition. The paper closed for 11 months (1979–80) in an attempt to put pressure on the unions, but this also failed. It was then sold to Rupert Murdoch's News International group, which has large media holdings in Britain, Australia and the USA. After further problems with the unions, Murdoch sacked his printers and moved *The Times* from Fleet Street to high-technology facilities at Wapping in east London. He employed only those workers who were prepared to operate the new machinery. These actions provoked bitter opposition, and the Wapping plant was heavily picketed by trade unionists. But other newspapers had to follow *The Times'* lead in order to survive.

New printing technology, improved distribution methods and cuts in labour and production costs have increased the profitability of the print industries. Despite the attraction of other media sources, they still have a considerable presence. But the business is very competitive, and papers can suffer from a variety of problems. However, the large risks involved have not stopped the introduction of new newspapers. The quality national daily, *The Independent*, was published in October 1986 and survives despite circulation losses. Sunday nationals, like *The Independent on Sunday* (1990), together with the *The European* (1990), have appeared in recent years. But other papers, such as *Today* (1986–95), have been lost. Britain's ethnic communities also produce their own newspapers and magazines, which are increasing in numbers and improving in quality. There is a wide range of Jewish, Asian, West Indian (Afro-Caribbean), Chinese and Arabic publications.

National papers are usually termed 'quality' or 'popular' depending on their differences in content and format (broadsheet or tabloid). Others are called 'mid-market', fall between these two extremes, and are tabloids (see table 10.1). The qualities (such as *The Times*) are broadsheets (large-sheet), report national and international news in depth, and analyse current events and the arts in editorials and articles. The populars (such as the *Sun*) are mostly tabloid (small-sheet), deal with relatively few 'hard news' stories, tend to be superficial in their treatment of events, and sensationalize and trivialize much of their material. It cannot be said that the British populars at the lower end of the market are deeply instructive, or concerned with raising the critical consciousness of their readers. But owners and editors often argue that their readership demands particular styles, interests and attitudes. 'Mid-market' papers, such as the *Mail* and *Express*, cater for intermediate groups.

Sales of popular papers on weekdays and Sundays far exceed those of the qualities. The qualities are more expensive than the populars and carry more up-market advertising that generates essential finance for the papers. The populars carry less advertising and cater for more down-market consumer material. The press (national and regional) in 1995 took 55 per cent of total advertising spending in Britain.

PLATE 10.2 Newspaper headlines *(Rex Features, London)*

There is no state control or formal censorship of the British press, although it is subject to laws of publication and expression, and there are unofficial forms of self-censorship, by which it regulates itself and its conduct. The press is also financially independent of the political parties and receives no funding from government.

Despite this critics argue that most newspapers are politically right-of-centre and sympathize with the Conservative Party. However, political slants can vary considerably over time and under the influence of events. For example, the small-circulation *Morning Star* has varied between Stalinist, Euro-Communist and Democratic Left perspectives. Papers may have a political bias

TABLE 10.1 The main national newspapers (average daily sales), 1997

Name	*Founded*	*Sales (Sept. 1997)*	*Owned/controlled by*
Popular dailies			
Daily Mirror	1903	2,442,078	Mirror Group
Sun	1964	3,887,097	News International
Daily Star	1978	631,853	United News and Media
Mid-market dailies			
Daily Mail	1896	2,344,183	Associated Newspapers
Daily Express	1900	1,241,336	United News and Media
Quality Dailies			
The Times	1785	821,000	News International
The Guardian	1821	428,010	Guardian Media Group
Daily Telegraph	1855	1,129,777	Telegraph Group
Financial Times	1888	326,516	Pearson
The Independent	1986	288,182	Mirror Group
Popular Sundays			
News of the World	1843	4,620,415	News International
The People	1881	2,001,978	Mirror Group
Sunday Mirror	1963	2,424,000	Mirror Group
Mid-market Sundays			
Mail on Sunday	1982	2,322,423	Associated Newspapers
Sunday Express	1918	1,261,690	United News and Media
Quality Sundays			
Observer	1791	498,086	Guardian Newspapers
Sunday Times	1822	1,449,113	News International
Sunday Telegraph	1961	938,253	Telegraph Group
The Independent on Sunday	1990	311,321	Mirror Group

Source: Audit Bureau of Circulation, September 1997

and support a specific party, particularly at election times, although this can change dramatically (as in the 1997 general election). A few, like those of the *Mirror* Group, support the Labour Party, some like *The Times* and *The Independent* consider themselves to be independent, while others, like *The Guardian*, favour a left-of-centre position. It appears in practice that the British public receive a reasonable variety of political views from their newspapers.

The press is dependent for its survival upon its circulation figures; upon the advertising that it can attract; and upon financial help from its owners. A paper may face difficulties and fail if advertisers remove their business. But a high circulation does not necessarily guarantee the required advertising and consequent survival, because advertisers today tend to place their mass-appeal consumer products on television, where they will benefit from a larger audience. Most popular papers are in constant competition with their rivals to increase their sales. They attempt to do this by gimmicks such as bingo games and competitions, or by calculated editorial policies that are intended to catch the mass readership. Owners may refuse to rescue those papers that make continuous losses. A number of newspapers in the twentieth century have ceased publication because of reduced circulation, loss of advertising revenue, refusals of further financial aid, or a combination of all three factors.

Regional newspapers

Regional, or provincial, newspapers are those that are published outside London. Excluding its national newspaper industry, London itself has one major central paper (the *Evening Standard*) with a daily circulation of some 440,000. There are also about 100 local weeklies, dailies and evening papers that appear in the Greater London districts.

Outside London, there are some 100 daily regional papers published in the cities and smaller towns in the mornings and evenings. They contain a mixture of local and national news and are supported financially by local advertising.

Some of the more famous daily regional papers, such as *The Scotsman* (Edinburgh) and the *Glasgow Herald* in Scotland, the *Western Mail* in Cardiff, Wales, and the *Yorkshire Post* (Leeds) in England, have considerable reputations and a wide circulation both in and outside their particular regions.

A recent development of some note in the regions has been the rapid growth of 'free newspapers', which are delivered direct to homes and for which the consumer does not pay. Some 800 are usually published weekly on a local basis, and they are financed by local advertising to such an extent that news is often outweighed by the advertisements. It is estimated that they have a weekly circulation of some 35 million.

Periodicals and magazines

There are 6,500 different periodicals and magazines in Britain, which are of a weekly, monthly or quarterly nature. They cover the vast majority of trades, professions, sports, hobbies and interests, and are aimed at different markets and levels of sophistication. It is very difficult to break into this established market with a new product. Some attempts, which manage to find a gap in the market, succeed, but most usually fail. For example, there are no illustrated news magazines in Britain, because they have been unable to compete with television and with the existing magazine coverage.

Among the serious weekly journals are the *New Statesman and Society* (a left-wing political and social affairs magazine); *The Economist* (dealing with economic and political matters); the *Spectator* (a conservative journal); and *New Scientist*. *The Times* publishes several influential weekly magazines, such as the *Educational Supplement*, the *Higher* (Education Supplement) and the *Literary Supplement*. The lighter side of the market is catered for by periodicals such as *Private Eye*, which satirizes and attacks what it considers to be the shortcomings of British society.

The teenage and youth magazine market is fiercely competitive, and whilst some new attempts to enter this specialist field succeed, others quickly fail. Women's periodicals, such as *Woman* and *Woman's Own*, have very large and wide circulations. But the best-selling publications are the weekly *Radio Times* and the *TV Times*, which contain feature stories and the scheduled programmes for BBC and independent television. Other magazines cover a varied range of interests, such as computers, rural pastimes, gardening, railways, cooking, architecture, do-it-yourself skills and a wide selection of sports.

The broadcasting media

Radio was the first broadcasting medium to appear in Britain. Experimental transmissions were made at the end of the nineteenth century, and the systems were further developed in the early twentieth century. After a period of limited public availability, national radio broadcasting was established in 1922, when the British Broadcasting Company was formed under the direction of John Reith.

In 1927, Reith became the first Director-General of the British Broadcasting Corporation (the present BBC) and set the tone and style for the BBC's future development. The BBC had a monopoly in broadcasting and tended to have a paternalistic image. Reith was concerned that the BBC should be independent of government and commercial interests; that it should strive for quality (as he defined it); and that it should be a public broadcasting service, with a duty to inform, educate and entertain. The BBC has since built up a reputation for impartial news reporting and quality programmes, both in its domestic services and through its worldwide radio and television broadcasting on the external services.

The BBC had a broadcasting monopoly in both radio and television (which had started in 1936 for a limited audience), but there was pressure from commercial and political interests to widen the scope of broadcasting. The result was that independent (commercial) television broadcasting financed by advertising and under the supervision of the Independent Television Authority (later the Independent Broadcasting Authority or IBA) was created in 1954, and the first programmes shown in 1955. In 1972, the Sound Broadcasting Act ended the BBC's monopoly on radio broadcasting and allowed the establishment of independent radio stations throughout the country, dependent on advertising for their financing.

A duopoly (two organizations) covered British broadcasting, which was shared between the public service of the BBC and the independent (commercial) service of the IBA. This division has now been expanded as cable, satellite and other broadcasting services have developed in recent years. British broadcasting is thus conditioned by the competition between the BBC and the independent organizations.

From 1988, the Conservative government made wide-ranging changes to British broadcasting. The aim was to provide greater deregulation and competition among broadcasters and to give greater choice to the consumer. The number of television and radio channels was increased, and the IBA was replaced by an Independent Television Commission (ITC).

The changes were controversial and were widely criticized for their alleged emphasis on competition and commercialism, rather than quality. In 1996, the Conservative government announced further deregulatory measures: all broadcasting and telecommunications services were to move to digital means of transmission, which will encourage the creation of many more national digital terrestrial television (DTT) channels. Viewers will be able to use DTT with a conventional television aerial and a set-top decoder. It also liberalized the restrictions governing the ownership of independent broadcasting licences.

A larger number of television channels may lead not to greater choice, but to rather inferior programmes as broadcasters chase bigger audiences. There is a finite number of people to watch television. In addition, advertisers' budgets cannot be stretched to cover all the available independent television offerings, and advertisers naturally gravitate towards those programmes that attract large audiences. Nevertheless, television in 1995 accounted for 28 per cent of total advertising spending.

The BBC

The BBC is based at Broadcasting House in London, but has studios and local facilities throughout the country that provide regional and national networks for radio and television. It was created by Royal Charter and has a board of governors who, under a chairman or woman, are responsible for supervising its programme structures and suitability. The governors are appointed by the Crown on the advice of government ministers, and are supposed to constitute an independent element in the organization of the BBC. Daily operations are controlled by the Director-General, who is chosen by the board of governors in consultation with the Prime Minister.

The BBC is financed by a grant from Parliament, which comes largely from revenue received from the sale of television licences (£1.6 billion per year). These are payable by anyone who owns a television set, and are relatively low in international terms (£89.50 annually for a colour set). The BBC also generates considerable income from selling its programmes abroad, and from the sale of a programme guide (*Radio Times*), books, magazines and videos.

The BBC in recent years has come under pressure from government to reform itself. It has struggled to maintain its position as a traditional public-service broadcaster, funded by the licence fee. Internal reorganization has led to a slimmer and more efficient organization, so that the BBC was given a 10-year extension of the Charter in 1996, based on the licence fee. But it has been encouraged to develop alternative forms of funding, such as subscription and pay services, and must include independent productions in 25 per cent of its television schedules.

The BBC's external services, which consist of radio broadcasts in English (the World Service) and some 39 other languages abroad, were founded in 1932 and receive direct financing from the Foreign Office. These services have a high reputation for objective news reporting and programmes. But, because of a declining radio audience, the BBC began television services in 1991 to Europe on cable subscription channels and by satellite links in Africa and Asia. It intends to develop the television service into a world leader.

The BBC is not a state organization, in the sense that it is controlled by the government, but it is not as independent of political pressures as many in Britain and overseas assume. Its charter has to be renewed by Parliament, and by its terms government can, and does, intervene in the showing of programmes that are alleged to be controversial or against the public interest. The BBC governors, although supposedly independent, are in fact government appointees. Governments can also exert pressure upon the BBC when the licence fee comes up for renewal by Parliament. The BBC does try to be neutral in political matters, to such an extent that all political parties have periodically complained that it is prejudiced against them. The major parties have equal rights to broadcast on the BBC and independent television.

Historically, the BBC was affected by the invention of television, which changed the entertainment habits of the people and created a dominant source of news. The BBC has two television channels (BBC 1 and BBC 2). BBC 1 is a mass-appeal channel, and its programmes consist of news, plays and drama series, comedy, quizz shows, variety performances, sport and documentaries. BBC 2 tends to show more serious items such as news analysis and discussion, documentaries, adaptations of novels into plays and series, operas, concerts and some sport. It is a minority channel and is watched by 10 per cent of viewers, although it is now increasing its audience; it is a crucial element in the provision of Open University courses.

BBC Radio has experienced declining audiences recently, but it still provides an important service. The BBC has five national radio channels; 39 local radio stations serving many districts in England; and regional and community radio services in Scotland, Wales and Northern Ireland. All of these compete for listeners with independent stations. The national channels specialize in different tastes. Radio 1 caters for pop music; Radio 2 has light music, news and comedy; Radio 3 provides classical and modern serious music, talks, discussions and plays; Radio 4 tends to concentrate on news reports and analysis, talks and plays; and Radio 5 Live (established 1990) provides sport and news programmes.

The ITC

Independent television and radio were considerably affected by government reforms under the Broadcasting Act of 1990. The ITC (Independent Television Commission) replaced the IBA; controls the activities of the independent television companies (including cable and satellite services); and consists of a government-appointed chairman or woman and other members.

The ITC does not produce or make programmes itself. In addition to supervising cable and satellite television, it grants licences to, and regulates, the transmitting companies who are responsible for making 50 per cent of the programmes (in addition to independent producers) shown on three advertising-financed television channels (the majority ITV/Channel 3, the minority Channel 4 and the new Channel 5 since 1997).

There are 15 ITV production companies at present, such as Granada (north-west England), Central (the midland counties of England) and Anglia (East Anglia). London has two companies holding one licence, with one providing programmes during the week (Thames) and the other at weekends (London Weekend). These companies make programmes for the 14 regions into which Britain is divided for ITV television purposes.

The licences granted to the present ITV companies are renewable every six years, and the companies have to compete with any other interested applicants. Although the licences are open to competitive tendering, it is by no means certain that a further licence will be granted to an existing company, or a new one to a new high-bidding company. Much depends on past performance, financial standing and commitment to provide quality and regional programmes. The programme companies receive nothing from the television licence fee, which is applicable only to the BBC. The companies are consequently dependent upon the finance they receive from advertising and the sales of programmes, videos, books, records and other publications.

ITV is the oldest independent channel and once seemed to provide only popular programmes of a light-entertainment and sometimes trivial type. But its quality has improved, because of competition from the BBC, and it now has a high standard of news reports, drama productions and documentaries. Under government legislation, ITV must provide programmes made in and about the region represented by the production company.

Channel 4 was established in 1982 in order to create an independent alternative to BBC 2. It is a public corporation, licensed and regulated by the ITC, which sells its own advertising time and retains the proceeds. It was intended to offer something different and challenging in an appeal to minority tastes, and it provides programmes in Welsh in Wales. Channel 4 initially had serious problems with advertising and the quality of its programmes, but has now developed a considerable reputation and is a success.

Channel 5 became operative in 1997 after a 10-year licence was awarded to Channel 5 Broadcasting Limited. It is funded by advertising, subscription and sponsorship, and covers some 63 per cent of the population. It had a shaky start in terms of the attraction of its programmes, but now has a 3.1 per cent share of the audience market, is improving its programmes and increasing its financial base.

Critics argued that the old IBA did not always keep a close watch on independent broadcasting developments; lacked sufficient regulatory powers and consistent policies; and sometimes acted arbitrarily in the granting of licences. There was also considerable concern at the rapid expansion and dubious quality of independent broadcasting as a whole. Its replacement (ITC) seems to be an improvement, but there has been controversy over the system of awarding ITV licences, which have often gone to the highest bidder with little apparent regard to quality and production efficiency.

The Radio Authority

A new Radio Authority now controls some 150 local and regional independent radio stations (ILRs) throughout the country, which are supported by advertising and provide mainly pop music, news flashes and programmes of local interest. They operate on a commercial basis, and revenue figures in 1993 suggest that radio is the fastest growing medium in Britain.

Three new commercial national radio stations have been created under government policy to expand radio broadcasting. The first licence was awarded to Classic FM in 1991, which broadcasts popular classical music and news bulletins. The second licence was awarded to Virgin 1215 in 1992, which specializes in rock music. The third licence was given in 1995 to Talk Radio UK, which is a speech-based service. Expansion will also occur at the city, local and community levels, because radio broadcasting has been deregulated by the government in its attempt to increase the variety of radio and include more tastes and interests.

Cable and satellite broadcasting

Television and other associated technological developments have become very attractive in Britain, and are a rich source of entertainment profits. At one stage, it was considered that cable television by subscription would considerably expand these possibilities. But cable in Britain, although growing slowly and potentially capable of further expansion and varied services, has been challenged first by video equipment sales and second by satellite programmes.

Television broadcasting by satellite has been available in Britain since 1989. The biggest satellite programmer is BSkyB (British Sky Broadcasting), which provides channels consisting of news, light entertainment, sport and feature films, through domestic receiving dishes. The choice of satellite channels is expanding steadily in Britain, although initially companies did have problems in attracting subscribers.

However, in those homes that had access to cable and satellite services in 1994, the share of television viewing was 31.6 per cent for cable and satellite; 23.6 per cent for BBC 1; 7.4 per cent for BBC 2; 30.5 per cent for ITV; and 6.8 per cent for Channel 4.

The role and influence of television

Television is an influential and dominant force in modern Britain. It is also a very popular entertainment activity. Over 98 per cent of the population have television sets in their homes, of which 95 per cent are colour sets, and over 50 per cent of homes have two sets or more. Some people prefer to rent their sets instead of owning them, because rented sets are repaired and maintained free of charge.

A large number of the programmes shown on television are made in Britain, although there are also many imported American series. A few programmes come from other English speaking countries, such as Australia, New Zealand and Canada. But there are relatively few foreign-language productions on British television, and these are either dubbed or sub-titled.

The range of programmes shown is very considerable, but they also vary widely in quality. Although British television has a high reputation abroad, it does attract substantial criticism in Britain, either because of the standard of the programmes, or because they are frequently repeated. News reports, documentaries and current affairs analyses are generally of a high standard, as are dramatic, educational, sporting, natural history and cultural productions. But there is also a wide selection of series, films, quizzes and variety shows that are sometimes of doubtful quality.

The competition between the BBC and independent television is strong, and the battle of the ratings (the number of people watching individual programmes) indicates the popularity (or otherwise) of individual programmes. But this competition can mean that similar programmes are shown at the same time on the major channels, in order to appeal to specific markets and attract the biggest share of the audience. It is also argued that competition has reduced the quality of programmes overall and resulted in an appeal to the lowest common denominator in taste.

Voices have been raised about the alleged levels of sex and violence on British television, particularly before the 'watershed' of 9 pm in the evenings, when young children may be watching. Some private individuals have attempted by their protests to reform and influence the kind of programmes that are shown. Recent research suggests that the public can be morally harmed by watching television for an average viewing time of 26 hours each week. The Conservative government considered that violence, sex and obscenity on television do affect viewers, and was concerned to 'clean up' television. A Broadcasting Standards Complaints Commission monitors programmes, examines complaints, establishes codes of conduct for the broadcasting organizations, and has recently tightened its rules concerning invasion of privacy by broadcasters. The sale and rent of 'video nasties' (videos that portray extreme forms of violence and brutality) have been banned, and rules for the sale of videos have been tightened. Some 69 per cent of homes now own at least one video-cassette recorder.

There is fierce competition among the increased number of broadcasters to attract viewers and advertising revenue. But the broadcasting debate is concerned with whether this entertainments expansion means more genuine choice or declining quality. Technological changes such as digital broadcasting will transform television into an interactive force that combines the Internet and personalized programming in a single package. On the other hand, broadcasters risk losing audiences and revenue as more people switch to the Internet itself. In 1997, 3.1 million people were connected to the Internet, and with a 94 per cent growth rate, 40 per cent of the population could be connected by 2000.

Media ownership and freedom of expression

The financial and ownership structures of the British media industry are complex, and involve a range of media outlets that include the press, radio and television. Sometimes an individual company will own a number of print products, such as newspapers and magazines, and will specialize in this area, but this kind of ownership is declining.

Today it is more common for newspapers to be owned and controlled by corporations that are concerned with wide media interests, such as films, radio, television, magazines, and satellite and cable companies. Other newspaper and media owning groups have diversified their interests even further, and may be involved in a variety of non-media activities. In Britain, only a

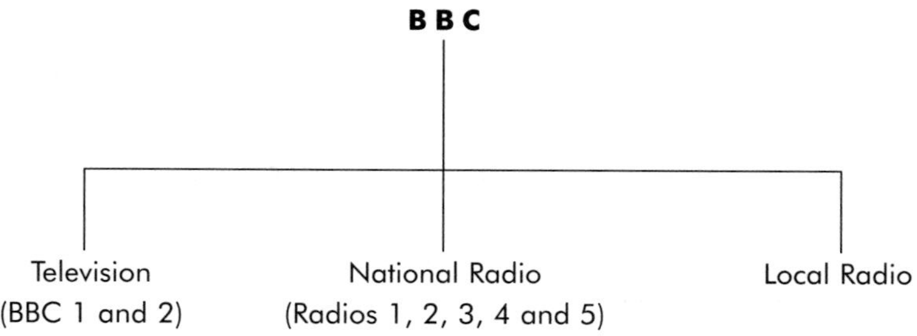

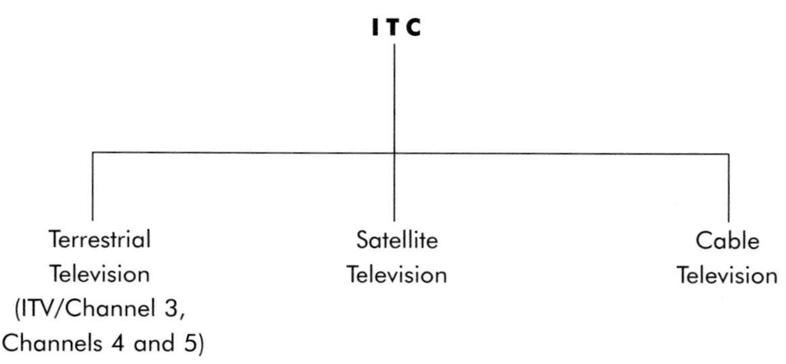

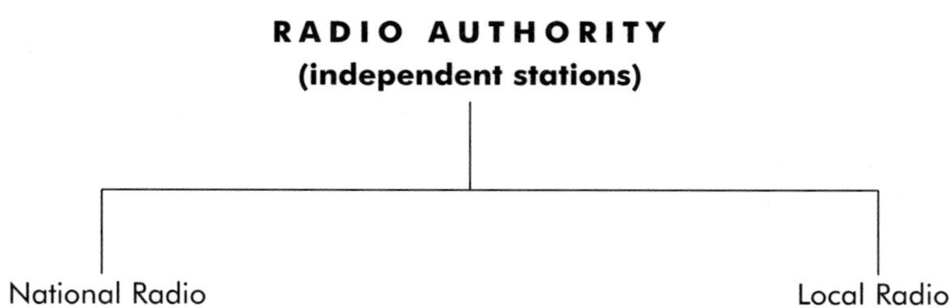

FIGURE 10.1 The structure of British broadcasting

few newspapers like the *Guardian* and the *Morning Star* have avoided being controlled by multinational commercial concerns.

This involvement of large enterprises in the media business, and the resulting concentration of ownership in a few hands, has caused concern. For example, more than 60 per cent of total newspaper circulation in 1997 was accounted for by News International and Mirror Group Newspapers. Although these concentrations do not amount to a monopoly situation, there have been frequent enquiries into the questions of ownership and control. Some critics argue that the state should provide public subsidies to the media industries in order to prevent them being taken over by big-business groups. But this suggestion has not been adopted, and it is felt that there are potential dangers in allowing the state to gain any direct or indirect financial influence over the media.

Today the law is supposed to guard against the risks inherent in greatly concentrated ownership of the means of communication. The purchase of further newspapers by an existing owner is controlled by law, and newspaper owners' shareholdings in independent radio and television stations are restricted. Further restrictions, such as independent directors of newspapers; guarantees of editorial independence from owners' interference; and trustee arrangements to allow newspapers to maintain their character and traditions, are usually imposed. These arrangements are intended to prevent monopolies and undue influence by owners. But such safeguards do not always work satisfactorily in practice, and takeovers of ITV television companies by rival companies and multi-media corporations are now permitted, within limits.

The question of free expression in the media continues to be of concern. Critics argue that the media do not have sufficient freedom to comment on matters of public interest. But the freedom of the media, as of individuals, to express themselves is not absolute. Regulations are placed upon the general freedom in order to safeguard the legitimate interests of other individuals, organizations and the state, so that a balance between competing interests may be achieved.

There are several legal restraints upon media freedom of expression. The *sub judice* rule means that the media may not comment on court proceedings, and must restrict themselves to the court facts. The rule is intended to protect the individuals concerned, and if a media organization breaks the rule, it may be found guilty of contempt of court and fined. Contempt of court proceedings may also be used by judges to obtain journalists' sources of information, or to prevent the media from publishing certain court details and documents.

The obtaining and publishing of state and official information is tightly controlled by the Official Secrets Act and by D-notices (information to the media concerning information that should not be divulged). The media are also liable to court proceedings for libel and obscenity offences. Libel is the making of accusations that are proved to be false or harmful to a person's reputation. Obscenity covers any action that offends against public morality. In such cases, the media organization and all the individuals involved may be held responsible.

These restrictions prevent absolute media freedom of expression. In some cases, it is argued that there is a need for reform if responsible investigative journalism is to do its job adequately. Britain is a secretive society, and the Labour government's proposed Freedom of Information Act may break down some of the secrecy and executive control.

On the other hand, the media can often act irresponsibly, invade individual privacy, behave in unethical ways, and sensationalize events for their own purposes. The media have won some libel cases brought against them, and gained important victories for open information, but they have also lost other cases because of their methods. Some media practices do cause concern, and the government may impose statutory restrictions on invasions of privacy, unless the media reform themselves in this area. But it is generally felt that freedom of expression could be less restricted than it is at present.

Another restraining media institution, the Press Complaints Commission (PCC), was created in 1990. It is financed by newspaper owners and is supposed to guard the freedom and

PLATE 10.3 **Paparazzi at a royal event** *(Stephen Parker/Rex Features, London)*

independence of the press; maintain standards of journalism; and judge complaints by the public against newspapers. Some critics argue that the PCC is not fighting as hard as it might for press freedom. Others maintain that it is not strict enough with newspapers when complaints against them are proved. A fear that the government might legislate against media abuses has led to a tightening of the PCC's rules about privacy invasion, harassment by photographers, and protection of children. Newspaper owners have also instituted an ombudsman system for each newspaper, through which public complaints can be made and investigated. It remains to be seen whether the PCC and the ombudsman system will be truly effective.

It is sometimes argued that the concentrated ownership patterns of the media might limit freedom of expression by allowing owners undue influence over what is included in their products. Ex-journalists have claimed that there is proprietorial interference in some of the media that is not being curbed either by editorial guarantees or by legal and government restrictions. On the other hand, editors and journalists can be very independently minded people, who will usually strongly object to any attempts at interference. Owners, in practice, seem to be careful not to tread on too many toes, because there are always competing media sources that are only too willing to publish the facts.

A further concern about limitations on media freedom has been the extent to which advertisers might dictate policy when they place their products. The question of advertisers' influence is complex, and might today be more applicable to the mass-consumer market of radio and television than the press. Advertisers dealing with the press are more concerned with the type or status of readers rather than their numbers. Arguably, the media have not succumbed in a substantial degree to the manipulations of the advertising agencies, in spite of the media's dependence upon advertising revenue.

Further stresses in the past were also placed upon the freedom of the media by the influence that the trade unions sometimes brought to bear. They frequently refused to print or broadcast material to which they objected, or forced owners and editors to insert their points of view. These pressures were sometimes backed by the threat of industrial action.

It is difficult to evaluate absolutely whether the media play a dominant part in influencing public opinion on a range of political and other matters. The left-wing view assumes that they do, and consequently disapproves of the alleged right-wing bias in the British media. But, while some people may have their attitudes directly shaped in these ways, it might be argued that a majority of readers and viewers have already made up their own minds, and react against blatant attempts at indoctrination. On certain occasions and for specific events (such as general elections), the media may have an important effect on public opinion.

However, many people learn to read between the lines of newspapers and broadcasts, and are conditioned early in life not to believe everything they 'read in the papers' or hear 'on the telly'. Since television in particular is often accused of being either right-wing or left-wing, depending on which government is in power, it would seem that the British people are receiving enough information from all sides of the political spectrum. In practice, most people object to having politics and other concerns 'thrust down their throats', and many take a sceptical attitude to such matters.

ATTITUDES

Attitudes to the media

According to opinion polls, the media are not a source of great concern to British people, although they do manifest their dissatisfaction or satisfaction with the various outlets. According to 1990 MORI polls, 39 per cent of people were satisfied with national newspapers and 40 per cent were dissatisfied; 63 per cent were satisfied with the BBC and 20 per cent were dissatisfied; 62 per cent were satisfied with independent television and 17 per cent were dissatisfied.

British Social Attitudes: 1988–89 asked whether media bodies were well run. Respondents rated independent radio and television at 83 per cent, the BBC at 67 per cent and the press at 39 per cent. But, in terms of who can be trusted for most of the time to serve the public interest, journalists on national newspapers scored only 15 per cent.

EXERCISES

■ **Explain and examine the following terms:**

media	circulation	'free newspapers'	Anglia
press	tabloid	*Private Eye*	'hot metal'
advertising	broadsheet	ownership	libel
The Times	*Sun*	Rupert Murdoch	*sub judice*
Fleet Street	John Reith	World Service	BBC
licence	ITC (IBA)	Channel 4	dubbing
PCC	mid-market	newsboys(girls)	duopoly

■ **Write short essays on the following topics:**

1 Describe and comment critically on the structure of British broadcasting.

2 Examine the problems of media freedom of expression.

3 Discuss the division of British national newspapers into 'populars' and 'qualities'.

Chapter 11

Religion

BRITISH RELIGIOUS HISTORY has been predominantly Christian. It has been characterized by conflict between Roman Catholics and Protestants, and by division into separate Protestant churches and sects. But it has also included non-Christian faiths, such as the Jews, and groups with humanist and special beliefs. Britain still possesses a diversity of religious denominations, which have been added to by recent immigrants.

Despite these features, the country appears to be largely secular in terms of the relatively low figures (20 per cent) for all types (Christian and non-Christian) of regular religious observance. However, religion remains an important factor in national life, whether for believers or as a background to national culture. It is reflected in active or nominal adherence to particular denominations; in general ethical and moral behaviour; and in the stabilizing functions of social institutions. Religiosity is greater in Wales, Scotland and (particularly) Northern Ireland than in England.

Religious history

There is little evidence of organized religion in very early British history, beyond archaeological discoveries that suggest various forms of heathen belief. Some Christian influences had reached England before AD 400 and during the Roman occupation, but they were not widespread or permanent.

However, Ireland was converted to Christianity around AD 432 by St Patrick, who had brought the faith from Rome. His followers spread Christianity to Wales, Scotland and northern England, and established religious centres, such as that of St Columba on the Scottish island of Iona. In AD 596–7, the Saxons of southern England were converted to Christianity by

St Augustine and other monks, who had been sent from Rome by Pope Gregory, and who also founded the ecclesiastical capital of Canterbury in AD 597. English conversion was encouraged by the Saxon kings, who considered that the hierarchical example of the Christian church would support their royal authority. The church also provided educated advisers and administrators, through whom the kings could control their kingdoms more efficiently. The connection between church and state was consequently established at an early stage in English history.

Southern English Christianity was based on the beliefs and practices of the Church of Rome. Although the faith of Ireland, Wales, Scotland and northern England was also founded on Roman doctrines, it had a more Celtic identification. Conflicts and divisions inevitably arose between the two branches of Christianity. But these were eventually resolved at the Synod (meeting) of Whitby in AD 664, where all the churches agreed to accept the Roman Catholic form of worship.

Christianity became a central and influential force in national life. The church was based on a hierarchy of monks, priests, bishops and archbishops. It was a part not only of religious culture but also of administration, government and law. But it was increasingly accused of worldliness and materialism, and was thought to be corrupt and too concerned with politics at the expense of religion. However, English kings maintained their allegiance to Rome and the Pope in spiritual matters, some with more conviction than others.

The relationship between England and Rome became difficult, and by the sixteenth century was at breaking point. English monarchs were jealous of the wealth and power of the church, and resented the influence of Rome in national affairs. Henry VIII argued in 1529 that as King of England he, not the Pope, was the supreme legal authority in the country, and that the church and its courts owed their allegiance only to him.

In 1534 Henry broke away from the supremacy of Rome and declared himself head of the church in England. The immediate reason for this breach was the Pope's refusal to accept Henry's divorce from his queen, Katharine of Aragon, who had not produced a male heir to the throne. But Henry also wanted to curb the church's legal authority and power. In 1536 he dissolved many monasteries and confiscated a large part of the church's property and wealth.

Although Henry had established a national church, that church was still Roman Catholic in its faith and practices. Henry did not regard himself as a Protestant, nor did he consider the English church to be part of the Protestant Reformation, which was affecting religious life in continental Europe. Indeed, Henry had defended the papacy against Martin Luther in 1521. The Pope rewarded him with the title of Fidei Defensor (Defender of the Faith), which British monarchs still bear today, and which can be seen on most British coins.

Nevertheless, the influence of the European Reformation caused the English, Scottish and Welsh churches to move away from Rome's doctrines. This development in England increased under Edward VI (1547–53), when practices and beliefs became more Protestant. John Knox in Scotland also accelerated the process by founding the separate Protestant Church of Scotland in 1560. Meanwhile, Ireland remained firmly Roman Catholic.

Henry VIII's daughter, the Roman Catholic Mary Tudor, tried to restore the Roman Catholic faith during her short reign (1553–8), but did not succeed. Her sister, the Protestant Elizabeth I (1558–1603), established the Protestant status of the Church of England by the terms of her Church Settlement. The Church's doctrine was stated in the Thirty-Nine Articles of Faith (1562), and its rituals and forms of church service were contained in the Book of Common Prayer, which has been revised in later centuries. English replaced Latin in church documents and services, and priests of the Church of England were later allowed to marry. The English church now occupied an intermediate position between Roman Catholicism and the Protestant churches of Europe.

However, this confirmation of the Protestant Church of England did not stop the religious arguments that were to affect Britain in later years. Many Protestants in the sixteenth and seventeenth centuries argued that the church had not distanced itself sufficiently from Rome. Some left to form their own religious organizations. Initially, they were called Dissenters, because they disagreed with the majority view; later they were known as nonconformists; and today they are the members of the Free Churches. Fierce religious conflicts between Protestants and Catholics, often resulting in martyrdom, continued during the seventeenth century. They culminated in the Civil War (1642–8) between the mainly Protestant Parliamentarians and the largely Catholic Royalists, which led to the protectorate of Oliver Cromwell.

The collapse of Cromwell's narrowly puritan regime after his death, and the restoration of the Stuart monarchy, did bring some religious moderation, but minority religions still suffered. The Roman Catholic Church underwent persecution and exclusion for 300 years after the English Reformation, and Jews and nonconformists also experienced discrimination. These religious groups were excluded from the universities, the House of Commons and public positions. It was not until the mid-nineteenth century that most restrictions placed on them were removed. Meanwhile, the Church of England solidified its dominant position in 1688, when the Protestant William III succeeded James II, the last Roman Catholic English king.

Further quarrels affected religious life in the eighteenth century, as groups reacted to rationalist developments in the Church of England. For example, the Methodists (founded 1739) stressed the emotional aspects of salvation and religion. They tried to work within the Church of England, but opposition to their views eventually forced them to separate. Nevertheless, an evangelical wing within the church was strongly influenced by Methodism. The evangelicals based their faith on a literal interpretation of the Bible and a humanitarian idealism. They accomplished many industrial and social reforms in nineteenth-century Britain. Today, the 'Low Church' wing of the Church of England is the successor to evangelical and other Nonconformist influences.

Other groups reacted to the Church of England in the eighteenth and nineteenth centuries, and founded a variety of nonconformist sects, such as the Baptists. On the other hand, the Oxford or Tractarian Movement, which developed in the 1830s, emphasized the Church of England's connections with Roman Catholicism. It followed Roman Catholic doctrines, and used elaborate ritual in its church services. It influenced succeeding generations, and today is represented by the Anglo-Catholic and 'High Church' wings of the Church of England.

There is religious freedom in contemporary Britain: a person can belong to any religion or none, and religious discrimination is unlawful. There is no religious bar to the holding of public office, except that the monarch must be a member of the Church of England. None of the churches is tied specifically to a political party, and there are no religious parties as such in Parliament.

In recent years, immigrants to Britain have added further religious diversity. Muslim mosques, Sikh and Hindu temples, and West Indian churches, such as the Pentecostalists, are common in areas with large ethnic communities. The growth of fundamentalist evangelical groups, 'enthusiastic' Christian churches and some 500 cults or religious movements have also increased the numbers of people active in religious life.

In Britain today the growth of religious observance and vitality is mainly found outside the big traditional Christian churches. The evangelical movement is the fastest-growing branch of Christianity, and is characterized by a close relationship among members and between them and God, Christ and the Holy Spirit. It breaks down the barriers of more traditional worship, places little reliance on church furniture, and has many different meeting places. It has basic Christian beliefs, but expresses them in different ways.

The Christian tradition

Christianity in Britain is represented mainly by the Church of England and the Roman Catholic Church (which are the largest), the Church of Scotland and the Free Churches. The Church of England attracts about one-fifth of religiously active Britons, and

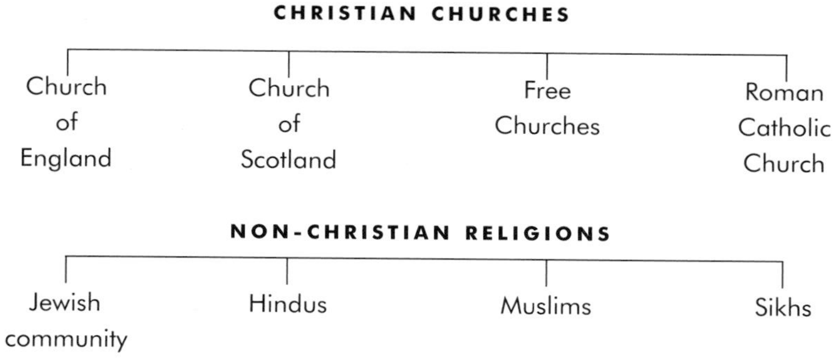

CHRISTIAN CHURCHES

Church of England	Church of Scotland	Free Churches	Roman Catholic Church

NON-CHRISTIAN RELIGIONS

Jewish community	Hindus	Muslims	Sikhs

FIGURE 11.1 Main contemporary religious groups

the Roman Catholic Church does only marginally better, but between them they account for 41 per cent of all regular worshippers. It is argued that these two competing churches built too many buildings for too few people in the nineteenth century. They have since used their resources to subsidize churches that should have been closed, and poorly attended services contribute to the decline.

The Church of England

The Church of England is the established or national church in England. This means that its legal position in the state is confirmed by the Elizabethan Church Settlement and Parliament. The monarch is the head of the church; its archbishops, bishops and deans are appointed by the monarch on the advice of the Prime Minister; and Parliament has a voice in its organization and rituals. But it is not a state church, like churches in some other European countries, since it receives no financial aid from the state, apart from salaries for public positions and help with church schools.

The church therefore has a special relationship with the state, although there are frequent calls for its disestablishment (cutting the connections between church and state), so that the church might have autonomy over its own affairs. In spite of low active

PLATE 11.1 Anglican village church, Northamptonshire *(Maggie Murray/Format)*

observance, it plays a central role in national life. Much of its membership is middle- and upper-class, and it is has been identified with the ruling establishment and authority. But there is conflict within the church at present between traditionalists, who wish to maintain old forms and beliefs, and modernists, who want a more engaged and adventurous church that would attract a contemporary congregation.

The structure of the church is based on an episcopal hierarchy, or rule by bishops. The two Archbishops of Canterbury and York, together with 24 other senior bishops, sit in the House of Lords and take part in its proceedings. Collectively, they form the senior branch of the church in its connection with Parliament.

Organizationally, the church is divided into the two provinces of Canterbury and York, each under the control of an archbishop. The Archbishop of Canterbury (called the Primate of

All England) is the senior of the two and the professional head of the church. The two provinces are subdivided into 43 dioceses, each under the control of a bishop. Many of the bishops' seats are very old and situated in ancient cathedral towns, such as Chichester, Lincoln, Durham and Salisbury.

The dioceses are divided into some 13,000 parishes, and each is centred on a parish church. Most parishes, except for those in rural areas, have a priest (called either a vicar or a rector) in charge, and a large parish may have additional assistant priests (curates). The priest occupies rent-free accommodation in a vicarage, but does not have a large salary, which in most cases today is paid out of central church funds.

The Church of England is considered to be a 'broad church' in which a variety of beliefs and practices coexist. Priests have freedom as to how they conduct their church services, which can vary from the elaborate ritual of High Church worship to the simple, functional presentation of Low Church services. The High Church or Anglo-Catholic wing (some 20 per cent of church membership) lays stress on church tradition and the historical influence of Roman Catholic practices and teaching. The Low Church or Evangelical wing (some 80 per cent of church membership) bases faith and practice on simplicity and often a literal interpretation of the Bible, and is suspicious of Roman Catholic influences.

The two wings of the church do not always cooperate happily, and between them there is a considerable variety of fashions. Some evangelical priests have introduced contemporary music and dramatic performances into their services, in order to appeal to younger congregations and more modern concerns. Today's priests have to deal with a wide variety of problems and pressures in their work, particularly in deprived and inner-city areas, and cannot easily be restricted to a purely religious role.

The main financial resources of the church come from its substantial property and investment holdings, and it is the third largest land owner in Britain, after the Crown and the Forestry Commission. The total assets of the church, which have been estimated at over £400 million, are administered by the Church

PLATE 11.2 Westminster Abbey *(John Oakland)*

Commissioners. This wealth has to finance many very expensive demands, such as salaries for the clergy and administrators, maintenance of churches and cathedrals, and a range of activities in Britain and abroad. In recent years, the finances of the church were seriously depleted because of investment failures, although the situation has now improved.

The membership of the Church of England is difficult to determine, because the church does not have adequate registers of members. Membership is assumed when a person (usually a baby) is baptized into the church, and some 40 per cent of the English population have been baptized. This membership may be confirmed at 'confirmation' at the age of 14 or 15, but it is estimated that only one-fifth of those baptized are confirmed, and that 1.8 million people are active members of the church. However, many other Britons may nominally identify themselves with the Church of England, even though they are not members.

Lay members of the parish are associated with church organization at the local level through parochial church councils. These councils send representatives to the local diocesan councils (or synods), where matters of common concern are discussed. Matters may then be sent to the General Synod, which since 1970 has been the national governing body of the church. It has spiritual, legislative and administrative functions, and makes the final decisions on subjects like the ordination of women priests.

Women in the past served as deacons (an office below the priest) and in women's religious orders, but could not be ordained as priests in the church. Debate and conflict still surround this question, although the General Synod approved the ordination of women, and the first women were ordained in 1994. The debate has split the church into factions, and driven some members and clergy into the Roman Catholic Church.

The Church of England is sometimes referred to as the 'Anglican Church', in the sense that it is part of a worldwide communion of churches whose practices and beliefs are very similar, and many of which descend from the Church of England. This Anglican Communion comprises some 90 million people in the British Isles (with Anglican churches in Wales, Scotland and

Ireland) and abroad, such as the Protestant Episcopal Church in the USA. Most of these churches have women priests and bishops. The Lambeth Conference, which is a meeting of Anglican bishops from all over the world, is held every 10 years in London, and is presided over by the Archbishop of Canterbury. It has great prestige, and its deliberations on doctrine, relations with other churches and attitudes to political and social questions can be influential.

In recent years, the Church of England has been more willing to enter into controversial arguments about social and political problems in contemporary Britain, such as the condition of people living in the inner cities, and has been critical of government policies. This led it into conflict with the Conservative government, and its popularity among politicians at present is not high. It has tended to avoid such issues in the past, and has been described as 'the Conservative Party at prayer' because of its safe, establishment image. It is still widely felt that the church, like the monarchy, should not involve itself in such questions, and historically it has favoured compromise. However, some critics argue that the church must modernize its attitudes, organization and values if it is to continue as a vital force in British life.

The Church of Scotland

The Church of Scotland (commonly known as the Kirk) is the second established church in Britain. Its position as the official national church in Scotland has been confirmed by successive legislation from 1707, which has asserted its freedom in spiritual matters and independence from all parliamentary supervision. The church is completely separate from the Church of England, has its own organizational structures, and decides its own doctrines and practices.

It was created in 1560 by John Knox. He was opposed to episcopal rule, and considered that the English church had not moved sufficiently far from Roman Catholicism. The Scottish church followed the teachings of Calvin, a leading exponent of the European Reformation, and developed a rather severe form of Presbyterian Protestantism. Presbyterianism means government by ordained ministers and elected elders (who are lay members of the church).

The church has a democratic structure. Individual churches are governed locally by a Kirk Session, which consists of the minister and elders. Ministers (who include women) have equality with each other. The General Assembly is the supreme organizational body of the church, and comprises elected ministers and elders. It meets every year under the presidency of an elected Moderator, who serves for one year and is the leader of the church during the period of office. There are some 790,000 adult members of the church.

The Roman Catholic Church

The Roman Catholic Church in Britain experienced much persecution and discrimination after the Reformation, and had difficulties in surviving. Although its organization was restored and the worst suspicions abated by 1850, reservations about it still continued in some quarters.

Today, Roman Catholicism is widely practised throughout Britain, and enjoys complete religious freedom, except for the fact that no Roman Catholic can become monarch. There are seven Roman Catholic provinces in Great Britain (four in England, two in Scotland and one in Wales), each under the supervision of an archbishop; 29 dioceses each under the control of a bishop; and over 3,000 parishes. The head of the church in England is the Cardinal Archbishop of Westminster, and the senior lay Catholic is the Duke of Norfolk. In Northern Ireland, there is one province with six dioceses, some of which overlap with dioceses in the Irish Republic.

It is estimated that there may be some 5 million nominal members of the Roman Catholic faith in Britain today, although the number of active participants is about 1.9 million. This figure makes it the largest Christian church in Britain in terms of observance. Its membership is centred on the urban working class, settlers of Irish descent, a few prominent upper-class families and some middle-class people.

PLATE 11.3 At prayer: Roman Catholic mass *(Judy Harrison/Format)*

The church continues to emphasize the important role of education for its children, and requires its members to try to raise their children in the Catholic faith. There are many voluntary schools specifically for Catholic pupils, which are sometimes staffed by members of religious orders, like the Jesuits and Marists. These and other orders also carry out social work, such as nursing, hospital duties, child care and looking after the elderly.

The Free Churches

The Free Churches are composed of those nonconformist Protestant sects that are not established like the Churches of England and Scotland. Some broke away from the Church of England after the Reformation and others departed later. In general, they refused to accept episcopal rule or hierarchical structures, and have ordained women ministers. Their history has been one of schism and separation among themselves, which has resulted in the formation of many different sects.

Their egalitarian beliefs are reflected in the historical association between political and religious dissent that was important in the formation of the Labour Party and the radical wing of the old Liberal Party. These churches have developed their own convictions and practices, which are often mirrored in their simple church services, worship and buildings. The Free Churches tend to be strongest in northern England, Wales, Northern Ireland and Scotland, and most of their membership has historically derived from the working class. The main Free Churches today are the Methodists, the Baptists, the United Reformed Church and the Salvation Army.

The *Methodist Church* is the largest of the Free Churches, with some half a million adult members and a community of 1.3 million. It was established in 1784 by John Wesley after Church of England opposition to his evangelical views obliged him to separate and form his own organization. Further arguments and division occurred within the Methodist Church in the nineteenth century, but most of the doctrinal and administrative disputes were settled in 1932. Today the Methodist Church in Britain is based on the 1932 union of most of the separate Methodist sects. But independent Methodist churches still exist in Britain and abroad, with a worldwide membership of several million. Attempts were made in the 1960s and 1970s to unify the Methodists and the Church of England, but the proposals failed. In practice, however, some ministers of these denominations share their churches and services.

The *Baptists* (formed in the seventeenth century) are today grouped in associations of churches. Most of these belong to the Baptist Union of Great Britain and Ireland, which was formed in 1812 and has a total membership of some 170,000 people. There are also independent Baptist unions in Scotland, Wales and Ireland (bringing the total Baptists to some 240,000), in addition to a worldwide Baptist fellowship.

The ancient Congregational Church in England and Wales had its roots in sixteenth-century Puritanism. It merged with the

Presbyterian Church in England (which was associated with Scottish Presbyterians) in 1972 to form the *United Reformed Church*, which now has some 120,000 members.

The *Salvation Army* emphasizes saving souls through a practical Christianity and social concern. It was founded in Britain by William Booth in 1865, and now has some 55,000 active members. It has spread to 89 other countries, and has a worldwide strength of 2.5 million. The Salvation Army is an efficient organization that has centres nationwide to help the homeless, the abused, the poor, the sick and the needy. Its uniformed members may be frequently seen on the streets of British towns and cities, playing and singing religious music, collecting money, preaching and selling their magazine *War Cry*.

Other Christian churches

Active membership of the large Christian churches has long been in decline, and now amounts to some 6.7 million people. But there are a considerable number of smaller Free Churches and nonconformist Christian denominations throughout Britain. The dissenting tradition has led groups in very varied directions, and they all value their independence and origins. For example, the *Religious Society of Friends* (Quakers), founded in the seventeenth century, has no ministers and no conventionally organized services. The Quakers' pacifism and social work are influential, and their membership has increased since the early twentieth century to about 18,000 people.

There has been a significant recent increase in 'enthusiastic' Christian churches. These are usually defined as independent Christian groups, which number half a million members and are characterized by their Pentecostalist or charismatic nature. They emphasize the miraculous and spiritual side of the New Testament rather than dogma, sin and salvation. Among them are churches such as the Assemblies of God and the Elim Pentacostal Church, which have many members of West Indian (Afro-Caribbean) descent. Fundamentalist evangelical groups have also been increasing, and there are many other religious sects in

Britain, such as the *Jehovah's Witnesses*, the *Seventh Day Adventists*, the *Mormon Church*, the *Christian Scientists* and the *Spiritualists*.

This diversity of groups produces a very varied religious life in Britain today, but one that is an important reality for significant numbers of people. Some of it illustrates a growth area in religious observance, marked by frustration or disenchantment with the heavy, formal and traditional style of the larger churches, and a desire to embrace a more vital, less orthodox and more spontaneous form of Christianity.

The non-Christian tradition

The non-Christian tradition in Britain is mainly associated with immigrants into the country over the centuries, such as the Jews and, more recently, Muslims, Sikhs and Hindus.

The Jewish community

Some Jews entered Britain during the Roman occupation, but the first large groups immigrated with the Norman Conquest, and were involved in finance and commerce. The present community dates from the mid-seventeenth century, following the expulsion of Jews in the thirteenth century. It now has 300,000 members and is estimated to be the second largest Jewish population in Europe. The community is composed of the Sephardim (originally from Spain, Portugal and north Africa) and the majority Ashkenazim (from Germany and central Europe).

In religious terms, the community is divided into the majority Orthodox faith (of which the main spokesman is the Chief Rabbi) and minority Reform and Liberal groups. The focus of religious life is the 250 local synagogues, and Jewish schools are attended by one in three Jewish schoolchildren. The majority of Jews live in London, where the East End has traditionally been a place of initial Jewish settlement, while others live mainly in urban areas outside London.

PLATE 11.4 Inside a synagogue *(The Hutchison Library)*

The community has declined in the past 20 years. This is due to a disenchantment with religion; an increase in civil and mixed marriages; considerable emigration by young Jews; a relatively low birth rate; and a rapidly ageing population of active practitioners. For some British Jews, their Jewishness is simply a matter of birth, and they are tending to assimilate more with the wider society. For others, it is a matter of deep religious beliefs and practice, and this fundamentalism seems to be increasing. But the majority still have a larger global identity with Jewish history.

Other non-Christian religions

Immigration into Britain during the last 50 years has resulted in a substantial growth of other non-Christian religions, such as Islam, Sikhism and Hinduism. The number of practitioners is growing because of relatively high birth-rates in these groups and because of conversion to such faiths by young working-class non-whites and middle-class whites.

There are now 1.5 million Muslims, of whom 1 million regularly attend mosque. Most of them come from Pakistan and Bangladesh, but there are other groups from India, Arab countries and Cyprus. The Islamic Cultural Centre and its associated Central Mosque in London are the largest Muslim institutions in the West, and there are mosques in virtually every British town with a concentration of Muslim people.

PLATE 11.5 Regents Park mosque, Central London *(Duncan Wherret/Barnaby)*

PLATE 11.6 A Hindu wedding *(K. Rodgers/The Hutchison Library)*

There are also large Sikh (390,000) and Hindu (300,000) religious groups in Britain. Most of these come from India, and have many temples scattered around the country in areas of Asian settlement. Various forms of Buddhism are also represented in the population.

Non-Christian religions amount to some 1.9 million practising members, and represent a significant growth area when compared to the Christian churches. But these communities constitute a relatively small proportion of the British population, the vast majority of which remains nominally Christian. However, they have altered the religious face of British society and have influenced employment conditions, since allowances have to be made for non-Christians to follow their own religious observances and customs.

They have also become vocal in expressing their opinions on a range of matters, such as the Muslim demand for their own schools supported by state funds; Muslim outrage against Salman Rushdie's novel *The Satanic Verses*, parts of which are considered to be blasphemous; and Muslim claims that British law and politicians discriminate against their religion.

Cooperation among the churches

The intolerance and bigotry of Christian denominations in Britain have gradually mellowed after centuries of hostility, restrictions and repression. There is now considerable cooperation between the churches, although this stops short of ecumenism (full unity). Discussions continue between the Roman Catholic Church and other Christian churches about closer ties, and an Anglican–Roman Catholic Commission explores points of possible unity. The old enmity between Protestants and Catholics has been reduced, but animosity continues in parts of Scotland and most demonstrably in Northern Ireland.

On other levels of cooperation, the Council of Churches for Britain and Ireland has representatives from the main Christian churches, is presided over by the Archbishop of Canterbury, and works towards common action and Christian unity. The Free

Church Federal Council does a similar job for the Free Churches. The Anglican and the main Free Churches also participate in the World Council of Churches, which attempts to promote worldwide cooperation, and studies common problems. The Council of Christians and Jews works for better understanding among its members, and the Council for Churches of Britain and Ireland has established a Committee for Relations with People of Other Faiths (that is non-Christian).

Such attempts at possible ecumenism and cooperation are seen by some as positive actions that might break down barriers and hostility. Others see them as signs of weakness, since denominations are forced to cooperate because of declining memberships and their lack of real influence in the contemporary world. Any movement towards Christian unity may also be threatened by the ordination of women priests in the Church of England, since the worldwide Anglican Communion accepts them, but the Roman Catholic Church is opposed.

Many churchmen at the grassroots level argue that the churches must adapt more to the requirements of modern life, or else decline in membership and influence. Religious life in Britain has become more evangelical and cooperative in order to reflect a diverse contemporary society and values. But some traditionalists wish to preserve the historical elements of religious belief and practice, and the tension between them and modernists in all religious groups is likely to continue.

Religion in schools

Non-denominational Christian religious education is legally compulsory in state schools in England and Wales. The school day is supposed to start with an act of collective worship, and religious lessons should be provided that concentrate on Christianity but also include the other main faiths. However, if a pupil (or parent) has strong objections, the pupil need not take part in either the service or the lessons. Religious services and teaching are not compulsory in Scotland.

In practice, few secondary schools hold daily religious assemblies. Custom differs for the religious lessons, particularly in areas with large ethnic communities. The lessons can take many different forms, and may not be tied to specific Christian themes. Frequent proposals are made that the legal compulsion in religious education should be removed, but it is still enshrined in the latest Education Acts. Some people see religious education and collective worship as a way to raise moral standards and encourage social values; others disagree. Many schools cannot meet their religious legal obligations, and question the point of doing so.

Religious membership and observance

The continuous decline in membership of the main Christian churches in the twentieth century has recently eased, and there has even been a slight growth. However, substantial increases have occurred in some of the Free Churches, non-Christian denominations and new or independent religious movements.

It is difficult to obtain precise information about religious membership and observance in Britain. Enquiries are not normally made about religious beliefs in censuses or on official forms, and denominations have their own methods of assessing membership figures. Some statistics suggest that 10 per cent of the population attend a Christian church, and less than 20 per cent of the total population go regularly to some form of religious service, whether Christian or non-Christian.

Yet it is estimated that 70 per cent of British people are married in a religious building and that about 90 per cent receive some form of religious burial or cremation. Thus it seems that a small minority attend religious services regularly, others go occasionally, but the large majority enter a religious building only for baptisms, weddings and funerals.

However, these figures should not necessarily be taken as a sign of British irreligion. A distinction can be made between formal religious observance of an institutional or organized kind and the private individual sphere of religious or moral feeling. Despite the appearance of a largely secular state, religion in its various forms is still an important factor in national life. Radio, television and the press concern themselves with religious and moral topics. Religious broadcasting on radio and television attracts surprisingly large audience figures, and recent reports suggest further demand for this type of communication.

Religion is also reflected in traditions and ceremonies, as well as being evident in national and individual morality. Religious denominations are relatively prominent in British life and are active in education, voluntary social work and community care. Religious leaders publicly debate doctrine, social matters, political concerns and the moral questions of the day, not always necessarily within narrow church limits.

ATTITUDES

Attitudes to religion and morality

While institutional observance may no longer be popular in Britain, people still have somewhat conventional religious beliefs. A MORI opinion poll in 1990 found that respondents believed in God (76 per cent); sin (69); a soul (68); heaven (60); life after death (49); the devil (37); and hell (31). These figures have been repeated in later polls, and indicate a considerable individual religious faith.

Such religious concerns seem also to influence matters of personal morality and civic responsibility. Although there are differences of emphasis between younger and older generations and between men and women, the British have strong views about right and wrong, though these are not necessarily tied to the teaching of any particular denomination. Opinion polls suggest that a majority of people think that the following are morally wrong: hard drugs like heroin; soccer hooliganism; soft drugs such as cannabis; scenes of explicit violence on television; adultery; scientific experiments on human beings; and scientific experiments on animals. Homosexuality and cinema pornography are also frowned upon by a large minority.

A majority now favour censorship of some forms of the media in order to preserve moral standards. But a large majority are in favour of euthanasia (allowing a doctor to end a patient's life) if the person has a painful and incurable illness. A majority also feel that it is worse to convict an innocent person (miscarriage of justice) than to let a guilty individual go free.

Poll interviews show that there is majority support for the institution of marriage and that most people have traditional ideas about love, family life and their moral demands. But there is a growing support for more equality within marriage, and faithfulness, mutual respect and understanding are seen as the most important aspects of marriage.

In terms of civic responsibility, polls suggest that attitudes to authority remain relatively conventional in some areas. A majority of respondents feel that children should be taught in the home environment to respect honesty, good manners and other people. Feelings have hardened towards those individuals who reject society as presently constituted, who demonstrate and protest and who encourage disobedience in children. A large majority would oppose any attempts by the trade unions to call a general strike in the country. Most respondents agree that schools should teach children to obey authority. But the number of people who consider that the law should be obeyed without exception has fallen, and more now believe that one should follow one's conscience, even if this means breaking the law.

These mixed views indicate that many British people now embrace an authoritarian posture in some questions of morals and social behaviour. 'Moral traditionalism', old values and civic responsibility are supported, and there is often a greater adherence to concepts of personal and social morality than to those dictated by official and legal restraints. This is also reflected in people's considerable concerns about drugs, law and order, crime, violence and vandalism, and their preference for strong action to be taken in these areas. In other matters, there seems to be a growing libertarianism.

Nevertheless, and according to a Leeds University survey in 1997, many Britons now do not trust other people, and see life as less predictable, more time-pressured, less secure, more materialistic and fast-moving, and their society as riddled with mistrust, cynicism and greed. Lacking traditional faith in conventional religion, people appear to put their trust in materialism and physical appearance, but there still seems to be a longing for spiritual understanding, other-worldly comfort and explanations. This search can lead in different directions. Apparently, people believe increasingly in the paranormal, telepathy (50 per cent) and second sight (55). Sixty-seven per cent believe that there is some truth in astrology, and 15 per cent believe that abduction by aliens is possible.

EXERCISES

■ Explain and examine the following terms:

Canterbury	Henry VIII	'Low Church'	confirmation
bigotry	Iona	Free Churches	General Synod
St Patrick	episcopal	Church Settlement	John Knox
Whitby	Quakers	vicar	Salvation Army
baptism	ecumenism	denomination	evangelism

■ Write short essays on the following topics:

1 What does the term 'Christianity' mean in relation to British religious history?

2 Discuss religious membership and observance in contemporary British life.

3 Critically examine the role of the Church of England.

Chapter 12

Leisure, sports and the arts

THE DIVERSITY OF LIFE in contemporary Britain is reflected in the ways in which the British organize their personal, sporting, leisure and artistic lives. These features reveal a series of different cultural habits, rather than a simple and unified image, though there are some activities that are associated with and tend to project a national identification. In many cases, pastimes are also connected to social class and minority participation. According to the authors of *We British* (Jacobs and Worcester, p. 124), the rich variety of leisure activities contradicts the notion of Britain as a country of philistines who prefer second-rate entertainment to the best.

Leisure activities

Leisure activities in earlier centuries, apart from some cultural interests exclusive to the metropolitan elite, were largely conditioned by the rural and agricultural nature of British life. Village communities were isolated, and transport was either poor or non-existent. People were consequently restricted to their villages and obliged to create their own entertainments. Some of these participatory activities were home-based, while others were enjoyed by the whole village. They might be added to by itinerant players, who travelled the countryside and provided a range of alternative spectator entertainments, such as drama performances and musical events.

Improved transportation and road conditions from the eighteenth century onwards enabled the rural population to travel to neighbouring towns, where they took advantage of a variety of amusements. Spectator activities increased with the industrialization of the nineteenth century, as theatre, the music halls and sports developed and became available to more people. The establishment of railway systems and the formation of bus companies initiated the pattern of cheap one-day trips around the country and to the seaside, which were to grow into the mass charter and package tours of contemporary Britain. The arrival of radio, films and television in the twentieth century resulted in a further huge professional entertainments industry. In all these changes, the mixture of participatory, spectator and home-based leisure activities has continued.

Many contemporary pursuits have their roots in the cultural and social behaviour of the past, such as boxing, wrestling, cricket, football and a wide range of athletic sports. Dancing, amateur theatre and musical events were essential parts of rural life for all classes, and were often associated with the changing agricultural seasons. The traditions of hunting, shooting and fishing have long been practised in British country life (not only by the aristocracy), as well as working-class blood sports, such as dog and cock fighting and bear baiting, which are now illegal. A feature of contemporary Britain is the continuing attempt to ban many kinds of hunting, such as fox hunting, and a MORI poll in 1997 showed that two-thirds of respondents favoured a complete ban. The countryside lobby is, naturally, opposed to this.

In addition to cultural and sporting pastimes, the British enjoy a variety of other leisure activities, since many diversified opportunities are now available and more people have more free time. Most workers have at least four weeks' holiday a year, in addition to public holidays like Christmas, Easter and Bank Holidays. The growing number of pensioners has created an economically-rewarding leisure market, while unemployment means that further substantial groups of people have more spare time. In 1993 some 14 per cent of total household expenditure was spent on leisure goods and services.

Consumer patterns associated with leisure activities are changing in Britain. These coincide with part-time and shift working and greater disposable incomes, particularly among the young. There is a demand for pubs and leisure services as well as shops, companies, businesses, doctors and schools to remain open longer or to be available for longer periods.

PLATE 12.1 A working men's club *(JaninaStruk/Format)*

The most common leisure pastimes are social or home-based, such as visiting or entertaining friends, trips to the pub (public house), watching television and videos, reading books and magazines, and listening to the radio, records, compact discs and cassettes. In winter, the most popular non-sporting leisure activity for the adult population as a whole is watching television (for some 26 hours a week), and for men television viewing is apparently the single most popular pastime throughout the year.

The British now occupy some two-thirds of their spare time using electronic equipment, and an increasingly large amount of money is spent on items such as television, radio (listened to for some 10 hours a week), video recorders, computers, compact disc players (owned by 46 per cent of households in 1995) and cable and satellite television. The home has become the chief place for family and individual entertainment in these respects, and poses serious competition to other passive activities outside the home, like the cinema, sports and theatre. Some 98 per cent of households now have a television set (95 per cent being colour sets), and some 76 per cent have at least one video recorder.

Despite the competition from television, the cinema and other electronic media, reading is still an important leisure activity for over half of men and women in Britain. There is a large variety of books and magazines to cater for all tastes and interests. The best-selling books are romances, thrillers, modern popular novels, detective stories and works of adventure and history. Classic literature is not widely read, although its sales can benefit from adaptations on television. The tie-in of books (of all types) with videos and television series is now a very lucrative business.

Do-it-yourself hobbies, such as house painting, decorating and gardening, are very popular, and home improvements and repairs amount to a considerable item in the total household budget. The practice of eating out has increased, and is catered for by an expanded variety of so-called 'ethnic' restaurants (particularly Indian and Chinese) and fast-food outlets.

Visiting the pub is still a very important part of British life, and more money is spent on drinking and other pub activities than on any other single form of leisure. Some seven out of 10 adults visit pubs, and one-third go once or more a week. The pub, as a social institution, has changed somewhat over the years, but still caters for a wide range of different groups and tastes. The licensing hours, which apply to opening times for the sale of alcohol, have been liberalized, and pubs now open from 11 am to 11 pm on every day except Sundays, though children under 14 are not allowed in the bar. Most pubs provide food in addition to drinks, and often have restaurants attached to them. In recent years, however, the establishment of wine bars, various forms of clubs, discotheques and dance halls has meant a considerable amount of competition for traditional pubs. Indeed,

PLATE 12.2 An English pub, Nottingham *(John Oakland)*

many pubs have had to change their formats in order to attract customers.

Holidays and where to spend them have also become an important part of British life, and have been accompanied by more leisure time and money for the majority of the people. They represent the second major leisure cost after pub drinking. While more Britons in recent years have been taking their holidays in Britain itself, where the south-west English coastal resorts, Wales and Scotland are very popular in summer, large numbers also go abroad in both winter and summer. The number of long holidays taken away from home by the British population amounted to 59 million in 1995, of which 33 million were taken in Britain

PLATE 12.3 Pensioners on holiday *(Rex Features, London)*

itself. Spain (27 per cent), France (10), Greece (8) and the USA (7) are the main attractions for holidaymakers, who buy relatively cheap package tours. The British seem to have become more adventurous, and are now travelling widely outside Europe on a variety of holidays.

Many other people prefer to organize their own holidays, and make use of the good air and sea communications between Britain and the continent. In Britain itself, different forms of holiday exist, from the traditional 'bed and breakfast' at a seaside boarding house, to hotels, rented houses, caravan sites and camping. Increased car ownership has allowed greater travel possibilities. Today, more than three-fifths of households have the use of at least one car, and 16 per cent have two or more.

Sports

There is a wide variety of sports in Britain today, which cater for large numbers of spectators and participators. Some of these are minority or class-based sports, while others appeal to majority tastes. The number of people participating in sports has increased, and sporting facilities and leisure centres in both the public and private sectors have expanded. This has coincided with a greater awareness of health needs and the importance of exercise. The 1993 *General Household Survey* estimated that 29 million people over 16 participate in outdoor and indoor sports or forms of exercise, with more men (72 per cent) than women (57 per cent) taking part. Spending on playing and watching sports, and buying sports equipment, amount to a considerable part of the household budget.

The most popular participatory sporting activity for both men and women is walking. Billiards, snooker and darts are the next most popular for men, followed by swimming and football. Swimming is the next most popular sport for women, followed by keep-fit classes. Fishing is apparently the most popular country sport.

Amateur and professional football (soccer) is played throughout most of the year and also at international level. It is by far the most watched sport, and today transcends its working-class origins. The professional game has developed into a large, family-oriented organization, but has suffered from hooliganism, high ticket prices, declining attendances and financial crises. However, enforced changes in recent years, such as all-seater stadiums, greater security, improved facilities and lucrative tie-ins with television coverage (such as Sky-Sport), have greatly improved this situation. Many of the top professional football clubs in the Premier League have now become public companies quoted on the Stock Exchange.

Rugby football is a popular winter pastime that is widely watched and played. It is divided into two codes: Rugby Union and Rugby League. Rugby Union was once confined to amateur clubs and was an exclusively middle-class and public school-influenced

PLATE 12.4 A crowd of people at a football match *(Jacky Chapman/Format)*

game. It became professional in 1995 (at least for the top clubs) and now covers a wider social spectrum. Rugby League is played by professional teams, mainly in the north of England, and still tends to be a working-class sport. Both types of rugby are also played internationally.

Cricket is a summer sport in Britain, but the England team also plays in the winter months in Commonwealth countries. It is both an amateur and professional sport. The senior game is professional and is largely confined to the English and Welsh county sides that play in the county championships. Attendance at cricket matches continues to decline, and the contemporary game has lost some of its attractiveness as it has moved in overly

PLATE 12.5 A football match: Derby County vs. Queen's Park Rangers *(Joanne O'Brien/Format)*

professional and money-dominated directions. It is now in danger of becoming a minority sport.

There are many other sports that reflect the diversity of interests in British life. Among these are golf, greyhound and horse racing, hunting, riding, fishing, shooting, tennis, hockey, bowls, darts, snooker, athletics, swimming, sailing, mountaineering, walking, ice sports, motor-car and motor-cycle racing and rally driving. American football and basketball are increasingly popular due to television exposure. All these sports may be either amateur or professional, and spectator- or participator-based, with car and motor-cycle, greyhound and horse racing being the most watched.

The professional sporting industry is now very lucrative, and is closely associated with sponsorship schemes and television coverage. Gambling or betting on sporting and other events has always been a popular, if somewhat disreputable, pastime in Britain, which is now much more in the open and so more acceptable. Most gambling (through betting shops or bookmakers) is associated with horse and greyhound racing, but can involve other sports. Weekly football pools (betting on match results) are very popular, and can result in huge financial wins. The new-found acceptability of gambling in Britain was reflected in the establishment of a National Lottery in 1994. It is similar to lotteries in other European countries, and considerable amounts of money can be won. Some of its income also funds artistic, community, leisure and sports activities that are in need of finance to survive.

It is interesting that many of these sports have contributed to institutionalized features of British life, and provide a certain degree of national identity. For example, Wimbledon is tennis; the Wembley Cup Final is football in England; St Andrews is golf in Scotland; Twickenham in England, Murrayfield in Scotland,

PLATE 12.6 Cricket in the city, Kennington estate, London
(Cleland Brims/Barnaby)

PLATE 12.7 Cricket in the country, Kent *(Alexander Brims/Barnaby)*

and Cardiff Arms Park in Wales are Rugby Union; Lords Cricket Ground in London is cricket; the Derby is flat horse racing; the Grand National in Liverpool is steeplechasing; Henley Regatta is rowing; Cowes Week off the Isle of Wight is yachting; Ascot is horse racing; and the British Grand Prix is Formula One motor racing. Some of these sports may appeal only to certain sections of the population, while others may still be equated more with wealth and social position.

Some people feel that the professionalization and commercialization of sport in Britain has tended to weaken the traditional sporting image of the amateur and the old emphasis upon playing the game for its own sake. But these values still exist to some degree, in spite of greater financial rewards for professional sport, the influences of sponsorship and advertising, and increasing cases of unethical behaviour in all sports. However, tobacco sponsorship of most sporting events has now been banned by the Labour government.

British governments have only recently taken an active political interest in sport. They are now more concerned to promote sport at all levels, and there is a Minister of Sport who is supposed to coordinate sporting activities throughout the country. It is also likely that a British Academy of Sport devoted to top-level sports performers and school sports, sponsored by the National Lottery and operating on a regional basis, will eventually be established. However, the national provisions for sport in Britain are not as adequate as they might be, and there is a lack of professional coaches, capital investment and sporting facilities compared with other countries. The government has privatized some local authority sports and leisure centres, particularly in inner-city areas, in an attempt to raise sporting standards and to provide more facilities, but critics fear that this policy will not succeed in attracting people.

The sporting notion of 'a healthy mind in a healthy body' has long been a principle of British education. All schools are supposed to provide physical recreation, and a reasonable range of sports is usually available for schoolchildren. Schools may play soccer, rugby, hockey or netball during the winter months, and cricket, tennis, swimming and athletics during the summer. Some schools may be better provided with sporting facilities than others, and offer a wider range of activities.

However, there have been recent complaints from parents that team games and competitive sports are declining in state schools. School reorganization and the creation of large comprehensives have reduced the amount of inter-school competition, which used to be a feature of education, and some left-wing councils are apparently opposed to competitive activities. There is also a shortage of school playing fields and a lack of adequate equipment. The position is particularly acute in the inner-city areas, and is of concern to those parents who feel that their children are being prevented from expressing their normal physical natures. They maintain that the state school system is failing to provide sporting provision for children, and some parents turn to the independent sector, which is usually well provided with sports facilities. The establishment of a British Academy of Sport may improve the availability and standard of state school sports.

The arts

The 'arts' once had a somewhat precious and exclusive image associated with notions of high culture, which were usually the province of the urban and metropolitan middle and upper classes. This attitude has lessened to some degree since the Second World War under the impetus of increased educational opportunities and the gradual relaxation of social barriers. The growth of mass and popular culture has increased the potential audience for a wider range of cultural activities, and the availability and scope of the arts has spread to greater numbers of people. These activities may be amateur or professional, and continue the mixture of participatory, spectator and home-based entertainment.

Some critics argue that the genuine vitality and innovation of the British arts are to be found in the millions of people across the country who are engaged in amateur music, art and theatre, rather than in the professional and commercial world. Virtually every town, suburb and village has an amateur group, whether it be a choir, music group, orchestra, string quartet, pipe band, brass band, choral group, opera group or dramatic club. In addition, there are hundreds of cultural festivals held each year throughout Britain, many of which are of a very high standard.

The funding of the mainstream arts in Britain is precarious and involves the private and public sectors. The public sector is divided between local authorities and the Arts Council of Great Britain. Local authorities raise money from the council tax to fund artistic activities in their areas, but the amounts spent can vary considerably between different areas of the country, and local authorities are attacked for either spending too much or too little on cultural activities.

Members of the Arts Council, who now operate on a regional rather than centralized level, are appointed by the Minister for Culture. They are responsible for dividing up an annual government grant to the arts that has to be shared among theatres, orchestras, opera and ballet companies, art galleries, museums and a variety of other cultural organizations. The division of limited funds has inevitably attracted much criticism. It means that many artistic institutions are often dependent upon the private sector to supply donations and funding, in addition to their state and local government money, in order to survive and provide a service. Some cultural organizations, such as the Royal Opera and museums, are now receiving much-needed finance from the National Lottery.

British theatre can be lively and innovative and has a deserved international reputation. There are some 300 commercial or professional theatres, in addition to a large number of amateur dramatic clubs, fringe and pub theatres throughout the country. London and its suburbs have about 100 theatres, but the dominant influence is the London 'West End'. The majority of the West End theatres are commercial, in that they are organized for profit and receive no public funds. They provide a range of light entertainment offerings from musicals to plays and comedies.

However, some of the other London theatres are subsidized from grants supplied by the Arts Council, such as the National Theatre, the Royal Shakespeare Company and the English Stage Company. These cater for a variety of plays from the classics to modern drama. The subsidized theatres in both London and the regions constantly plead for more state financial aid, which the government is loath to give, even though the government subsidy is considerably less than that given to most comparable theatres in continental Europe. But there is a feeling in some quarters that these theatres should be more competitive and commercially-minded like the West End, although Arts Council grants have been recently increased.

Many of the theatres in the regions outside London are repertory theatres, which means that they provide a number of plays in a given season, and have a resident theatre company and organization. The repertory companies have traditionally been the training ground for British actors and actresses. They present a specific number of classical and innovative plays and a variety of other artistic offerings in a season.

Most theatres in London and elsewhere have had difficult times in recent years in attracting audiences and in remaining solvent. They have had to cope with increased competition from alternative and new entertainment activities. New commercial theatres in some cities are proving popular and are taking audiences away from the established repertory companies. These commercial theatres provide a wide range of popular entertainment, shows and drama, as well as plays performed prior to a London run. There are now signs that audience figures for all types of theatres are picking up again.

Opera in Britain occupies a similar position to that of the theatres, and is divided into subsidized, commercial and amateur companies. The Royal Opera House in London is home to the Royal Opera, which supplies London seasons and occasional regional tours. The English National Opera Company provides a similar mid-market service from the Coliseum Theatre in London. In future, it and the Royal Opera may share the refurbished facilities of the Covent Garden Theatre. There is a range of other opera companies, both in London and the regions, such as the English Opera Group, the Welsh National Opera and the Scottish Opera Company. There are also several light opera groups, and ballet companies such as the Ballet Rambert, the London Festival Ballet, the Scottish Theatre Ballet and the Royal Ballet, which operates in London and Birmingham. A number of contemporary dance companies have also been formed in recent years.

Britain has many quality orchestras, although most of them are based in London, such as the London Philharmonic, the Royal Philharmonic and the BBC Symphony Orchestra. There are regional symphony orchestras, such as the Halle in Manchester, and a number of chamber groups in London and the regions. Most of the opera, ballet and orchestra activities have their greatest appeal in London and still cater for only a minority of the people. But more popular forms, such as brass bands, choral singing and light music, have a large following. The more exclusive entertainments are heavily dependent upon Arts Council subsidies, local government grants and private donations. The country's operatic, dance and classical music offerings can compete against international rivals.

British popular music also led the world from the 1960s and was both an economic and a cultural phenomenon. Since the Beatles, the domestic market for music sales has multiplied more than sixfold. However, in recent years, there has been a staleness in the popular field that has affected mainstream, avant-garde and 'ethnic' music alike. Some critics attribute this to commercial manipulation and standardization, and others to a lack of substantial and consistent talent.

However, British popular and rock music today has regained its domestic and international following, is attractive to the overseas youth market, and constitutes Britain's fastest growing industry. Music is worth £2.5 billion a year, and the value of UK single and album sales rose by 6 per cent in 1996. Compact discs, now selling 160 million copies a year, are the most popular music format and have led to the phasing out of vinyl records. The music business has grown bigger than shipbuilding, electronic components and the water supply. It constitutes a sizeable amount of British exports in the form of recordings, concert tours, clothing and books. Polls suggest that 81 per cent of Britons between 16 and 24 spend their leisure time listening to CDs, tapes or records at least once a week. This comes second only to television as a leisure pursuit.

There is a wide range of museums and art galleries in Britain that provide for a variety of tastes. Most of them are financed and controlled by local authorities, although some are commercial ventures and others, such as national institutions like the British Museum and the National Gallery in London, are the province of the Minister of Culture. In the past, entry to most of the public museums and art galleries was free of charge, but in recent years entrance fees have been charged for some institutions. This development has led to protests from those people who regard such facilities as part of the national educational and cultural heritage, which should be available to all without charge. But museums and art galleries are also finding it difficult to operate on limited funds, and are dependent upon local government grants, Arts Council subsidies and National Lottery donations.

The history of the cinema in Britain has shown a big decline since its early days as a very popular form of mass entertainment and from 1946 when annual visits reached a total of 1.6 billion. The domestic film industry had virtually ceased to exist, because of lack of investment and government help, although British films with British actors continued to be made abroad and in Britain with foreign financial backing. More government and National Lottery finance (£80 million) is now being provided to support British film making.

Many cinemas have now either gone out of business completely, or have changed to other activities such as dancing and bingo. In 1960 there were over 3,000 cinemas in Britain.

PLATE 12.8 The Royal Albert Hall, London *(John Oakland)*

Today there are 2,000 cinema screens which are situated either in single buildings or in multi-cinemas. Annual audience figures dropped from some 501 million in 1960 to 193 million in 1970. This decline was hastened by the arrival of television, and continued as new forms of home entertainment, such as videos, have increased. However, although admissions sank to 55 million by 1984, there has been an increase to 124 million (or currently 2.5 million a week). This improvement in audience figures has been encouraged by cheaper tickets, a wider range of films, responses to competition, and the provision of an alternative leisure activity within more modern surroundings, such as multi-screen cinemas. But apparently more than 30 per cent of the population never go to the cinema, and 47 per cent of those aged over 35 never go.

As in sport, certain arts activities and their associated buildings have become virtual institutions, such as the West End, repertory companies, the Last Night of the Proms, the Royal Opera House in Covent Garden, the Albert Hall, the Royal Festival Hall, the National Theatre, the Tate and National Galleries, and the Shakespeare Memorial Theatre at Stratford-Upon-Avon.

ATTITUDES

Attitudes to leisure, sports and the arts

MORI public opinion polls in 1990 showed that Britain's cultural life was thriving and that a large number of people participate in a variety of available pastimes, sometimes with surprising priorities. One poll asked interviewees 'which, if any, of the these have you been to in the past twelve months?', with the following results: library (49 per cent), cinema (32), museum (27), theatre (25), art exhibition (17), football match (14), pantomime (13), orchestral concert (10), pop concert (10), modern dance (8), opera (3) and classical ballet (2).

A second poll asked interviewees 'which of these things have you done in the past month?', with the following results: watched television or a video (89 per cent), read a book (64), had friends round to your home for a meal or a drink (51), been to a restaurant (49), been to pubs (46), general exercise and keep fit (42), gardening (40), do-it-yourself (39), been away for a weekend (23), been to a sports club (20), been to a cinema (16), competitive sport (16), been to a nightclub or disco (15), been to the theatre (15), been to a social or working men's club (15), been away on holiday (13) and been to a wine bar (12). The interesting point in this list is the popularity and second place of reading.

Later polls in the 1990s suggest that these findings still apply, although there have been decreases in some activities. According to the Audit Commission in 1996, there were 336 million visits to libraries (despite a reduction of 19 per cent in the previous 10 years and a library cash shortage) and 440 million books were issued, nine for every person in Britain. Only readers in Finland, Denmark and The Netherlands borrow more library books per head of population. In comparison, 140 million people visited local swimming pools and sports centres, and the number of visits to local museums and art galleries was 10 million.

The authors of *We British* (which includes the first two polls above) concluded from their investigations that 'we can report that the nation is in no telly-induced trance. Its tastes mix watching and doing, "high" and "low" cultures, with a richness that contradicts the stereotypes of the British as divided between mindless lager louts and equally money-grubbing consumers. The mix we have found will not please everybody. Not enough football for some, not enough opera for others. But that is what we should expect in the culture of a whole nation' (*We British*, p. 133).

EXERCISES

■ Explain and examine the following terms:

do-it-yourself	the pub	rugby football
package tour	National Lottery	sponsorship
bear baiting	darts	'bed and breakfast'
high culture	cricket	the Arts Council
'West End'	brass bands	repertory theatres
football pools	'ethnic' restaurants	multi-screen cinemas

■ Write short essays on the following topics:

1 What do the above opinion polls reveal about the British people? Should one trust the polls?

2 What is your impression of the British people, in terms of their leisure, sporting and artistic activities?

Bibliography

Annual Abstract of Statistics, Central Statistical Office, London: HMSO.

Autoglass/Audience Selection, opinion poll, London, 1997.

Bristol University, education research report, Bristol, 1997.

Britain: An Official Handbook, annual, Central Office of Information, London: HMSO.

British Crime Survey, annual, Home Office, London: HMSO.

Criminal Statistics, England and Wales, annual, London: HMSO.

Education Statistics for the United Kingdom, annual, London: HMSO.

Eurobarometer, European Union occasional polls, Brussels.

Gallup public opinion polls, occasional and annual, Surrey.

General Household Survey (The), Office of National Statistics, London, 1993.

Harris public opinion polls, occasional and annual, London.

ICM, occasional polls for *The Guardian*.

International Crime Victimization Survey (The), annual, Government Publications Centre, London.

Jacobs, E. and Worcester, R. (1990) *We British: Britain under the Moriscope*, London: Weidenfeld and Nicolson.

Jowell, R. (ed.) (1988) *British Social Attitudes: 1988–89*, Aldershot: Gower.

Jowell, R. (ed.) (1991) *British Social Attitudes: 1991–92*, Aldershot: Dartmouth Publishing.

Jowell, R. (ed.) (1992) *British Social Attitudes: 1992–93*, Aldershot: Dartmouth Publishing.

Jowell, R. (ed.) (1993) *International Social Attitudes: 1993–94*, Aldershot: Dartmouth Publishing.

Jowell, R. (ed.) (1995) *British Social Attitudes: 1995–96*, Aldershot: Dartmouth Publishing.

Jowell, R. (ed.) (1996) *British Social Attitudes: 1996–97*, Aldershot: Dartmouth Publishing.

Jowell, R. (ed.) (1997) *British Social Attitudes: 1997–98*, Aldershot: Ashgate Publishing.

Key Data, annual, Central Statistical Office, London: HMSO.

Leeds University/Ogilvy and Mather Direct, research poll, London, 1997.

Manchester University, education research report, Manchester, 1997.

Market and Opinion Research International (MORI), for *The Times* and *The Sunday Times*, regular surveys.

National Institute of Economic and Social Research, education report, London, 1997.

National Opinion Poll (NOP), occasional surveys, London.

NatWest Insurance Services and Crime Concern, opinion survey, Bristol, 1997.

Office for National Statistics, education report, London, 1997.

Population Trends, quarterly, London: HMSO.

Regional Trends, annual, Central Statistical Office, London: HMSO.

Research Surveys of Great Britain, poll, London, 1997.

Social Trends, annual, Central Statistical Office, London: HMSO.

The Commonwealth Year Book, annual, London: HMSO.

The Economist, weekly magazine of record, London.

The Sunday Times, weekly newspaper of record, London.

The Times, daily newspaper of record, London.

UK Media Yearbook, annual, London: Zenith Media.

Whitaker's Almanac, annual publication, London: Whitaker.

World Economic Forum (The), education report, Geneva, 1997.

Suggested further reading

Survey books on British civilization

McDowall, D. (1993) *Britain in Close-up*, London: Longman.

Sevaldsen, J. and Vadmand, O. (1993) *Contemporary British Society*, Copenhagen: Akademisk Forlag.

Storry, M. and Childs, P. (1997) *British Cultural Identities*, London: Routledge.

The environment

Clapp, B.W. (1994) *An Environmental History of Britain*, London: Longman.

Gray, T. (1995) *UK Environmental Policy in the 1990s*, London: Macmillan.

Rose, C. (1991) *The Dirty Man of Europe*, London: Simon and Schuster.

History

Davies, J. (1993) *A History of Wales*, London: Penguin.

Haigh, C. (1990) *The Cambridge Historical Encyclopaedia of Great Britain and Ireland*, Cambridge: Cambridge University Press.

James, L. (1994) *The Rise and Fall of the British Empire*, London: Abacus.

Kearney, H. (1990) *The British Isles: A History of Four Nations*, Cambridge: Cambridge University Press.

Mackie, J.D. (1978) *A History of Scotland*, London: Pelican.

Marwick, A. (1996) *British Society Since 1945*, London: Pelican.

Morgan, K.O. (1986) *The Oxford Illustrated History of Britain*, Oxford: Oxford University Press.

Pounds, N.J.G. (1994) *The Culture of the English People*, Cambridge: Cambridge University Press.

Society

Abercrombie, N. and Warde, A. (1992) *Social Change in Contemporary Britain*, Cambridge: Polity Press.

Goldthorpe, J.H. (1989) *Social Mobility and Class Structure*, Oxford: Oxford University Press.

Hamnett, C., McDowell, L. and Sarre, P. (1989) *The Changing Social Structure*, London: SAGE/Open University.

Hutton, W. (1996) *The State We're In*, London: Vintage.

Johnson, P. (1994) *Twentieth-Century Britain: Economic, Social and Cultural Change*, London: Longman.

Obelkevich, J. and Catterall, P. (1994) *Understanding Post-War British Society*, London: Routledge.

Smith, D. (1994) *North and South*, London: Penguin.

Multiracial Britain

Gilroy, P. (1992) *There ain't no black in the Union Jack*, London: Routledge.

Hiro, D. (1992) *Black British: White British*, London: Paladin.

Holmes, C. (1991) *A Tolerant Country?: Immigrants, Refugees and Minorities in Britain*, London: Faber and Faber.

Layton-Henry, Z. (1992) *The Politics of Immigration*, Oxford: Blackwell.

Solomos, J. (1989) *Race and Racism in Contemporary Britain*, London: Macmillan.

Politics

Hennessy, P. (1995) *The Hidden Wiring*, London: Victor Gollancz.

Jenkins, S. (1995) *Accountable to None: The Tory Nationalization of Britain*, London: Hamish Hamilton.

Jones, B. (ed.) (1997) *Politics UK*, Hemel Hempstead: Prentice Hall.

Marr, A. (1995) *Ruling Britannia*, London: Michael Joseph.

Moran, M. (1989) *Politics and Society in Britain: An Introduction*, London: Macmillan.

Pearce, M. and Stewart, G. (1992) *British Political History 1867–1990: Democracy and Decline*, London: Routledge.

Sked, A. and Cook, C. (1990) *Post-War Britain: A Political History*, London: Pelican.

Local government

Leach, S., Stewart, J. and Game, C. (1994) *The Changing Organization and Management of Local Government*, London: Macmillan.

Stewart, J. and Stoker, G. (1995) *Local Government in the 1990s*, London: Macmillan.

Wilson, D. and Game, C. (1994) *Local Government in the United Kingdom*, London: Macmillan.

European Union

George, S. (1991) *Britain and European Integration since 1945*, Oxford: Blackwell.

George, S. (1994) *An Awkward Partner: Britain in the European Community*, Oxford: Oxford University Press.

Nugent, N. (1994) *The Government and Politics of the European Community*, London: Macmillan.

Northern Ireland and Eire

Aughey, A. and Morrow, D. (1996) *Northern Ireland Politics*, London: Longman.

Bardon, J. (1992) *A History of Ulster*, Belfast: Blackstaff Press.

Boyle, K. and Hadden, T. (1994) *Northern Ireland: The Choice*, London: Penguin.

Kee, R., (1982) *Ireland: A History*, London: Abacus.

McGarry, J. and O'Leary, B. (1995) *Explaining Northern Ireland*, Oxford: Blackwell.

Law and civil liberties

Feldman, D. (1993) *Civil Liberties and Human Rights in England and Wales*, Oxford: Clarendon Press.

Robertson, G. (1989) *Freedom, the Individual and the Law*, London: Pelican.

Spencer, J.R. (1989) *Jackson's Machinery of Justice*, Cambridge: Cambridge University Press.

Economics

Buxton, T., Chapman, P. and Temple, P. (1997) *Britain's Economic Performance*, London: Routledge.

Donaldson, P. and Farquhar, J. (1988) *Understanding the British Economy*, London: Penguin.

Glynn, S. and Booth, A. (1996) *Modern Britain: An Economic and Social History*, London: Routledge.

Michie, J., (1992) *The Economic Legacy 1979–1992*, London: Academic Press.

Welfare state

Deakin, N. (1994) *The Politics of Welfare*, London: Harvester Wheatsheaf.

Ham, C. (1992) *Health Policy in Britain*, London: Macmillan.

Hill, M. (1993) *The Welfare State in Britain: A Political History since 1945*, Guildford: Edward Elgar.
Johnson, N. (1990) *Reconstructing the Welfare State*, London: Harvester Wheatsheaf.
Mohan, J. (1995) *A National Health Service?*, London: Macmillan.

The media

Curran, J. and Seaton, J. (1991) *Power without Responsibility: The Press and Broadcasting in Britain*, London: Routledge.
McNair, B. (1994) *News and Journalism in the UK*, London: Routledge.
Negrine, R. (1994) *Politics and the Mass Media in Britain*, London: Routledge.

Index